Also A Mother

Also A Mother

Work and Family as Theological Dilemma

Bonnie J. Miller-McLemore

Abingdon Press
Nashville

ALSO A MOTHER:
Work and Family as Theological Dilemma

Copyright © 1994 by Abingdon Press

This book is printed on acid-free recycled paper.

Library of Congress Cataloging-in-Publication Data

Miller-McLemore, Bonnie J.
  Also a mother:work and family as theological dilemma / Bonnie J. Miller-McLemore.
    p.   cm.
  Includes bibliographical references.   *2001557q*
  ISBN 0-687-11020-3 (pbk.)
  1. Feminist theology.   2. Motherhood—Religious aspects—Christianity.   3. Work—Religious aspects—Christianity.   4. Working mothers.   5. Work and family.   I. Title.
BT83.55.M55   1994
261.8'358743—dc20   93-44713

Most Scripture quotations are from the New Revised Standard Version Bible, Copyright 1989 by the Division of Christian Education of the National Council of the Churches of Christ in the USA. Used by permission.

Those noted RSV are from the Revised Standard Version of the Bible, copyright 1946, 1952, 1971 by the Division of Christian Education of the National Council of the Churches of Christ in the USA. Used by permission.

"Propanganda Poem: Maybe for Some Young Mamas" is from *The Mother/Child Papers* by Alicia Suskin Ostriker, Copyright © 1980 by Alicia Suskin Ostriker. Reprinted by permission of Beacon Press.

Excerpt from Mary Guerrera Congo, "The Truth Will Set You Free, But First It Will Make You Crazy" from *Sacred Dimensions of Women's Experience*, edited by Elizabeth Dodson Gray, copyright 1988, is used by permission of Roundtable Press, Wellesley, Mass.

Painting on front cover, "Out of Reach, Daughters of Eve" by Francis Bernard Dicksee, is used by permission of the Bridgeman Art Library, London.

95 96 97 98 99 00 01 02 03 04—10 9 8 7 6 5 4 3 2

For Mark, and

for Chris, Matt, and Dan,

without whom this book would not be

CONTENTS

❧ ❧ ❧

ACKNOWLEDGMENTS

❦ ❦ ❦

I often read acknowledgments for what they tell me about the author and how the author pulled off an endeavor that usually is hidden in the book itself. But this book does not really hide what most books acknowledge in their acknowledgments. Its most central instigators— Mark, Chris, Matt, and Dan—are, in one way or the other, appreciated throughout for changing my heart and mind, and for continuing to hammer out with me the gritty, cumbersome details of work and family. I do not need to say more on this score.

I do need to recognize an excellent friend and editor, Ulrike Guthrie, who tested firsthand the dilemmas of my text and my conviction that a "good enough" mother indeed also can be a "good enough" worker by birthing a child in the middle of this. I also want to recognize, simply and in general, the many, many people who made this book what it is—my parents, grandparents, family, friends, mentors, teachers, students, supervisors, counselees, colleagues, neighbors, babysitters, readers, church members, editor and child—you know who you are. I heartily thank all of you upon whom I depend.

PREFACE

❦ ❦ ❦

A woman . . . either has children or writes books.
Robert Briffault, *The Mothers*

This book has gestated for about five years—at least since the conception of my second son in 1988—maybe longer in less explicit ways. And it has assumed many different shapes.[1] But the Thursday I quit procrastinating and sat down to try to put it into final shape, I forgot that that day, the first Thursday in April, was also the day I had signed up to be "Library Mom" at my middle son's preschool. I remembered it when Matt came home from preschool empty-handed. He didn't care much, but I felt sick. And I pondered.

I ponder again when, just as I write this, at this very moment, the phone rings, and Carol tells me that my youngest son, Dan, is crying with a fever. Isn't this—this *hesitation* to stop my work to go and get him—what this book is all about?

This book ponders the virtues of the good mother/good worker that frame these sometimes trivial, yet revelational moments. These are moments, I have come to believe, that repeat themselves endlessly, not only in my life but in the lives of many, many women, in less and more significant ways, often further complicated by poverty, abuse, racism, chronic illness, and other life-changing factors. And ultimately, this book defies rules that a good person just does not go around defying lightly. It defies the virtue of never hurting another person, which defines the "good girl," and the virtue of unconditional love, which defines the "good woman" and the "good mother." It defies the virtues of self-fulfillment and self-assertion, which define the "good feminist"; the virtues of independence, self-reliance, and achievement which define the "good man" and the "good worker"; and, ultimately, the virtues of objectivity and detachment which define the "good scholar."

But I have not, I tell myself, done anything wrong. I, a mother who

13

writes, would not risk such defiance if I did not believe that theology has some better virtues which it ought to be offering in place of these and that they can materialize only if theology debunks some old and very powerful myths in the first place. This book seeks the rightful place of the virtues of self-respect, mutuality, shared responsibility, interdependence, justice, and passionate objectivity—in work and in families. More exactly, this book is about being "good enough" together, caring for one another in the midst of our imperfections, instead of being "good" or "perfect" alone, and the ripple effects of such an ethic in our worlds of work, family, and religion.

My bookshelves also have their own story to tell about the evolution of this project. Each time I went into the large, winding bookstore in the basement of the seminary where I work, I walked out with yet another book on family, mothers, and work. Many of them begin the same way—with the complications of being a fully participating parent while being a member of the workplace. Like a bee to honey, I was drawn to these books and collected them rather indiscriminately on the shelves of women's-studies literature in my office and at home. Although almost all were by women outside my field, their commonality of theme and purpose led me to pile them together with books on feminist theology. My increasingly laden bookshelves mixed theology with psychology, philosophy with sociology, ethics with political science.

And in most cases, the authors of these books also crossed their own disciplinary boundaries, some with little awareness. New psychologies of women, work, and family did not just describe female emotional development. Every social-scientific study of women's experiences advocated, prescribed, judged, and recommended ethical, philosophical, and even religious changes for a better society. At the same time, feminist theology is quite often good psychology. In fact, in contrast to much contemporary theology, people like Rita Nakashima Brock and Catherine Keller read and integrate the best of current social-science research on human experiences. But I was critical of feminist theology. No one in feminist theology, I believed, was writing about family and work. Or at least, only one book I knew of began with confessions of the conflicts.

Then one day, either to delay the formidable task of actually trying to write the book or, more positively, to prepare myself mentally, I began to reorganize my shelves. Out of the mix, I pulled theology. I took those books by people in theology, mostly women, and I gave them their own special shelf. It was a critical act of new intention. In each book, I discovered heretofore hidden nuggets of truths about work and family that I somehow had overlooked in my first readings. In the more recent publications of women theologians of color, I found distinct, but more closely related, concerns about mothers and families.

I returned to my two-year-old text and laboriously began to pick out the threads of theology woven quietly throughout, until a new design began to appear in the same old cloth. And almost to my surprise, despite my own professional identity, I saw that it was an important design—both one that my feminist theologian friends need to realize they have already been weaving, even if no book title has yet read *Family and Work,* and one that others in women's studies and in studies of work and family need to consider if they are to comprehend the full picture of contemporary dilemmas. Beneath the mundane anxieties of "Library Moms," and the more serious apprehensions about the well-being of all women and all our children, is the reality of work and family as a theological and creative dilemma. What is the promised life for which God created us and for which we should strive? What is a generative life? We must deliberate on this if we really hope to make much headway.

I have only scratched the surface, I am convinced. I have not "done it all." I can't. I have to go pick up Dan. But besides, I, for one, want to hear other voices, voices different from my own. This is, after all, a "good enough" book as it is, precisely because it recognizes these quite essential limits.

PROPAGANDA POEM

❦ ❦ ❦

Maybe for Some Young Mamas

. . . I am telling you and you can take me for a fool there is no
good time like the good time a whole mama
has with a whole little baby and that's
                              where the first images
of deity come from—sister you know it's true
you know in secret how they
cut us down

            because who can bear the joy that hurts nobody
            the dazzling circuit of contact without dominance
            that by the way might make you less vulnerable
            to cancer and who knows what other diseases
            of the body
            because who can bear a thing that makes you happy
            and rolls the world a little way
                              on forward
                              toward its destiny

            because a woman is acceptable if she is
             weak
            acceptable if she is a victim
            acceptable also if she is an angry victim ("shrew," "witch")
            a woman's sorrow is acceptable
            a deodorized sanitized sterilized antiperspirant
            grinning efficient woman is certainly acceptable

but who can tolerate the power of a woman
close to a child, riding our tides
into the sand dunes of the public spaces.

Alicia Suskin Ostriker,
The Mother/Child Papers

A Good Mother Who Can Find?

A good wife who can find?
She is far more precious than jewels. . . .
Strength and dignity are her clothing,
and she laughs at the time to come.
Proverbs 31:10, 25 RSV

A good mother who can find? This is not a new question. From its initial inception in Proverbs 31 to recent permutations, it has been given various answers for centuries, answers often laden with religious sentiment. But the way this question has been asked and answered is changing. Until recently, it was asked mostly by men and some male-identified women, out of a hidden fear of women and out of a desire to control their reproductive powers. It was answered in terms of what a woman should provide her husband and her children, and this answer was given religious sanctions.

Now I raise this question as one that must be asked by mothers themselves—particularly mothers in my own field of religion. We must ask it out of protest against the "deodorized sanitized sterilized antiperspirant grinning efficient" images of mothers. We must answer it with courage to dispel the clouds of silence that enshroud the complexities of mothering, and with first-hand knowledge of the "power of a woman close to a child."[1] And it must be answered in terms of what women require in order to mother well enough and still provide for themselves in a society that no longer knows exactly who should provide for whom in reproducing the world. An adequate answer requires new religious ideals and stories both for women and for men.

This book stands as my own beleaguered response of sorts. I am a white, middle-class, Protestant seminary professor and feminist theologian; I am also a wife and a mother of three sons—eight, five, and three years old. It is the clash of these commitments that provoked this book. It was literally born along with my children, almost as inevitable, and yet as precarious as their lives. One would not have happened without the other; at the very same time, the book barely survived the children as they survived its unforeseen demands. Or so it sometimes seemed.

It is in the eye of this storm over my attention that the core ideas germinated, crystalized, and cried to be picked up and heard. The child, or more accurately, the children, the ideas that emerged—that mothers of all kinds perform an enormous amount of indispensable caring labor and must support one another; that the acts and thoughts of mothering are a unique and largely untapped resource for theological reflection; that men must begin to master caring labor; that children themselves deserve greater voice—necessitate nothing less than a radical transformation in religious sanctions about family and work for men and women.

Christian ideals of motherly self-sacrifice and fatherly hard work, as they have been interpreted by church tradition and promoted in society at large, not only fail the lives of many people today, but misrepresent both the intent of God's creation and the promise of the gospel message itself. This book proposes a Christian feminist maternal theology which draws on maternal knowing to challenge the mores of a society that has selectively divided the burdens and rewards of family and work along gender lines. It calls for a rereading of the biblical and theological traditions that have been poorly used to uphold these divisions, and it attempts to reclaim the values of caring labor for both men and women.

A good mother who can find? Today we must hear this question differently. It is no longer a matter of *finding* and possessing a good wife or mother who will fulfill all the roles assigned to her by society. Today it is a matter of fostering a postpatriarchal environment that will make good mothering possible, of redefining what we mean by the term *good*. It is a matter of catching a glimpse, in the figure of Woman Wisdom in Proverbs 31, of the survival of the Goddess and a prepatriarchal world in which women's experiences were central and women's inherent strength and dignity valued, and of chasing that glimpse until it yields new virtues for today—"good enough" work and love.

This mission presents at least two kinds of reconstructive challenges: What would new motherhood (and hand in hand, new fatherhood, new families) look like? What would a new work world look like? These simple questions unfold into a vicious series of questions: How can we adjudicate the nurturing standards of the 1950s and the rigid standards of our fiercely competitive workplaces, or should we overthrow them? If we overthrow them, how is one to make a life that has no precedent and that, seemingly, robs one of the support, validation, and guidance of the disparate traditions of both motherhood and feminism? Can one be a mother and still retain one's intellectual, professional personality?

On the other hand, how does the ideal of equality in the workplace fare next to the reality of the delight that many mothers take in their relationship with their children? Can the dehumanizing parameters that have confined private and public life—the segregation of women, and family, and men, and work along gender lines—be refashioned, or are they indelibly cemented into the human psyche and society? What exactly is an enhanced life in postmodern America for women and men alike, and for children? And what, if anything, have theology and church traditions had to say, and what might they say about all this? These are questions deliberated here.

This book began several years ago as an academic exercise. Feminist convictions left me with an instinctive intellectual disenchantment with psychological theories of development and the religious models of human vocation and family based primarily on the experiences of men. I began to reevaluate cultural ideals of *generativity,* a term first proposed by psychologist Erik Erikson to talk about the challenges in adulthood of finding adequate avenues of work and love. But once I found myself inhabiting a pregnant body, once I began to really hear my new name uttered by a child who thought of me as "mother," once I encountered firsthand the fundamental opposition in my own adult life between the demands of family life and the demands of the labor market, this became a different project. It took on new life, a life of its own.

At the heart of this book lies angry frustration with silence regarding conflicts between working and family about which I was naively oblivious before I had children and for which I was unprepared in many ways. Close to that is alarm at the narrow analysis and simple solutions of many recent popular voices. Under the truncated motto of "family values," many have made family "decline" or "crisis" sound like some kind of new problem that feminists have failed to consider or that deserves unprecedented and isolated attention. Feminists have been talking about family values of a different sort for longer than many suppose.

Here I search psychological theory, feminist theory, scripture, theology, ecclesial practice, and primarily, my own experiences, for a broader analysis that counters the ignorance and moralism I share with much of the society in which I live. The first part of the book holds the dilemma of work and family up to the light to examine a few significant angles of its crystalization. It explores representative interpretations of some of the problems in psychology (chapter 2), in feminist theory and the women's movement (chapter 3), in feminist theology (chapter 4), and in the culture at large. While powerful voices in psychology, feminist theory, and feminist theology suggest significant advancements on previous readings of work, love, and family, each leaves us with unanswered questions about the place of mothers and caring labor.

The second part of the book searches the wisdom of mothers as a source for new visions. Women of all colors and classes continue to carry out an enormous amount of indispensable, unremunerated caring labor, which at once undergirds human life and is peripheral to it, as men have defined it, and therefore is without value. Part II protests this definition of work and value, asserts the values of caring labor, and strives to make mothers and children more economically and theologically visible, while urging fathers, men, and the wider community to become more accountable. Moving from reflections on my own attempts to "make up a story to live by" (chapter 5), to the revelations of bearing children (chapter 6), and on to the revelations of living according to the pace of children (chapter 7), the second section professes experiences of mothering and working fresh ground for the normative and religious reconstruction of the nature of human "generativity."

Erikson first proposed the term *generativity* as a central task for the next to last stage of life. While this concept is neither familiar nor easy to grasp, it remains an apt one for our consideration. In this single word, we find embodied the human aspiration for a fulfilling adulthood which includes at least two aspects of human life that various theological traditions have long honored: (1) meaningful vocation; and (2) fruitful procreation. In a nutshell, generativity means an encompassing orientation to a life of productivity, creativity, and procreativity. Although Erikson understood the term strictly psychologically and discussed it primarily as one particular adult stage in the eight phases of the human life cycle, the term has important kinship with theological doctrines of creation, procreation, vocation, and redemption.

Introduction

In the next few chapters, I will say a good deal more about generativity and its limits as previously conceived. I use this more encompassing term specifically to underscore my contention that beneath the middle-class scuffle over gender roles and child care lies an essential religious crisis of work and love, or generativity and care. Although it might be simpler to ponder "work" or "love," or even "the family," in isolation, as sometimes has been the case in theology, these three arenas are integrally related. Right next to the question "A good mother who can find?" stand the questions "A good job who can find?"; "A good family who can find?"; "A good community who can find?"

Implicit in all these questions is a fundamental religious question about the nature of the generative life and of care that carries implications for American society as a whole. How might theological doctrines of love, self-sacrifice, creation, procreation, vocation, and community better respond to women and men who want to work in fulfilling ways and love in intimate relationships, including those that involve raising children? Is this the promised life for which God created us and for which we should strive?

Motherhood may no longer be the main source of female identity. Nor need it be. But 90 percent of American women have and care for children at some point during their lives. Feminists, including feminist theologians, justifiably have questioned the romanticization of motherhood. Now it is time to consider what, beyond tolerance of instability and diversity, we propose to put in its place. Theology develops doctrines of creation, procreation, and vocation, or what it means to be created by God to live on this earth, and doctrines of salvation, or what it means to receive God's grace. But in speculating on the meaning of creation and human fulfillment, theology seldom pulls the life experiences of mothering into its arena for anything but limited, and even oppressive commentary. And it certainly never has entertained seriously what mothers think, feel, desire, and know about creation and revelation. At this particular junction in Christian history, it is critical to do so.

It is not just a matter of recognizing the ongoing place of motherhood in the lives of many women and reconsidering the identity of motherhood. It means refusing the self-destructiveness of previous ideals of self-sacrificing love and hard work, and reclaiming women's experiences of mothering as fresh ground for reflecting on the nature of human fulfillment, and as sources of revelation about creation and salvation.

This book has at least three interrelated purposes, then. In it, I grope for words to describe some of the conflicts of work and love in two-earner families—one of the many "new families" of today.[2] Second, I try to listen to the inner discourse of a mother. Third, I attempt to listen theologically and ethically to the voice of the mother. My gropings have their natural and imposed limits. I talk primarily from my own experience as a white professional woman, with the conviction that white women have some critical internal problems to resolve in the arena of motherhood before we can go on the road and presume to have reasonable dialogue with women of other ethnic groups and classes. But also, the constraints of my life imposed some limits on this project.

While I draw on recent research, I have not talked to the extent I would have liked with poor women, racial-minority mothers, single mothers, or to mothers of older children. Second, although I do not look at problems peculiar to stepfamilies, gay and lesbian families, single-parent families, and other specific family structures, I do discuss issues broadly shared by many people. Third, at this point, I am less eager to attempt the kind of social, political, and economic analysis that is needed and that is best done by those within these fields than I am to work through the relevant ethical and theological analysis, as befits my own expertise. However, I am anxious to hear what people in these fields propose, as well as to listen to those who have been silenced. This is not a finished project for any of us.

I find in Adrienne Rich's hesitation to talk about her own conflicts the best expression of my own:

> I have hesitated to do what I am going to do now, which is to use myself as an illustration. For one thing, it's a lot easier and less dangerous to talk about other women writers. But there is something else. Like Virginia Woolf, I am aware of the women who are not with us here because they are washing the dishes and looking after the children. Nearly fifty years after she spoke, that fact remains largely unchanged. And I am thinking also of women she left out of the picture altogether—women who are washing other people's dishes and caring for other people's children, not to mention women who went on the streets last night to feed their children.[3]

I agree with her conclusions: It is divisive and destructive to think of ourselves as "special women" as long as we all know women whose gifts are buried or aborted. "Our struggles can have meaning and our privileges—however precarious under patriarchy—can be justified only if they can help to change the lives of women whose gifts—and whose very being—continue to be thwarted and silenced."[4]

Listening to the mother stirs up new theological and ethical questions. We must ask ourselves: What kind of theological premises are required to sustain a family life that fulfills the need for security, commitment, and continuity of its members, without destroying a woman's self-identity in the process (chapter 5)? What, if anything, does a woman learn existentially and theologically from carrying a nascent developing embryo-child inside herself? Can the two evils, the demonization *and* the idealization of women's sexual and maternal bodies, be countered by a renewed appreciation of the human worth of the pregnant body, the one who bears, the nursing woman (chapter 6)?

What do people learn existentially and theologically from relating intimately to a child who is both dependent, needy, vulnerable, and responding, giving, teaching? What do children require and deserve? God created humans to love and to work, to be fruitful and multiply, to till the earth and keep it. But what does this mean today for women and men? Jesus blessed the children. The needs of children are primary and immediate. But has this blessing been adequately understood (chapter 7)? What kind of ethical, religious, and ecclesial frameworks can reconcile egalitarian relationships with the demands of the workplace and the demands of the homestead (chapter 8)? These are not easy matters with simple solutions. Part II of this book does not pretend to provide definitive or exhaustive answers, but it does suggest initial responses to these kinds of questions and parameters for a kind of existential, religious, ethical, and ecclesial conversation that must continue.

In exploring these questions, I am talking to at least three audiences: my colleagues in theology and pastoral care; the broader academic public; and the people next door. For the most part, neither my academic colleagues nor my friends who practice pastoral care and counseling have paid sufficient attention to problems in the current practices and theological ideals of family, work, and love. And yet the broader academic public, particularly those in public policy and the social sciences, needs the critical minds of those of us in the fields of theology and culture, pastoral care and psychotherapy. No strategy of child care or parental leave will resolve all the conflicts. Policies and sciences sensitive to the ethical and religious pulse of the people and the complex nuances of human faith, love, and aspiration will go further in comprehending the dilemmas than those determined solely by facts, figures, statistics, and social analysis.

The last audience is perhaps closest to my heart: those who face these problems daily. Around me, I see women and men negotiating untried roles and complex schedules in which a single change throws everything and everyone out of sync. I see women testing the limits of various jobs, dissatisfied with the demands of still predominantly male-run institutions and families, and yet unable to find a way to transform the problems. I see people struggling to determine how to spend their limited time and energy, arbitrating competing demands, often tired of the burdens. Many are "doing it all," for the sheer lack of any other way of living during this transitional time in human history, guided only by the determination that something in the midst of the conflicts and hassles feels right about what they are doing.

The growing commitments of this book about what feels right about "doing it all," as well as the growing alarm about what seems wrong, are not intended as some new proverb-like dogma to recreate an image of righteous mothering. Rather, it is foremost an invitation to take up a conversation on the dilemmas of work and family, which, in one way or another, touch all our lives and bear upon the shape of the future of human society. This discussion has crucial implications for theology because it challenges the ways theology has portrayed human fulfillment and images of God; it questions the ways theology has called humans to live and work as individuals, as families, and as communities; and it reconsiders the ways we gather as church. We cannot wait any longer to have it.

The first chapter initiates the discussion. It samples the dilemmas, demonstrates the ways women provide essential ingredients in holding up the world, and then considers traditional or dominant theological recipes for "motherhood and apple pie." These are the first steps in creating new recipes.

❧ ❧ ❧

Part One

DILEMMAS OF WORK AND FAMILY

CHAPTER ONE

Motherhood and the Theological Pie

God blessed them, and God said to them, "Be fruitful and multiply, and fill the earth and subdue it; and have dominion over the fish of the sea and over the birds of the air and over every living thing that moves upon the earth."

Genesis 1:28

Working mothers are enhancing their children's lives in many ways that nonworking mothers are not.
Blurb on Anita Shreve, *Remaking Motherhood*

A Sampling of the Dilemmas

As a "working mother," I read the blurb on the back of Anita Shreve's *Remaking Motherhood* eagerly: "Working mothers are enhancing their children's lives in many ways that nonworking mothers are not." These are fighting words. Why doesn't most of white middle-class North America believe this? Why do some of us want so strongly to believe it? Why do others, from Phyllis Schlafly to Mrs. Dan Quayle, want as desperately to prove otherwise? Who set up this opposition anyway? Aren't women being divided and conquered precisely at a moment in history when we really need one another's support? And why must women worry so much about enhancing their children's lives?

Can you imagine an alternative marketing blurb: "Working fathers are enhancing their children's lives"?

One thing is certain: The claim sells. As the twentieth century closes, we sit smack in the middle of a revolution in practices and ideals of work and love. Rearrangement of relations between the sexes tugs a thread that is unraveling the weave of an entire culture. This revolution carries as much consequence for women as the Industrial Revolution did for men when it separated the workplace from the home and moved men out. Many men and women now stand at arms over who takes care of what. Roles that used to be obvious have become debatable choices. "Am I doing the right thing?" wonders Shreve, as she goes from child to work, from work to child. Women cannot, it seems, "fail at child-rearing and sleep at night."[1]

According to the "Dr. Spock of the 90s," Harvard pediatrician T. Berry Brazelton, lots of people bring nonmedical anxieties to his office after many sleepless nights, tossing and turning, trapped in "Families Without a Culture," as one of his chapter titles reads.[2] His colorful naming of the confusion of modern parents is only partially accurate, however. Many people are not so much *without* a culture as caught *between* cultures that have widely divergent, frequently clashing, strikingly compelling standards.

As a white feminist mother with Protestant convictions, I stand upon several thresholds, caught between cultures. I am neither inside nor wholly outside the traditions and cultures that have held me and those that have liberated me. On one hand, despite my best intentions, I still wrestle with the resilient ideals of the "Father-Knows-Best" family that gripped the heart of America in the 1950s. At the same time, I live, albeit uneasily, with the new, still sketchily drawn ideals of working women. I feel caught in a vicious circle that the women's movement identified: women's stories have not been told and have not shaped cultural myths; without them a woman is lost; in order to forge ahead, women need stories that value their experiences.

For the most part, the task of arbitrating the contradictions between cultures has been up to individuals. My own efforts have been strained at several points. Daily, I become entangled in the ambiguous oppositions between so-called public and private life. On the one hand, my "private" vocation as devoted mother collides head on with my religious and feminist hopes for justice and equality in a "public" world not structured for, and even hostile to children. On the other hand, my "public" vocation as professor clashes with my religious and maternal desires for creation, nurturing, and sustenance in the "private" world of child play and domestic routine. My life refuses to fall into the traditional dichotomy between private and public arenas that Western society has fostered.

I face a double bind. My heritage as a Christian feminist mother involves a forceful dual disinheritance. First I question marriage and motherhood and fear the entrapping snares of domesticity, and then I find myself questioning tactics for success in a male-defined workplace. Coming of age in the 1970s, I was acutely aware of the entrapments of home and children. But the birth of children reinforced my disinclination to become an "honorary man" in a world organized and run by men, the power of money, and the lure of status. Both the conventional "marriage plot," which assigns women the script of taking care of the private world, and the "quest plot," with its script of heroic adventures in public life, have valid appeal but serious flaws.[3] Yet, if neither narrative fits today's world, what's the new plot for women and for men alike?

Resolution of the daily conflicts leads inevitably to contradictions, frustrations, ambiguous solutions, and hard choices. One day while trying to revise a manuscript during the naptime of one of my sons, I recall feeling torn between a desire for total uninterrupted silence and horror at my fantasy that a capricious god might grant my impulsive wish and I would lose my children forever. That moment, indelibly stamped upon the memory of time, illustrates vividly the dilemmas of creativity and procreativity I seek to portray: at one moment, I want to drop the whole project to turn to household matters of grave importance; at the next, I want to see it through for its own value and for my love of the work. A hundred times—and not for the last time by any means—I have wondered, am I attempting a self-defeating task, trying to "conceive" in professional and familial ways at the same time? No matter how a mother designs her life—whether she stays home, works at home, works outside the home—most would admit that conflicts plague their attempts to resolve the questions of working and loving.

Women Provide the Goods

This sampling reflects in part the particular turmoil of the white, educated, and middle-class at the close of the twentieth century. But concerns about mothering are not concerns only for white, middle-class women. And the question of who cares for children appears as—even though it should not be—simply the mother's problem. This has been a powerful illusion cast by a post–World War II mindset which idealized the breadwinner husband and his homemaker wife at the culmination of a century of increasing isolation of the suburban housewife. Theology simply confirmed this illusion by giving it religious backing and otherwise ignoring the female experiences of reproducing the world as quite peripheral to authentic theological reflection.

White middle-class women have much to learn from the struggles of women in other racial and economic groups who have experienced this ideal in different ways. Some women "don't see conflicts" when stated as an either/or between "nest and the adventure," or motherhood and work. "We, black women," Toni Morrison declares, "do both. We don't find these places, these roles, mutually exclusive."[4] At the same time, on the first page of her historical study of African American women, work, and the family, Jacqueline Jones identifies the connections and tensions between black mother and black employee as central to the personhood of black women in American history.[5]

Many women have not encountered an overt opposition of public and private roles for a variety of reasons. Working-class women have had no choice but to manage reproductive and productive labors side by side in order to survive. Mothers of color have had to wage complicated battles on several fronts. They face not just gender bias but racial and economic discrimination. As a result, they have had to be independent centers of strength, essential for the survival of the group and seldom confined to the private domain.

Like purple is to lavender, in Alice Walker's words, the demands on many African-American mothers make the demands on most white women pale by comparison. White claims on black mothering have taken many women out of their own homes. The slave mother was perpetually caught between demands upon her mothering, internal and external to her own family. The emancipated mother, like Katie Cannon's great-grandmother, "walked hundreds of miles, from plantation to plantation, looking for the children that had been taken from her and sold as slaves . . . until she found all her children and brought the family back together."[6]

This pattern of working beyond the call of human duty to secure the survival of children and family, as well as caring for white children while leaving her own to be guarded by family, kin, and stranger, persists today.[7] The early feminist protests about the entrapments of the house-wife do not make much sense to those robbed of chances to establish safe, strong homes, or to those fighting to prepare their children for survival in a hostile, racist, discriminatory environment.[8] Rather, moth-erhood must be cherished to persist at all, even for the sake of the endurance of the larger group. Loss of self on the part of mothers has been a crucial factor in sustaining the African American community and cannot be entirely dismissed as sexist and exploitive.

A more fundamental oppressive experience, according to Toinette Eugene, is that of "being deprived at some time of a mother's attention because of the inordinate demands of a racist society competing for possession of her person."[9] From this vantage point, the relationship between African American men and women is also different. Male-female roles are less rigid. Equality often is more prevalent. Instead, the strength of the black female itself sometimes becomes the issue. Ultimately, solidarity between black women and black men is essential, over against the white feminist separatist strategies that set women against men.

In some important ways, then, the burdens of mothering and the dilemmas of work, love, and family of black women are different from those of white women. Consequently, many of the struggles and solu-tions have been and may continue to be different. At the same time, in the larger struggle of liberation, women—stay-at-home mothers, "work-ing" mothers, liberal, radical, social feminists, womanists, lesbians—must try not to undermine one another in our different but related struggles. For only in understanding the divergent forms that domina-tion assumes will the exploitation of all women and mothers end. On the one hand, the American ideal of "motherhood and apple pie"—the mother who stays home and bakes cookies—has a grip on the mindset of the American people that often reaches beyond class and race differ-ences. On the other, it is also critical to point out that it is an image that is itself built directly upon, and even sustained by, class and race distinc-tions.

Women and mothers do share at least one essential characteristic that crosses over the differences and becomes most apparent in the lives of poor women and women of color: "What all women have in common," asserts Hilda Scott, "is that they share most of the unpaid work of the world." The vast majority of women, whether mothers or not, are "poor in the absolute sense that they carry out an enormous amount of indispensable work without any remuneration whatsoever."[10] Dubbed "labors of love,"

> woman's unpaid work, her productive and reproductive labor for which she receives no remuneration, underpins the world's economy, yet it is peripheral to the world's economy as men define it, and therefore has no value. It is this that makes women a category of persons who are economically invisible, whose work is non-work, who have no experience or skills, who don't need a regular income because their husband supports them.
>
> How did men come to be the ones who define work and value? Is there something eternal and scientific about these definitions? Are they based on a "natural" division of tasks between women and men? Do women have different definitions than men, and how might work and value be defined in a non-sexist society?[11]

As unpaid reproductive labor is redistributed and given a minimal wage, it simply lands on the backs of poorer women and women of color. A society that relegates caring qualities to women and caring tasks to oppressed classes and races presents a complicated problem that touches everyone in distinct ways.

As one book title puts it, America as a society is struggling to figure out *Who Cares?*[12] Just as women have begun to claim some of the fruits of self-fulfillment and individualization, everyone, from politicians to scholars and studies like *Habits of the Heart,* have decried the dangers of rampant individualism and the decline of commitments to the common good and family values.[13] While these judgments may be partially justified, we must wonder about their accuracy in terms of the course of the lives of women and other oppressed groups in our society. Heretofore, unbridled, competitive self-interest has been allowed, even encouraged, but primarily on the part of certain privileged men in the public world of work. It has not been allowed other specific groups in our society.

It is not until others, women in particular, cross this boundary between self-fulfillment and self-sacrifice that we recognize the problems. Someone needs to keep a check on self-love, to keep tabs on the good of the community, to volunteer to help out, someone needs to clean up the messes, wipe bottoms, drooling mouths, and otherwise care for those who cannot care for themselves. But who? It has been mainly women and the underclasses that have borne the burden of domestic responsibilities. While the individualistic spirit of much of American society does pose problems, one must wonder how much of the uproar over individualism is about the collapse of a public-private dichotomy as women and minorities cross taboo dividing lines. And one must question whether a return to "family values," or community living as formerly understood, is an adequate or viable solution.

Dehumanizing codes of domestic labor denigrate all of us. Anxiety about "good housekeeping" and "keeping the peace" may be the primary anxieties of many white women. But these anxieties have mushroomed into a new list of anxieties that affect almost all American women: strife over domestic and economic responsibilities and security; divisive segregation of public work from private love; exploitation of reproductive labor; destabilization of the family; demise in community life and its underpinning structures. Poorer mothers and mothers of color confront these anxieties with fewer economic and social supports. For oppressed groups that rely on strong families as potential springboards for political action, for resistance to dominant culture, and for community organization and individual mobility, the destabilization of the family and community is a particularly acute problem.[14] As the workload of women worldwide grows heavier, it grows even more for the poor and the working class. And it grows heavier for mothers of all kinds.

On the Theological Platter

At this particular point in religious history, American religious traditions in general are struggling to reckon with the imperative of gender equality. No denomination in the United States has escaped unscathed, whether the reaction is a scramble to reassert the headship of husbands in some evangelical circles or repeated unsatisfactory attempts to issue a new pastoral letter on women, in the case of Roman Catholic bishops. Many mainline congregations accept women in more equal positions of leadership than was usual three decades ago, but offer little relevant discussion about much of the gender-related strife that has accrued in the intervening years in the lives of most members.

Even if religion is no longer a central determining force in shaping public morality, this general state of affairs in religion has consequences for society. In society at large, the attempts to move women into work and men into families, with little reconstruction of the religious doctrines that shape ideologies of work and love, have failed in many respects. Try as we might, American society cannot secure a full generative life for men and women without serious reconsideration of prevalent religious models and definitions of generativity. Religious metaphors of work and family continue to influence most people more than they realize.

Broadly speaking, Roman Catholicism has sanctioned procreation—"be fruitful and multiply" (Gen. 1:28)—and Protestantism has sanctioned vocation—"fill the earth and subdue it . . . till it and keep it" (Gen. 1:28; 2:15). Roman Catholic tradition has long affirmed the procreative capacities and requirements of human existence, associating these almost totally with physical reproductive processes. At the same time, genuine religious life required a celibacy untainted by acts of procreativity. With the Reformation, Protestant traditions countered the priority placed upon celibacy by sanctioning the special religious vocation of all of life's work, including domestic toil, and by fashioning a powerful work ethic which bestowed salvific powers on human labor. Work was understood as a direct expression of a unique human dignity and as an affirmation of divine election. Ironically, this sanctification of all of life's work as holy left women with less rather than more access to a specifically religious vocation than under Catholicism.

But for many reasons, doctrines of both procreation and vocation, and their corresponding ethics, have largely lost power and meaning in the last several decades of this century. Abiding by their commands no longer assures the promised abundant life. The Protestant work ethic has been taken over by a corporate and largely male industrial work force. In the process, it has degenerated from a communal ideal into an individualized compulsive workaholism, focused on this-worldly productivity and acquisition. And since the 1960s, the Roman Catholic procreative ethic that made physical reproduction so central to Christian marriage has had to reckon with the equal, if not greater, importance of the personal relationship of mutuality and fidelity between spouses. The practices of conception and contraception of many Roman Catholics are far removed from those dictated by doctrinal decree.

In both cases, part of the problem has been the almost total dismissal of the sanctity of women's experience as women and as mothers. Both traditions have long collapsed a woman's vocational and procreational roles into a single monochromatic function: the social, biological role of motherhood. And the religious ideal of biological motherhood simply excludes to some extent working women, lesbians, and single women. A woman's work and love are restricted to husband and children; a man's, to his work. Under the resilient reign of these religious metaphors of human fulfillment, many people in the twentieth century have simply parceled up the generative tasks of public vocation and private procreation between men and women, to the dangerous point of impoverishing and endangering the domains of both work and home, as well as themselves and society at large.

Mainline Protestant traditions have been especially quiet about generative responsibilities. In contrast to more conservative traditions, many people in mainline congregations now admit that fathers do not always know best. But they have not determined who does, if fathers don't, or, more precisely, they no longer know exactly what is best. Many people in the pews, especially those under age fifty, consider theological doctrines of male headship and female submission, narrowly extrapolated from Ephesians 5:22, to be wrong. When these household codes appear as part of the worship lectionary, if they are read at all, one can practically feel the dissent, as telling looks between mothers, daughters, and sometimes husbands and fathers, ripple through the congregation. Women and men, most seem to agree, are equal before God.

But exactly what this means for the common life of work and love in churches, in families, and in jobs is less clear. Contrary to early feminist efforts, the ambiguous meanings of equality surface not so much around still-unresolved questions about inclusive God language, or even female leadership, but most explicitly when concrete chores arise, whether within the home or within the church community itself. Women are elders, even ministers, and we may have slightly fewer prayers directed to "Our Father," but who runs the Sunday school program now?

Protestant heritage has undoubtedly shaped convictions about the elements of a faithful generative life. I can readily identify four premises that have crept into my living and being: (1) family and parenthood are valued as vocations in their own right, as worthy, or even more worthy, than the celibate religious life; (2) love and children are signs of God's gift and blessing; (3) work is valued as a way for people to sustain themselves, provide for others, and otherwise collaborate with the living community—never simply as a means for making money; and at the very same time, (4) the call to follow God relativizes all familial and vocational commitments as secondary to the reign of God, the coming of the kingdom, and the new ecclesia, with its reconstituted family of another sort.

As powerful as these ideals are, I know them as much from my academic study of religion as from any graphic memory of lessons taught and learned in churches. And there is little in current mainline practice that offers guidance to the way these ideals are best embodied in the midst of life's daily throes. Even worse, a great deal that I have learned about exhaustive self-sacrifice, sinful self-assertion, the trappings of embodiment, and the place of women and mothers in biblical stories and religious traditions—even the Protestant dismissal of Mary's role as mother of God and of feminine images of the deity—serves me very poorly indeed.

Most male theologians who have speculated about religious symbols and the nature of human fulfillment have been far removed from the experiences of mothers and the immediate demands of the youngest generation. The very success that gives these theologians voice and prestige depends precisely upon their leaving child care and home care to others. Domestic and family demands enfeeble, it has been thought, genuine creativity. The conflicts between these demands and creativity seldom make their way into theological writing. The "special relations" and particular affections between mother, father, and child detract, it is claimed, from the general distance needed to reflect theologically upon universal relationships of love and justice. Most religious images of work and love reflect this detached state. The foremost religious thinkers have seldom taken seriously the knowledge that a mother and child might have about divine and human love, justice, power, and grace, or the complexities that accompany their attempts to realize these values.

New Recipes, New Ingredients

People are hungry for stories that belong to more encompassing, believable narratives about the course and meaning of life. The accounts of fifty-two feminist mothers in London, Leicester, and Helsinki, interviewed by sociologist Tuula Gordon, illustrate this well. Embarked upon careers, these women reject motherhood as traditionally defined, and then, upon commencing motherhood, they reject careers as traditionally defined. Challenging both spheres, while attempting to redesign an adequate life purpose, fosters a perpetual sense of transgression and failure. These women talk about the hazards of crossing the forbidden boundaries of social expectations and the structurally established distinctions between public and private, man and woman, work and love, production and reproduction. This trespassing produces parallel feelings of "failure as a mother" and "failure as a feminist." Possessing no strategy or story to reconcile the public world of work and the private world of mothering, many women have the "feeling of always doing something wrong."[15]

Designs for new stories abound. Plenty of books—books aimed at capturing popular sales, like Shreve's, and books of a more serious nature—mark the moment. Besides *Remaking Motherhood,* we have *Recreating Motherhood; Inventing Motherhood; Hard Choices; Loving and Working;* and *Women Changing Work.*[16] Alongside these are a number of books about men: *New Men, New Minds; How Men Feel; Working Wives, Working Husbands;* and *The Nurturing Father.*[17] The lists go on. Many books interview and report. Some analyze and make pessimistic predictions. A few, like Shreve's, forecast positive outcomes to the current turmoil in gender roles. Almost all endorse similar strategies to alter the anguish—increased gender-role consciousness and flexibility, greater participation of men in home and family life, better day-care and leave policies, flextime, shift work, shortened hours, after-school programs.

As helpful as these alternative blueprints for survival are—and they are a good beginning—they are partial. They do not usually speak directly to the moral and philosophical anguish experienced by Gordon's interviewees and many other women. Ultimately, the problems studied in most of these books are not just pragmatic problems of job and gender strategies, but moral and spiritual quandaries about how to live life. Many books simply scratch the surface of these quandaries—the hopes and guilt over vocation and duty; the resilient faith in human becoming, and the failures and the loneliness of choosing a different path; the joy in creation and in the gift of children; the despair of attending to constant demands and forsaking the gift; and the perpetual moral, religious, and even soteriological ambiguity of all gender strategies. This book seeks to delve below the surface and touch upon some of these issues.

Below the surface, I pick up the warning signals of a pending danger: The reproduction of the species is becoming so burdensome that individuals cannot solve all the problems. Having and taking care of children in a hostile environment becomes a heroic option. The bearing and the rearing of children takes considerable energy and presence; it is not to be lightly dismissed. A theology that does not make room for the demands, responsibilities, and joys of relating to children as a fundamental part of life is a theology on the verge of its own demise. A theology that begins to listen more attentively to its mothers and children will gain insight into the demands and dynamics of nurture, the creation of personhood, the blessings of mutuality, and the values of the gift of life. And until theology begins to speak with a mother's voice, initial efforts to alter public policy, or innovative schemes to consolidate new gender roles, remain partial and limited. Hearing the challenge of the mother's voice to distorted ethical and religious definitions of love, self-fulfillment, self-sacrifice, work, vocation, and the generative life, is a requisite step in the longer-term project of broader social change.

❦ ❦ ❦

CHAPTER TWO

Generativity in Male Theory and Men's Lives

A LESSON IN EXCLUSIVE LANGUAGE

[God] said, "Take your son, your only son Isaac, whom you love, and go to the land of Moriah, and offer him there as a burnt offering on one of the mountains that I shall show you."

Genesis 22:2

We are told in Deuteronomy 8:18, "Thou shalt remember the Lord thy God, for 'tis he that gives thee power to get wealth."

Cotton Mather

The headlines have been about women's liberation, but the changes for men . . . are no less real. . . . Men have not always responded gracefully and happily to these changes.

Don Welch, *Macho Isn't Enough!*

A few notable biblical stories provide a precedent for fathers to treat their children, their sons, as expendable. Although God stops Abraham as he prepares to sacrifice his son Isaac, church tradition still has commended Abraham for his unwavering fidelity. And God Himself—and here the pronoun reflects the perceived reality—gives up his Son to save the world. Although not intended, perhaps, these narratives convey an implicit message about the expendability of children and relationships for a greater ultimate cause.

When the story of father Abraham is imaginatively retold from the mother's perspective, such as in the work of Ellen Umansky, Sarah angrily protests Abraham's gross miscalculation of what God requires.[1] Heedless, or even thoughtful, sacrifice of children, she already knows, is not what God requires. Is Abraham's religious delusion the first popular example of generativity gone awry?

Women like Sarah, Rebekah, Rachel, Hagar, and Tamar, who have quite significant roles in less familiar biblical narratives, might say so. It is these women who act in religious history to convert sacrifice into a means to gain a more ultimate end, the providing of connections. They provide connections between men, and ultimately, through procreation, assure the continuation of the Israelites. In many cases, these matriarchs engage in overtly less noble acts of trickery or deception, in order to further the prospects of their sons or husbands. But on some level, God blesses the trickery as a prophetic challenge to the well-laid, but distorted generative plans of finite men.[2] It may be time to listen to new narratives.

In the 1950s, when life-cycle theorist Erik Erikson first articulated his timely idea of "generativity" and "stagnation" as a primary conflict of mature adult development, he happened upon a psychological concept that has wider normative implications than he ever intended. Freud had once declared that the sane, or nonneurotic, person was someone able to work and to love. Erikson, never satisfied with Freud's claim that the potential for this development was set in the first few stages of life, spent years attempting to elaborate and fine-tune Freud's deceptively simply prescription. In its place, he proposed that healthy, mature adults must successfully adjudicate the tensions of two focal developmental crises—first, the clash between intimacy and isolation, and then the clash between generativity and stagnation. He chose the term *generativity* as a metaphor to encompass several facets of adult work and love: procreativity, productivity, and creativity. Yet the expression has far greater range than any one of these activities alone.

As compelling as the idea of generativity may be, however, there are problems, problems in Erikson's original conceptualization, in its enactment in contemporary society, and in the religious values which frame that enactment—values Erikson himself never fully understood. This calls for a second reading.

That task begins with psychology and with Erikson, the originator of the idea of generativity, because modern psychologies are powerful players in shaping the way people today think about themselves and their hopes in life. When it comes to questions about mothers and work, love and intimacy, psychology has operated as a quasi-religious culture-forming body of knowledge. When people need help in solving dilemmas of work and love, they turn not so much to church and synagogue, not to sacred scriptures and theologians, but more often to the self-help bookshelves, popular talk shows, and the therapeutic interventions that the modern discipline of psychology has spawned. So, what has psychology, and, more specifically, Erikson, told us about generativity and human fulfillment?

The "Norm" for Development: A Man's Expert Definition

Generativity, in its first appearances in psychological theory, was generativity for and by men. This was not the result of malicious intent on the part of prominent psychoanalysts and psychologists; it was simply the accepted view at the time modern psychology took root. Male generativity was the norm and the central subject for exploration; female generativity was a subset with narrower, specialized boundaries, an exception to the rule of male generativity, and subject to male whims and definitions. Female generativity came up for discussion when it became a problem that affected and related to men.

Female generativity did become a more obvious problem as Western society entered the industrial age. Prior to the Industrial Revolution, women possessed indispensable skills and roles, particularly as midwives and respected healers of the family and community, despite the hierarchical and patriarchal structures that defined the place of women below men. They produced clothes; planted, pickled, and preserved food; manufactured medicines, soap, and candles. Their participation in human society, while under the rule of men, assumed an authority of its own, essential to the survival and well-being of the community. Women had vital work to do and contributions to make, however much this was directed by the edicts of men.

The Industrial Revolution displaced this authority and created what Barbara Ehrenreich and Deirdre English call the "woman question" or "woman problem" that troubles psychologists and others to this day.[3] The market economy that created a new world of work for men shattered the previous unity of work and home, public and private, and forged a line between them taut with moral tension. As women's productive activities were engulfed by the factory system, they lost a sphere of significant influence. Expelled to the increasingly restricted private domain of home, many women lost their last few threads of connection to public life. Without the former roles they had played in the community's survival, they found themselves bound anew to the seeming trivialities and insignificances of daily bodily existence. Not surprisingly, the "woman question"—What would become of women in the modern world?—suddenly captured the modern urban imagination and became a gripping public issue. What are women going to do with themselves now?

But who responded initially? Men of the establishment—physicians, philosophers, scientists—took up this question and produced a surge of books and articles. Freud's particular version—What do women want?—continues to resound through the halls of the academy and the offices of analysts. His answer, like the majority of the modern scientific answers, rested upon the expropriation of the ancient powers of women and the denial or destruction of the "accumulated lore of generations of mothers" and former "networks of skill-sharing."[4] In place of these autonomous sources of women's knowledge, we have what Ehrenreich and English call *For Her Own Good: 150 Years of the Experts' Advice to Women.*

The intense resistance of mainstream science to the actual voices of women persists. Research on health continues to ponder the oddities of female nature, all the while excluding women and the lore of mothers, both as subjects and as authors. From this vantage point, the differences between theories of human, or more exactly, *male* development and women's experience have signified a problem in women, not an oversight or error in male theory. Only in recent years have women begun to challenge this biased assumption, claimed the validity of women's experience, and pointed out the differences as omissions in male developmental theory.

Erikson, and behind him, Freud, exemplify the pattern. They number among the more powerful modern "experts" who sought to solve women's "hysteria," in Freud's case, or to explain the emptiness of their "inner space," in Erikson's. In place of religious guidelines, they established psychological standards for healthy development and a "normal" life cycle which continue to captivate the American public. Despite their interest, and even their extensive therapeutic experiences with women, the assumed subject of most of their writings remains men. When discussing women, they presume to define their "true nature" over against male standards, with a "certainty and a sense of . . . infallibility rarely found in the secular world."[5]

Freud conflates the generic with the masculine and mistakes the woman's lack of a penis as an inborn defect. With man as the measure and woman the deviation, a woman's pleasure in pregnancy and children can be none other than a desire to have a penis. Any other desire represents a refusal to accept the fact of her castration. To the ears of the mother caught up in the fullness of her pregnancy, or those of women with other creative talents, this sounds absurd. But Freud heard but a few themes in the complex symphony of women's lives.

Women's major fulfillment in adulthood, in Freud's analysis, involves by necessity a frustrated quest to receive from males, whether father, husband, or son, what they lack by nature. In her work and love, says Freud, an adult woman has three choices: (1) neurosis; (2) a "masculinity complex"—that is, a refusal to accept the female's castrated state; or (3) optimally "normal femininity."[6] This latter category, the best for which women can hope, is actually a regressive, fixated stage in the "normal" or, more precisely, male development. "Normal femininity" entails the passive acceptance of a biological fate, and even a masochistic, narcissistic resignation to a secondary, dependent destiny as a vessel of male activity and a vicarious appendage of male offspring. Such are the characteristics of "definitive femininity." In a word, women can never attain full, mature humanity.

Freud's interpretation gives no more credibility to a woman's ability to develop as an autonomous, rational individual, capable of the higher realms of intelligence and moral discipline, than did the early church

Fathers, Aristotle, Aquinas, and other classic figures. Psychological facts about women's lower nature replaced classical theological and philosophical doctrines, but with the added vengeance of the claim to objective, scientific truth. Equally troubling, they replaced religious values, which at least formally espoused the created worth of every human being, regardless of gender and other distinctions, with a value "neutrality" that evaded normative considerations.

The pregnant mother, perhaps one of the most powerful symbols of human creativity and transformation, is stripped of her potency. Perhaps, we might surmise, Freud overlooked this symbol because he unconsciously felt his inability to bear children as his own inborn deficiency. Not surprisingly, general literature on the wishes of boys and men to bear, suckle, and rear babies has been "repeatedly lost," largely as a result of "male analysts' defenses against their own womb and breast envy."[7]

But no amount of speculation about Freud's repressed envy will undo the damages of his degrading depiction of childbearing and women's other generative possibilities. Early on, several within the field of psychology—Helene Deutsch, Alfred Adler, Karen Horney, and others—challenged these orthodox Freudian notions, acknowledging the existential framework of penis envy as envy of social (not ontological or natural) domination. Such appeals, however, did little to alter the bias against women that lies at the heart of modern psychology. Although psychoanalytical ideas about the role of the unconscious and of sexuality certainly have offered women a unique methodological tool with which to dismantle oppressive views of women, the basic psychoanalytic constructions, unfortunately, also have served to perpetuate the idea of women's inherent inferiority. The mother, when she appears in psychoanalytic theory at all, is primarily an "object" or "self-object" in the child's psychological world, and both a source of and an example of pathology.

Generativity and the "Inner Space"

Does Erikson simply join Freud in perpetuating this sexist sociocultural consensus as biological and psychological fact? In some ways, yes, even when he departs from Freud. Yet, in other important ways, no. True to America in the 1950s, the crux of female identity according to

Erikson involved giving up her attachments to her own parental family and committing herself to a man and to the care of his children. Her well-being therefore rested upon her outward appearance, the success of her "search for the man . . . by whom she wishes to be sought," and finally, the particular characteristics of her children.[8] A woman's generative identity depended upon the private world of intimacy, children, and home, whereas a man's self-verification came from "labor's challenge" and a *"love for his works and ideas."*[9] A woman gave and received through the labors of love, and had few other loves; a man gave and received through the love of labor.

As the debate over gender roles challenged this division even as Erikson issued it, he himself observed in 1974 that as a man and a Freudian, "I couldn't possibly be anywhere else and . . . considering where I came from, I was doing all right being where I was."[10] In his own way and in the manner of his time, he wanted to include women: "When I speak of man," as he put it, "I emphatically include woman."[11]

At the same time, however, Erikson does include women in a new way. He deserves credit for admitting man's strong envy of maternal capacity, even if his depiction of this capacity is a bit romanticized and simplified. At some point, he notes, every boy and man is disquieted by women, who "produce what in all its newborn weakness, is and remains, after all, the most miraculous human creation in the universe: and it breathes!"[12] While his marvel at a woman's pursuit of the activities "consonant with the possession of ovaries, a uterus, and a vagina" blinds Erikson to other sources of female identity, it also opens up new possibilities.[13] Where Freud strips the pregnant body of its potency, Erikson almost gets carried away with it. But in getting carried away, he at least moves beyond Freud.

Erikson not only checks the distortions of Freud's reading: Where Freud saw a lack—penis envy—and damned the potential of women to develop fully, Erikson saw a gain—the "existence of a productive inner-bodily space safely set in the center of female form and carriage."[14] Although the depiction of female generativity in terms of an empty cavity central to her being has obvious limitations, Erikson at least attempts to correct the failures of psychoanalytic theory to grasp the nature of female identity.

Merely asserting a capacity rather than a defect begins to affirm that women have possibilities for a mature womanhood, other than the passive, masochistic existence and "ubiquitous compensation neurosis" of Freud's women. Although motherhood has enslaved women, the solution, Erikson believes, is not "to claim that there is no instinctual need for parenthood and that parenthood is *nothing but* social convention and coercion."[15] Instead, he gives this particular generative act a certain priority. As Pamela Daniels observes when she applied for a position as a teaching fellow in Erikson's undergraduate course on the life cycle, "motherhood somehow enhanced," rather than detracted from her qualifications.[16]

While a variety of generative activities contribute to society, parenthood affords the first and the most primal generative encounter for many. Anatomy is not destiny, but it cannot be disregarded, for it enriches human horizons. Without this experience or a comparable generative involvement, many people fall prey to the "mental deformation of self-absorption," and society falls prey to the darker sides of modernity's technological advancements.[17] For Erikson, an "ecology" built around the "fact that the human fetus must be carried inside the womb for a given number of months, and that the infant must be suckled or, at any rate, raised" provides the strongest challenge to a modern male ecology built around conquering the outer spaces through escalating, self-aggrandizing materialistic acquisition.[18] The superficialities and destructiveness of this kind of generativity, Erikson believes, has brought the Western world to the brink of disaster. He romanticizes what the "mothers of the species" can do to redirect this downward spiral of modernity's productivity. But he is not wrong to hope that mothers might bring a new kind of vision.

On the one hand, therefore, with a only a slight change of phrase from Freud, Erikson says that a woman's fulfillment rests upon filling her "inner space" with the seeds of the offspring of "chosen men." But on the other hand, with this inner space comes "a biological, psychological, and ethical commitment to take care of human infancy."[19] Despite the parallels with Freud in the former phrase, the latter represents a distinctive contribution.

For the commitment to care, according to Erikson, is not a duty placed upon women alone, but an essential and highly prized virtue for all human beings. The "strength of the generations," and "by this I mean a basic disposition underlying all varieties of human values systems" depends on it. Care—learning how to care, enacting care, fostering care—these human activities ground life and keep the cycle of generations secure in its spiraling axis. All mature adults must acquire the virtue of care, the "widening concern for what has been generated by love, necessity, or accident," and overcome the ambivalence that naturally adheres to the work one has generated. Generativity, or the "concern for establishing and guiding the next generation," defines adult maturity for both women and men.[20]

The Ideal of Generativity

Given the generative dilemmas of modernity, Erikson declares, nothing less than a "new religious context," or "guiding vision," with "new and convincing duties as well as rights" will suffice.[21] In making such assertions, Erikson departs more from orthodox psychoanalysis than he himself cared to admit. He concedes that although originally, psychoanalysis strove to differentiate itself from theology and philosophy, psychology itself must now confess that it often functions as a positive ethical science. It does define "normality" and influence history and culture, and it must be recognized and judged on that basis.

Although Erikson saw *generativity* as simply the primary focus of mature adult development, there are ways in which the term begins to take on a vital life of its own, both in the work of Erikson and as others adopt the idea. The work of practical theologian Don S. Browning is a good example. In *Generative Man*, Browning lifts the idea of generativity out of its embeddedness in the life cycle. He claims that it is an implicit moral and religious assumption that operates at the core of Erikson's psychology. Moreover, it is a more ethically adequate mandate than the ethical premises of comparable modern psychologists.[22]

In other words, the ethical and quasi-religious values behind Erikson's descriptions of generativity as a life stage infiltrate and shape his otherwise psychological discussion of human development. Generativity is not just a phase of adult growth. It is an encompassing orientation to life that is particularly well-suited to the problems of modernity. The imperative to take care of what and who one has produced is the foundation upon which the earliest life stages are built and sustained. Without adequate generative activity on the part of adults, the young will suffer and the life of the human community itself will wither and die. Erikson firmly believed this, whether or not he stated it explicitly as a belief, and out of this belief emerged many of his compelling psychological observations about trust and mistrust in infancy and identity confusion for adolescents.

The virtue of care and the idea of generativity, then, is at once the second to last stage in the "eight ages of man" and the ethical axis of the cycle of generations as a whole. As a stage in adult development, all those who successfully weather the conflict between generativity and stagnation in the second to last stage, then move to life's final phase, having acquired the new "virtue" or "ego strength" of care. As the ethical axis of the cycle of generations as a whole, Erikson implicitly promotes a broader orientation to life, described by Browning as a "culture of care" and a "generative ethic," which governs each step in ego growth.[23] This ethic requires an initial receptivity to care, and then an emerging capacity to care for others in families, communities, and, ultimately, succeeding generations.

On the one hand, Erikson never specifically articulates this view. He frequently sees generativity as merely one phase in adult maturity and defines its tasks in gender-restrictive ways. But the vision of generativity behind the specific generative tasks has broader significance. The highest good, whatever the specific act, is the "maintenance of life," or the "regeneration of the cycle of generations." On occasion, Erikson discusses generativity in terms of "mutuality," "an ecology of mutual activation," or even as a modern version of the Golden Rule: "Truly worthwhile acts enhance a mutuality between the doer and the other—a mutuality which strengthens the doer even as it strengthens the other."[24] Human action, male and female, is judged in terms of its accountability to the other human beings brought into this world.

"His Work Was His Life"

At this point in Erikson's conception of the generative act, his theory has some affinity with feminist theologies and, with the addition of a feminist critique, implications for contemporary dilemmas of family and work. He was certainly not a feminist before his time. He was even a bit troubled by the "new 'feminist' alarm" over generative possibilities. But in his attempt to reclaim the power of human relationality that evolves in inner, rather than outer spaces, he was on to something.

But the term, and the ideal of generativity itself, seem ripe for misappropriation. Although Erikson readily perceives the heart of America's "identity crisis," and even discusses the problems caused by *"generative frustration,"* he does not anticipate the extent of the current generative crisis. Nor did Browning begin to suspect that, as a theoretical stance, a generativity that is removed from first-hand knowledge of domestic labor and child care is distorted and weak indeed. Given the pervasive condescending attitude toward women during his era, Freud's rationalization of oppressive social structures as inherent flaws in female biological nature should not surprise us. And given his social and historical location, Erikson could not have done other than amplify the idea of generativity along sex-stereotyped lines. More troubling, however, is the perpetuation of these patterns in human lives. In the concrete actualities of life, male-defined generativity is still the norm.

Studies of the enactment of generativity in the lives of men are quite revealing. According to developmental psychologist Daniel J. Levinson and his colleagues, and others who rely on Erikson's theory, when the norm of generativity is translated into men's lives, we find a steady drive for vocational productivity, with concern for care, procreativity, children, and home as an afterthought. For most men, generativity, in its fuller sense, does not truly determine action until much later, after a "mid-life crisis," if at all. The typical pattern for "normal" persons involves "becoming one's own man," or climbing the ladder of success in the hierarchical public world of labor.

In a word, male-dominated psychological and moral theory, as well as male-run institutions, have come to think about and value generativity largely in terms of *producing*. Rearranging gender roles is one thing; transforming the power of this view of generativity in our corporate institutions and the dominant culture is another. Browning tempers this view somewhat by emphasizing that generativity ultimately means a *taking care of* what (although not particularly who) one has produced. Erikson himself argues that he uses the term broadly, as a metaphor for an adulthood centered on relationships, not simply as another term for career advancement. Generativity includes productivity and creativity, but these popular synonyms, he insists, cannot and should not replace it.[25]

But, in fact, they have. As Browning and Erikson insinuate, and as Levinson's study, *Seasons in a Man's Life*, demonstrates, there is a progressive restriction of the ideal. Levinson's empirical survey of the patterns of male development, based upon biographical interviews of forty men, age 17 to 47, illustrates that most men pursue generating at the cost of preserving, and they pursue producing at the cost of caring. While the analysis of the interviews is based partly on Erikson's life-cycle theory, the actual lives of men contradict some of the ideals of Erikson and Browning's abstract theories. Both Erikson and Browning might have critiqued this distortion of the ideal of generativity in the lives of men, but neither attended to gender disparities in the enactment of generativity.

Levinson's study captures an essential feature of the pattern of male development: In our society, as early as age 17, the product of a man's work is *the* foremost "vehicle for the fulfillment or negation of central aspects of the self."[26] Adulthood means *generativity*, but is now defined largely in a technical, product-oriented sense. The men studied pass through Erikson's phase of generativity by placing its focuses in the sphere of work, and not in connection with others, whether friends, colleagues, wife, or children. Adult men have few intimate relationships. When they choose to pursue relationships, they are byproducts of mature adult development, and often a means to another end, but seldom the ideal, point, or goal. Relationships are viewed instrumentally. They help support "the Dream," but are not essential to its fulfillment. The wife, "special (loved and loving) woman," is the "true mentor," principally because she tries to further her husband's advancement:

> Her special quality lies in her connection to the young man's Dream. She helps to animate the part of the self that contains the Dream. She facilitates his entry into the adult world and his pursuit of the Dream . . . shares it, believes in him as its hero, gives it her blessing, joins him . . . and creates a "boundary space" within which his aspirations can be imagined and his hopes nourished.[27]

That a man might learn to give comparable support and create "space" for a woman's or a child's dreams seems almost ludicrous. Or at least it does not appear an essential aspect of development in the lives of the men studied. While women strive to foster such space and base their self-image around the question, "Am I giving enough?" men ask, "Am I a doer?" Giving becomes an "added luxury" after a man has paid his dues in productivity, according to psychologist Jean Baker Miller.[28] While most women "drift" as they struggle to find a way to interweave family and work in their life Dream, the Dream for men is often pursued single-mindedly and remains almost indistinguishable from occupational goals.[29]

Other researchers, like developmentalist Douglas C. Kimmel, author of the textbook *Adulthood and Aging,* and George Vaillant, in *Adaptation to Life,* join Levinson as examples of the increasing constriction of Erikson's term and Browning's normative ideal. Kimmel defines generativity as a "sense of productive accomplishment," sought in work or as a parent, "so that there will be something one has done that will outlive oneself." But is a child "something one has done"? Odder still, he does not even mention generativity in his chapter on "Families and Singles." He actually places rearing children and managing a home in parentheses when listing factors that help resolve the crisis of generativity, such as success and satisfaction in one's job.[30] Raising children, ordering the home, preserving family traditions, securing friendships, and community are subsidiary. They are undervalued, parenthetically reserved for women.

For Vaillant, generativity simply refers to a mid-life stage of "Career Consolidation," focused upon achievements and rewards.[31] The idea of caring for the "production," much less caring for children, drops out of the picture completely.

A Test Case: New Reproductive Technologies (NRTs)

The debate over NRTs offers an interesting test case for these observations. In the scenario painted by Levinson and others, part of men's desire to have their own biological offspring would seem to arise more from the need to make and acquire a production uniquely one's own, to enhance one's sense of achievement, than from a need to create and take care of a new life. We must wonder how well men who participate in NRTs, whether as researcher or as spouse, can empathize with the generative anxieties of women, or can assume the necessary generative responsibilities.

The discussion of generativity and NRTs is situated in the broader context of a long tradition of men's control over women's sexuality and reproduction, which continues to this day. Some feminists have interpreted reproductive research, developed and applied primarily by male physicians, researchers, and businessmen, as one more step in the use and abuse of women's generative abilities. As early as 3100–600 BCE, as villages became agricultural communities, according to Gerda Lerner in *The Creation of Patriarchy*, women became resources as commodities of exchange, able to work and to create intertribal family ties.[32] It is women's sexuality and reproductive capacity that is the valued commodity. Although many people may not overtly see a woman's biological potential as a commodity, it is within this cultural context that interest in NRTs developed and where discussion of reproductive generativity often occurs.

Not surprisingly, evaluations of reproduction and NRTs have tended to focus upon the "product of pregnancy and childbirth (the foetus, the infant) over the mother herself."[33] Note how easily the woman carrying the child is ignored in well-known court-ordered obstetrical interventions. In the case of Angela Carder, a 28-year-old woman, 26 weeks pregnant and dying of cancer in June of 1987, the product—the baby—becomes central. Contrary to the wishes of husband, parents, obstetrician, and her attorney, and in the midst of Angela's own ambivalence, the court ordered delivery of the baby by caesarean section. The baby died two hours later; Angela, two days later.[34]

Or consider the labels "*test-tube* babies," "*artificial* insemination," and "*surrogate* mother." Each term diminishes the real work required of women: babies may begin in the test tube, but the time spent there remains insignificant compared to that spent in the womb; the only artificial aspect of insemination is the restriction of the man's participation, since the woman's participation is far from artificial; and surrogacy still involves heavy burdens upon the woman and is less a substitution than a shared labor.[35] In all three cases, apart from relatively minor laboratory manipulations, the demands upon the woman's body, psyche, and spirit while bearing a fetus and conceiving a baby still occur, not to mention the months or years of breast-feeding and days of toilet training to follow. How many men fret over the latter? No doubt public policies might receive a different hearing if they did.

In a society so heavily committed to high productivity, the idea of caring for the "production" can drop out completely. In the case of Baby M, in which the Sorkow decision upheld the validity of surrogate contracts and awarded custody to Bill Stern, the sperm donor and biological father, it is Betsy, his wife, who will stay home and take care of the child.[36] It is women who bear an inordinate degree of responsibility for "maintaining and regenerating" the cycle of generations. The tasks of generativity remain unevenly divided, granting men the power to produce and the entitlement to products, but leaving women with the demanding responsibility of caring for what or who is produced.

In the focus on performance and results, people risk equating the birth and rearing of a child with product-oriented manufacturing, a metaphor that will never do. Indeed, hasn't the "climbing the ladder" motif already crept into the fascination with NRTs, subtly transferring to motherhood the sense that all women can or should perform the achievement of having a child, to acquire a product of their own? In one sense, however, not even biology can determine ownership, although it may have an important role in determining responsibility. Current discussions about reproduction mislead persons into believing otherwise.

This whole discussion takes on immediate relevance as the battle over abortion heats up to a new level of antagonism and even life-threatening violence on the part of those "pro-life." Many justifiably assert, as does Catholic moral theologian Richard McCormick, the "claims of nascent life upon us."[37] But they assert these claims without authentic regard for the more complicated but equally valid claims of the lives of children and mature adults. That is, persons believe that they can abstract the moral debate about the life of a fetus from the troubling questions of caring for the children, once born.

At the present moment, mothers bear the major onus. In the last several decades, the range of this responsibility has grown from physical provision to emotional, social, and intellectual development. The "myth of maternal omnipotence" and the "fantasy of the perfect mother"—apt phrases coined by sociologists Nancy Chodorow and Susan Contratto— put almost all blame or credit for the child's behavior and well-being on the mother.[38] Fathers do not typically share this responsibility, except perhaps financially, and in the case of many aborted fetuses, economic support would not have been forthcoming for the children. Women know the weight they bear and the blood they shed. In a real sense, men do not. They do not experience the "claims of nascent life" or the claims of young children's lives. In quantitative measures of time alone, women do.

55

Cogs in the Wheels

For better and for worse, men have been both the avid disciples and the primary cogs in the wheels of production. In terms of actual power and money, capital accumulation has rewarded men far more than women. On another scale, it has precluded a humane life. Drugs, heart disease, suicide, homelessness, reduced life expectancy, workaholism, isolation from family by the pressures of work and the circumstances of divorce—all afflict men, especially minority and lower-class men, at higher rates than women, although women are close behind.

In the two decades since Erikson's forebodings about the destructive side effects of modernity, conditions in America's workplace have only worsened. Since 1974, real wages have stopped rising. Maintaining the life-style enjoyed on one income in the 1950s now requires two incomes. Contrary to the initial hopes that modern technology would bring a shorter work week, the average work week, according to a Lou Harris poll, had lengthened from 40.6 hours in 1973 to 46.6 hours in 1987. For professionals, the work week is even longer: 52 hours.[39] One commentator observes that the growing time crunch is "a major social problem that has reached crisis proportions over the past 20 years."[40]

There are ways in which the advanced technology of today oddly turns against us. Contrary to the hopes that technology would make life easier, it often speeds it up and makes it more complicated. New gadgetry like FAX machines, car phones, voicemail, electronic mail, and call waiting deceptively intensify the daily workload, rather than lessen it.

There are many reasons why the proclivity toward productivity and workaholism has only intensified. Americans have inherited a deeply ingrained work ethic but seldom stop to question or reevaluate it. If they did stop to consider the way they think about work, they might discover that a work ethic is not just some outgrown eighteenth-century Puritan relic, but an integral, ongoing reflection on work's meaning as part of life. They might discover that the infamous Protestant work ethic of the Puritans has degenerated from a view of work as a means to ensure the well-being of the human community to an excuse to seek one's own personal profit.

This work ethic spawned the American dream, which promises a better life to those who work hard. This dream, however, is relevant to a shrinking number of people. For many, both the ethic and the dream have backfired. While the Protestant work ethic began as a communal ideal that saw industrious labor as a sign of one's divine election within a religious context, it has ended instead by providing a piety and cultural context that condones self-righteous individual achievement, selfish self-sufficiency, and ruthless ambition.[41]

The work ethic made work a calling and a source of human self-worth, thus making idleness a sin. In this view, however, it was all too easy to forget the delicate balance between work and the contemplations of sabbath rest, the essential relationship between work and one's vocation before God. It became easy to blame the jobless and poor rather than seek to help them. The American dream worked during periods of rapid economic growth, hiding the division of wealth and labor that allots 80 percent of the riches to the top 20 percent of society. It fares poorly, however, during periods of slower economic growth. The hard work of many women and minorities has had little effect on making the dream a reality. Success is more contingent upon others than the dream and its ethic admit.

Yet the fire of the American dream burns on, fanned to new heights by popular culture, the media, and an economy predicated on ever-increasing profits. A capitalistic economy, driven by the creation of new desires, plays on the infinity of human desire and rides right over the well-being of the worker and the community. Movies such as *Indecent Proposal* and *Pretty Woman,* and advertisements for cars or perfume tempt us with the apparent delights of money. Money, it seems, can even be used to acquire relationships.

Meanwhile, the gap between the rich and the poor and unemployed grows. Those in the middle simply work harder, consume more, and try to reclaim their assumed birthright of upward mobility. The dream burns on, but now without the company of some of its former central tenets—the condemnation of greed and the love of money, the call to love God alone, and the command to use one's talents and gifts for the betterment of the community and the building of the kingdom. The latest and most fervent believers in the American dream are young women. Many of the women, age 12 through 25, studied by Ruth Sidel pursue a female version of "rags to riches," even if it is only a false dream, one that defines success narrowly in terms of what one can purchase.[42]

Different views of work—work as service, work as curse, work as a basic human right, or work as the direct expression of a unique human dignity and a way of collaborating with others—are a well-kept secret.[43] Unfortunately, most people seldom think about alternative philosophies or theologies of work, in which the substance of work as such, and not its product, receives serious consideration. If the way we work together largely determines the way we live together, even the 40-hour work week might come under reconsideration.

The decree of the 40-hour week, 50 weeks a year, now carries a certain quasi-religious immutability. Most businesses would stiffly oppose any other way. The proclivity toward productivity has been aggravated in recent years by several significant global shifts: shifts in world economic power and our new status as the world's biggest debtor nation, fierce worldwide competition, and fears of Western decline. Yet people in almost every other industrialized nation, except Japan, work fewer annual hours, take longer vacations (from 3 to 8 weeks, and 5 weeks by law in some countries like Spain and Sweden), enjoy better family-leave policies and innovative time-scheduling opportunities such as sabbaticals.[44]

The corporate gospel, it seems, has secured its definitions of success and productivity in the minds, watches, and economic pocketbooks of the American people. Those who make it to the top, acknowledge management gurus like Tom Peters and Nancy Austin, must give up so-called nonproductive activities—"family vacations, Little League games, birthday parties, evenings, weekends, and lunch hours . . . and most other pastimes." Taking care of others or enjoying oneself is a pastime? Work with material results is "productive"? Reading a book, raising a child, silence, meditation are "nonproductive"?

Between a Rock and a Hard Place

The twentieth-century "men's movement" also bemoans the tell-tale effects of industrialization. Many men stand between a rock and a hard place. The conventional generative avenues of earlier times, which grounded male identity in the ability to provide and protect, have deteriorated while men were paying the price for trying to live up to them. Little attention has gone to those debilitating effects, or, until recent stirrings in a growing men's movement, to the difficulties of reshaping new modes for men's generative identity.

Neither the religious community nor the larger culture is sure exactly what to make of the men's movement. The current "mythopoetic" movement that has received incredible media hype is not the only recent movement. One must wonder why only one has received the attention it has, since there are at least three distinct faces of the contemporary men's movement: (1) a profeminist activist movement that began in the 1970s and includes such phenomena as Jon Snodgrass's *For Men Against Sexism,* John Stoltenberg's *Refusing to Be a Man,* the National Organization of Men Against Sexism (holding annual Men and Masculinity conferences since 1975), the White Ribbon Campaign in Canada, organized by men to stop male violence after the Montreal massacre of fourteen women, and so forth; (2) an antifeminist movement actively working against equality for women, either denying the existence of inequality or embracing male domination; and (3) a mythopoetic men's movement, with Robert Bly as the most prominent figure, disclaiming "soft men," proclaiming dominator archetypes such as the warrior and king, and, at the same time, claiming a more generally just and equitable society.

The ambiguity of this last face of the movement, lying somewhere between the first two, and the hoopla that surrounded its gatherings and pronoucements (Bly's *Iron John* was on the *New York Times* best-seller list for all twelve months of 1991[45]) raise significant questions for women and feminists: Does the third group deserve a category different from the second? Is this movement uprooting the politics of patriarchy, or just giving it a new face? Will it make men sensitive nurturers, defenders of all people's liberation, or will men continue to blame women for their problems and defend their own privileges?

What is most troubling in Bly's work is the almost totally depoliticized emphasis on white male intrapsychic self-affirmation. Men need to attend to new understandings of "masculinity," better mentoring, and the lost rituals of becoming a man. But they cannot adequately do so apart from acknowledging, as a few people in the men's movement have, the underlying economic, social, and political structures that cause the malaise and the injustice of their own historical privileges as males. Economic definitions of success that invalidate the "nonproductive" activities of home, women, and children will need to be addressed.

Just as women ought not to put all the blame on men, mature masculinity cannot be reached by distancing itself from or placing blame on mothers, women, or feminists. The complaint about father absence needs to be situated in a patriarchal culture that has been built on the backs of women and mothers. Genuine masculinity requires a social activism that prevents paternal violence and teaches actual parenting skills to boys and men. It is questionable whether the images of the new warrior within or the king contribute to, rather than exasperate, these causes. Whether the ultimate intent of the current men's movement is to undo the damage patriarchy has done to the man-soul, or to revive a "kinder, gentler" patriarchy, the pain out of which the movement arose will not quietly disappear.

Too Little, Too Late: A Lesson in Exclusive Language

Not surprisingly, given the narrow perception of generativity centered around obtaining and owning products, many men experience some kind of crisis, popularly understood at the time of Daniel Levinson's research as a "mid-life crisis." Whether sparked by an unexpected failure, by disenchantment with the actual consequences of success or, in the case of *The Bonfire of the Vanities*, by sheer chance circumstance, some men abruptly question the emptiness of the path they have chosen. Some may reconsider the value of various relationships heretofore neglected. *The Bonfire* epitomizes the worst outcome: a self-perpetuated downward spiral of self-annihilation that ends with the uncaring exploitation of the one's misery for another's profit.

Whatever the outcome, according to more recent studies by psychologist Jan Halper in *Quiet Desperation*, theologians James E. Dittes in *The Male Predicament*, and James B. Nelson in *The Intimate Connection*, men have begun to experience the strain of their formulaic career patterns and what Nelson calls "masculinization," or the ideology of "hegemonic masculinity."[46] The four thousand executive men that Halper interviewed have become increasingly disillusioned by the "fruits" of their "success."

Although neither Halper, Dittes, Levinson, nor Nelson stress this conclusion, I would contend that the crisis results directly from a strong cultural value that pushes men to ignore generative relationships and focus upon acquisitions of vocational success. At forty, an age that seems long delayed in light of women's development, only a kind of "crisis" may force many men to recognize the importance of various attachments previously devalued or ignored as marginal. Some men in Levinson's investigation attempt "a more equal weighing of attachment and separateness."[47] At last they realize that others are not "products" and do not exist solely for the promotion of their own dream. Success of the dream becomes less critical. Some of the men Halper studied respond to their "quiet desperation" by changing their lives and redefining what it means to be a man in today's world. Generativity in a fuller sense may become a possibility.

But how will it become possible? Levinson, Erikson, and Browning all assume that the virtue of care for what one has generated cannot emerge fully until one reaches the final stages of adulthood. Even if it were true that authentic generativity must await the late forties and fifties, they fail to account for just how such a capacity to produce, care, and nurture can emerge out of a series of stages that clearly prioritize other divergent values, such as self-assertion, independence, and even overt disregard for what one has created. If "only the initial stage of trust versus mistrust suggests the type of mutuality that Erikson means by intimacy and generativity," as Harvard professor Carol Gilligan observes, how can intimacy or generativity appear suddenly in adulthood?[48] All the stages in between promote separateness and, in Levinson's study, have "individuation" as their ultimate goal. Erikson explores the antecedents and consequences of identity and autonomy, but neglects the genesis and import of intimacy and attachment.[49]

Don S. Browning does emphasize the way each stage contributes to the virtue of care and generativity. He argues that the essence of generativity is *"just as fundamental"* at life's earliest points as at life's conclusion: "The capacity for higher generativity (which is the very essence of ethical living) has its foundations in the very beginning of life."[50] But neither Browning nor Erikson makes entirely clear how generativity is actually woven into a childhood centered around autonomy and will, initiative and purpose, industry and competence. In the latter stage, for instance, the child, or actually the boy, focuses on "industry" or "work roles," in "line with the *ethos of production*," learning to master the technical tools of the trade.

But is this the case for girls? At the same age, it is not uncommon for girls to begin to focus instead on cooperating and caring for life's smaller beings, such as younger children, dolls, stuffed and live animals. Although Erikson acknowledges the significance of intimacy in a woman's resolution of the identity crisis, he does not draw upon women's experience to broaden his definitions. His general chart of the life cycle remains unchanged.

Women's experiences suggest some new questions. How do infants, young children, and adolescents acquire the ability to understand the way others feel and think? How does the empathic imagination essential to authentic care and human response develop? How do people become able to form and maintain bonds? How do they move from receiving care to giving care, to caring in ever-widening circles of commitment? Questions like these receive at best peripheral attention, not just in Erikson's theories, but in most modern accounts of human development.

Levinson's reported mid-life shifts in what and whom to care for, and how to care, come too little, too late, and with too many restrictions. I question whether most men can truly achieve such a dramatic alteration in their fundamental priorities at this point. How can men ultimately reconcile values for care and mutuality with the deep-seated status given to "becoming one's own man," or a separate, self-sufficient authority not subject to dependence upon or influence from others? How can men relinquish ingrained patterns of climbing to the top rung of the ladder? This has always demanded that attachments be surrendered, or at least regarded as secondary or tertiary. How can one change such a basic orientation to life and begin to develop, in mid-life, attributes of generativity? In few instances does Levinson actually provide examples of meaningful attachments that do occur and endure beyond the crisis. Ambivalence about intimacy prevails. Even if the men do realize significant values of care and connection at some point, this realization still symbolizes more a failure or loss of "success," as society has defined it, than a redefinition of the meaning of the word itself.

Browning and Erikson perceive the hazards of a success defined by unrelenting productivity. Browning's grounding question on the opening page of *Generative Man* asks how we can slow down the "runaway economic and technological expansion of Western society" that is destroying our ecology, our health, our lives.[51] Erikson expresses a concern that people will relieve their "generative frustration" by seeking technical, materialistic solutions, whether NRTs or nuclear arms. He recommends an alternative route: People ought to turn their anxieties about personal productivity and survival into "a more *universal care* concerned with a qualitative improvement" for every child born.[52]

But Erikson and Browning avoid the troubling question of the dramatic changes necessary to make genuine generativity for men *and* women a realizable possibility. For the most part, they ignore the powerful dynamics of gender and sexism. Even though his book is more current, Levinson does not deal with the dramatic changes that have occurred as women enter the public work world, or as society debates new definitions of masculinity and femininity. Browning does express concern that modern society, so busy in its technological generation of products, has lost the rudimentary means to conserve, preserve, maintain, and generally take care of itself and the highly advanced technological creations it continues to generate. Erikson, he believes, identifies the "problem of modern *man*" as "*his nongenerative mentality—his* inability to care for what *he* creates." "Man" remains nongenerative "in the way *he* treats *his* children, builds *his* buildings, conducts *his* science, experiments with *his* technology, and ravishes *his* environment."[53]

Here I believe it is important to retain the masculine pronoun. Although not the source of all the problems in contemporary generativity by any means (technology, individualism, capitalism are equally culpable ideologies, as we have seen), Browning fails to perceive the masculinist roots and overtones of the problem. I do not consider it surprising that, in his book on Erikson, Browning initially names Erikson's normative ideal "generative *man*." Although partly a technical blunder that has Browning now apologizing for his exclusive language, it remains a slip that subtly reveals the predominant orientation of Erikson's ideal, Levinson's interviews, Browning's study, and most of the dominant understandings of work and family in Western society—man.

❦ ❦ ❦

CHAPTER THREE

Generativity in Feminist Theory and Women's Lives

WHAT'S A FEMINIST MOTHER TO DO?

Wives, be subject to your husbands as you are to the Lord. For the husband is the head of the wife just as Christ is the head of the church.

Ephesians 5:22-23

The history and fate of feminism are intimately tied to the history of the family.

Judith Stacey,
"Are Feminists Afraid to Leave Home?"

In his own limited way, Erikson himself desired and called for a second reading of generativity. What will happen, he wondered, when women "cultivate the implications of what is biologically and anatomically given"? Will women and mothers correct the imbalances of the "self-made man" and his unrelenting pursuit of technological expansion and exploitation?[1] Is the disposition for the female commitment to human offspring the core of the Women Question, as Erikson presupposed? Erikson himself could not begin to fathom the debate that has occurred around these questions since he raised them.

Generativity in Feminist Theory and Women's Lives

Feminists have been divided over the "female disposition for commitment to human offspring," and indeed, over the function and role of families and mothers. The hot debate over sexual difference and equality is just one example of the way some of the discussion is played out. Sexual difference is easily one of the most controversial issues in current feminist talk. Are women equal to men? Are women different, in terms of their reproductive activities? Feminists are often labeled accordingly. How did American feminism arrive at this kind of impasse and, more recently, impasses over the state of the family? Where does this leave women?

The issues are far from simple. This chapter traces and situates some of the debates and tensions that have colored feminist deliberations on generativity, mothering, and families. The analysis makes clear the divided and divisive character of these deliberations, as well as the cause for hope.

Is Motherhood the Problem Feminism Can't Face?

Is motherhood the problem feminism can't face? One of the more outspoken critics, economist Sylvia Hewlett, has said so. In *A Lesser Life,* she wields facts and weaves tales to substantiate her scathing lament about the "myth of women's liberation in America." Her own contribution to the cause of women's liberation, however, becomes questionable when she turns her ire back on the very women who inspired the women's movement and fans the flames of feminist infighting and self-blame. Hewlett ranks among the finest of America's backlash "movers, shakers, and thinkers," according to Susan Faludi. Alongside Hewlett's revelation of the setbacks suffered by U.S. women in this century, a second and more problematic thesis reverberates throughout her book: Feminists pushed mothers and children into this squeeze, but for all their ideological support, they do not really care what happens to either group. She does not mince words:

> The feminists of the modern women's movement made one gigantic mistake: They assumed that modern women wanted nothing to do with children. As a result, they have consistently failed to incorporate the bearing and rearing of children into their vision of a liberated life.[2]

She continues, "The women's liberation movement has not just decided to ignore children . . . feminists rage at babies; others trivialize, or denigrate them." Not just anti-men, the movement has been "profoundly anti-children" and "anti-motherhood." In a word, *"Motherhood is the problem that modern feminists cannot face."*[3]

Hewlett is wrong here in several ways. To make a sure impression, she grossly oversimplifies the feminist stance. She sorely misplaces the blame. But she does raise a crucial question: If women have gained, why are mothers and children worse off?

Wave upon Wave:
Motherhood and the Flow of Feminist Waters

When Martha Weinman Lear first coined the term "second wave," in reference to the period of feminism dating from approximately 1966 and the founding of the National Organization for Women, she indirectly named a challenge to the perpetuation of a women's revolution.[4] Again and again, feminist claims have had to ride the stormy seas of culture and have ebbed and flowed in response to the repressive backwash of politics. Swimming against dominant cultural tides, succeeding generations have struggled to catch the drift of those who have gone before, and often have lost the memories in the receding waters of time, making another "wave" necessary. Indeed, the broader heritage of feminism goes back at least to Mary Wollstonecraft's *Vindication of the Rights of Woman,* published in 1792. Further research shows that even her work did not spring up out of nowhere, but belonged to a deeper ripple of feminist voices that were actively suppressed and redirected by social walls and dams.[5]

In the "first wave" that gathered momentum with Wollstonecraft's masterpiece of Enlightenment discourse and flowed into the nineteenth century, women's rights activists like Elizabeth Cady Stanton and Susan B. Anthony took initial steps toward freeing white middle-class women from the oppressions of secondary citizenship. In the early twentieth century, women rallied around the cause of enfranchisement. After a long, harrowing seventy-two-year fight that involved many, many campaigns to influence male legislatures, male-run political parties, and male voters, women's right to vote was obtained in 1920 with the passage of the nineteenth Constitutional amendment.

With the good news came the bad: Once the vote was granted, the movement's momentum subsided. Diverse factions behind the cause resurfaced, and although many factors converged, one source of the movement's dispersion was its trouble in tackling the problems of the family and domestic life. The women activists themselves were divided over the import of motherhood and domesticity, some claiming its centrality, others impatient with domestic distractions. For the most part, they represented an elite group of women and had less sense of the problems of female poverty, racial oppression, child care, or parental leave that seem so familiar today.

Although a unified fight for abolition had fueled consciousness early on about the equal worth of women, Stanton and Anthony had used rhetoric about the moral superiority of white mothers as a basis for claiming the importance of white women's suffrage over black suffrage. The movement therefore lost touch with the critical stream of thought and experiences of working-class mothers and mothers of color. For many of the leaders themselves, combining a career and family was nearly an impossible prospect. When Lucy Stone married late in life, for example, she ceased her work in the women's movement. Their emphasis had been placed more on legal and political rights of white women and less on changing the relationship of men and women, or family and work patterns.

As disturbing, however, is our general cultural amnesia. While legal and political changes tend to stay with us, new ideas about social and emotional relations have a way of drifting off into spinning eddies and remote tidal pools. Stanton, for example, argued that the harmony of households depends upon equal responsibility of men and women, and she advocated specific domestic reforms that would assure this. Frances Willard, a leader in the temperance movement, made a strong case for active, devoted fatherhood and gender-equal partnerships in the home, and also detailed concrete proposals about coeducation and property rights, for instance, to assure this.[6]

But did anyone heed these words of wisdom? For those born after the 1920s, the fresh ways in which these women did begin to answer questions of equality and parenthood were quickly submerged in the lore of idealized motherhood and femininity that captured the American imagination in the 1950s with unheralded vigor. Few children born from the 1920s through the 1950s heard about Stanton, Anthony, or

Willard, either in classroom history lessons or in stories told around the dinner table. In the dominant images of the post-Depression and post–World War II years, motherhood became a profession all its own. Girls took classes in home economics and, later, interior decorating. Alternatives were submerged, and prospects for equal domestic partnerships nearly drowned.

The "second wave" in the 1960s succeeded in stirring the waters of women's collective memory and bringing to the surface the next rallying point beyond the vote: a repudiation of autocratic ideologies of domesticity and the pursuit of unqualified entrance into male-dominated institutions. White middle-class women who had had the mixed fortune to achieve the benefits and boredom of surburban living became acutely aware of the traps of wife and motherhood in the nuclear family of the 1950s. Betty Friedan's *Feminist Mystique,* alongside Simone de Beauvoir's *Second Sex,* were instrumental handbooks in this shift in women's consciousness.[7] Women protested the oppressive liabilities of homemaking and babymaking, and pressed for authentic opportunities in the job market and the pay scale.

In both waves, feminist theory and the women's movement had a great deal to say about generativity and female dispositions. Broadly stated, the women's movement effected at least three quite powerful changes in cultural and religious perceptions of adult generativity: (1) Marriage and children may be rewarding, but they no longer are a viable career for women, although many people are loath to admit this.[8] (2) In addition, fatherhood may be executed from a growing distance or squandered in destructive proximity, but the consequences of paternal absence and paternal abuse for families and society will no longer go unnoticed, although this too has been hard to accept. (3) Equally unsettling, women expect, even if they do not receive, equality of opportunity. Even women who do not actively demand equity at work or at home bristle at Pauline-like imperatives: "Wives, be subject to your husbands."

American society and religion have struggled to deal with the fallout from these three changes. Whereas the first wave sometimes relied on church structures and religious tenets to further the cause of women's rights, the second wave turned on both church and religion for providing a fundamental undergirding ideology for female submission. In the first wave, some Protestant churches—Quakers, for example—encouraged women to assert their rights, based on the equal importance of all humans before God. In the second wave, the use of biblical passages, such as Ephesians 5:22 to condone male headship and female servitude, or the Genesis creation story to establish women's lesser, even evil, status, came under direct attack. So did male God images and ecclesiastical structures that excluded female participation.

When feminists in theology arrived on the scene, a bit late, they lent their skills of historical and theological analysis to deepen the critique. Later, as many feminist theologians continued to affirm society's need for religion and the place of religious symbols, myths, and rituals, the critique was qualified by reconstructions of religion's viable contributions, although these reconstructions seldom had to do explicitly with new normative theories of the family or motherhood. Most feminists in mainline Protestant denominations have toiled at the margins of their traditions. When and where possible, they have effected changes in language and representation, more than in familial or maternal images and norms. Mainline congregations have followed the cultural tide that has mixed feminist proposals in the increasingly muddy waters of social and personal relations, changing some ecclesiastical practices and religious language, but in the main, ignoring the tensions that brew beneath the surface.

Log Jams and Dams:
Abandoned Mothers? Destroyed Families?

In promoting new rallying points and alternative views of generativity, both first- and second-wave feminists have encountered countless log jams and dams, of which Hewlett's work is only one example. Second-wave feminists, in particular, have been accused of abandoning mothers to the double burden of family and work. They have been blamed for promoting racist views, using "women" as a category that failed to include poorer women and women of color. Most poignantly, they have been accused, first by the evangelical right and then by others, of destroying the family.

An equal relationship is not the biblical view of the family, said some conservative American Christians. Social theorists and politicians of wider persuasion, and the media joined the ground swell, invoking Hewlett and suggesting that the feminist view was not the American view of the family. The "feminism-has-been-a-disaster" scenario appeared on "Nightline," on "Phil Donahue," and on the pages of several best-sellers. The desperate working mother, the childless spinster, the worsening test scores of our nation's children, the impoverished child, the blight of the pregnant teen, and the single mother—all these have been too hastily laid on feminism's doorstep.

The realities are far more complex and ambiguous. The one criticism that has been taken the most seriously by feminists—that they failed to include all women—is the most valid. The second wave did break and ride over serious concerns of many mothers and women. Although the attack on job discrimination met the needs of most women, the critique of domestic oppressions and idealized motherhood left high and dry those women who had no choice but to work for low wages simply to survive, and who relied on a different sort of motherhood, unrecognized by the movement, to secure the continuity of the family and the community.

In its efforts to liberate women from domestic oppressions, neither the first nor the second wave foresaw some of the indirect negative effects on many future mothers and children, including the counter-effects of the failure to obtain genuine equality. Nor could these movements anticipate the larger social, economic, and cultural roadblocks that would further complicate the life of home and family. The feminist attack on domesticity was not the only force at work. Nor is it true that feminism failed to offer any alternative possibilities for families.

The demands of life in an industrial and postindustrial capitalist society made almost irrelevant many differences between genders that had been necessary in a preindustrial, agrarian economy. The increasing technical sophistication and rationality, the service orientation, and the individualism of a postindustrial economy have changed forever the character of work and home for both men and women. With industrialization, parents spend less and less time with children in the household, the percentage dwindling from most of their adult lives to only one-third. Lost to big industry were the important jobs women had done in the home economies that sustained families and communities. Parenthood and family relationships lost some of their ascribed status and began to occupy an ever shrinking place in people's lives.

Certainly, feminism made a difference. It played the role of "unwitting midwife," helping to expedite the massive social transformations of the workplace and family life that had incubated throughout the twentieth century and came to a head in the postwar era. But as sociologist Judith Stacey suggests, gender changes were "coincident with the rise of second-wave feminism," rather than caused by it.[9] The modern nuclear family, with its rigid, narrow gender roles, would have come under increasing stress, with or without a feminist critique.

As historian Flora Davis puts it, the truth boils down to the fact that over the years, feminists "did what seemed doable."[10] Feminist politics of the mid-1960s removed several obstacles to women's equal treatment in the workplace, although countless obstacles remain. When their demands for child care, child-care tax deductions, leaves, and other benefits met with resistance, they redirected their efforts. Less attention was paid to how to live with the changes—particularly the changes in personal, familial, and community life—for the many women who live very different lives.

Again, Distortions in the American Dream

So why are mothers and children worse off in some ways, although not in all ways? The answer is far more complex than Hewlett allows. Feminists are part of a much larger social, economic, and political picture that surrounds mothering and children. The feminist revolution falters less over feminism's failures than over the economic and cultural trends that extend beyond this debate. Other crucial factors have had an equally powerful role: politicians who have ignored or resisted European policy solutions; America's rugged individualism and long-standing traditions of self-reliance; backlash in the media and elsewhere; and politics itself.

In extensive interviews and observations with couples in a dozen homes, from the late 1970s to the late 1980s, Arlie Hochschild and Anne Machung discover a major discrepancy between the change in women and the almost complete lack of change anywhere else. More specifically, the revolution is "stalled," according to their reading, in terms of the friction between "faster-changing women" and "slower-changing men."[11] Whether this friction is the crux of the problem or not, attacks on the oversights of feminists distract attention from some of the other impinging causes of women's worsening situation: a shifting economic and political climate; a decade of conservative government; the attack on liberalism; the rise of the New Right; overt bigotry and women-hating—in a word, the rigors of life in a period of backlash. From this perspective, predictions of the demise of liberalism or of a postfeminist era are not only premature, but may even be fear tactics.

Or so argues Faludi, the person who raised "backlash" to formal public awareness in the title of her book. Faludi's *Backlash: The Undeclared War Against American Women* presents quite a different analysis of the problems from that of Hewlett. In contrast, Faludi refuses to blame feminism. Backlash, according to Faludi, is the powerful attempt in the last decade to retract the "handful of small and hard-won victories that the feminist movement did manage to win for women," partly by blaming feminism as women's enemy. Backlash even operates as a "preemptive strike": historically, moves that create the backlash which challenges women's achievement appear just before women actualize these accomplishments, propelled by fears of what they might portend.[12]

Mary Hunt describes the emerging contours of backlash for theology and the church:

> Gains made in seminaries, churches, and universities are quietly being eroded. Some seminaries report being back at square one on inclusive language. Hiring, tenure, and promotion for women in church and academy still lag way behind men. *Feminism* is a dirty word for some entering seminarians who nevertheless take for granted what have been hard-won gains for women. Certain liberation movements have been slow to incorporate a feminist critique.[13]

According to two different government studies, theology and religious studies continue to lag behind many disciplines in awarding doctorates to women.[14] Statistics on women desiring positions in ministry reveal a similar pattern. Such reports are cause for concern. This period of guarded retrenchment threatens to undo some of the advances made by women.

To be sure, feminists have not found a way to integrate children into the "fabric of a full and equal life," as Hewlett argues. But for that matter, neither have men or anti-feminists. Contradictions do not characterize just feminist responses to mothers and children; a nicely concealed contradiction distorts America's treatment of mothers and children in general. Popular psychology touts the import of the early years, and T. Berry Brazelton's books rise on the bestseller list according. Candidates for political office kiss babies and promise policies that support the family. Motherhood and apple pie go together.

Yet the labors of love essential to the welfare of children hold little real value. Statistics on health, poverty, education, drugs, mortality rates, abuse, homelessness, and suicide reveal an incredible insensitivity to the actual demands of children and mothering. Child- and mother-centered ideologically, we are; child- and mother-loving in reality, we are not. As Stacey puts it, "Americans seem to love *The Family* far better than families."[15] More to the point, Americans love *The Child* and *The Mother* far more than children and mothers.

In *A Lesser Life*, Hewlett does not yet understand this. As she tells her story, in the late 1960s she came to the "Promised Land" of justice and greater economic opportunity from a depressed mining community in South Wales, in pursuit of the American dream.[16] It is the larger cultural framework of this dream, built largely for and by certain men, that she and others who turn upon feminists seldom question, and it is that dream that needs radical overhaul. Although Hewlett chooses a biblical image, this is the extent of her religious sensibilities. She seeks no further insight into the power of religious ideals to shape economic needs and desires. Hewlett and those who blame feminism often do not question America's definitions of success and the religious ideologies behind them. Failure to broaden their analysis in this direction weakens the analysis.

If Hewlett better understood the contradictions of raising children in a culture that ultimately devalues them, she would be less shocked by the lack of enthusiasm she receives when she tries to arrange a family-policy panel at the Economic Policy Council of the United Nations Association, with members from the "topmost ranks" of business, academe, and organized labor.[17] We must wonder about a society in which those who do make it to the "topmost ranks" have little to do with children, out of the sheer necessity of their "success."

Hewlett herself has since acknowledged a necessary change in her thinking: "One of the questions I posed in *A Lesser Life* is why the modern women's movement hadn't put children center stage. . . . When I got to *When the Bough Breaks*, it became easy to explain . . . *no* group in this society puts them center stage."[18] The misdirected anger behind *A Lesser Life* searches for a better target. *When the Bough Breaks*

73

argues that the private and public neglect of children in America is unique among developed nations. We spend nine times as much on the elderly as on children, and twice as much on military pensions as on AFDC.

We fund costly coronary bypass surgery for those over sixty-five, but cut back on the small sums of money necessary to inoculate those under five against measles. While America has made significant advances in caring for the elderly, something is awry when we spend 24 percent of our budget on the old, but just 4 percent on families with children; when we spend $100 billion on health care for the elderly, but just $14 billion on children; when we underwrite multiple heart-bypass surgery for seventy-year-olds, but fail to provide prenatal care for poor women.[19] As Marian Wright Edelman claims, if we keep this up, we are on the verge of losing our African American, white, Latino, Native American, and other children to the dangers of "drugs, violence, too-early parenthood, poor health and education, unemployment, family disintegration," and ultimately, to the "meaninglessness of a culture that rewards greed and guile, and tells [children that] life is about getting rather than giving."[20]

In her analysis of motherhood and American society, Barbara Katz Rothman identifies three deeply ingrained ideologies that determine how we think about working and loving: the ideology of patriarchy, the ideology of technology, and the ideology of capitalism. (1) Patriarchy, as a basic worldview, runs deeper than male dominance. Patriarchy is a system in which paternity is the central social relationship, men use women to bear children for men, and mothers are vessels through which men must pass their seed. (2) The ideology of a technological society thinks about the world in mechanical, industrial terms, about ourselves as objects, about people as made up of machines and being part of larger machines, and about work and love in terms of control and efficiency. (3) The ideology of capitalism sees life according to the profit motive. Based on assumptions analogous to those one makes in connection with private property, we "own" our bodies, we want children "of our own," and we make related decisions based on cost-benefit analysis.[21]

These ideologies interweave to form the infrastructures of a high-tech, product-oriented, "commodification of life."[22] As a recent bumper sticker reads, "Life is a game, and the one with the most toys at the end wins." According to one study, the proportion of young people who see financial success as a major life goal has doubled since 1970, with a related decline in the proportion concerned with finding meaning in life.[23] People talk about parenting in economic and psychological language. In economic language, children are the "products of conception," the family is a unit of consumption, the pregnant body is the "quality control" on the assembly line of life, and parenting is a temporary service rendered. In popular psychological language, children are the means to the end of self-gratification; pregnancy and childbirth are self-fulfilling experiences. But when viewed economically and psychologically alone, parenting quickly becomes a costly and frustrating experience.

Hewlett is not alone, then, in her endorsement of a limited definition of success, where "milk and honey" equal the bottom line, or in her confusion about who to blame for the shabby state of family affairs. In the hearts of men and women, the faded form of an American dream of a Promised Land lives on—a dream in which one can work and have a fulfilling family life—but more often than not, it turns into a nightmare of anxiety, tension, and strife. Social, economic, and even legal structures punish women who choose procreation and nurturance over production alone, and they discourage men from becoming more than marginally involved in activities that give and sustain life. Alternative moral and religious views do not seem to hold much influence at all.

Breakthroughs,
or New Currents Running in Old, Muddy Channels?

During the last decade, however, even this has changed. Religious feminists, working within the constraints of evangelical Protestant, Jewish, and more orthodox Roman Catholic traditions, have endeavored to revise narrow theological readings of gender roles, family relations, and biblical passages from Genesis, Ephesians, and elsewhere.[24] Although the respective denominational structures have yet to see feminist work as central to the reshaping of religious doctrines and orders, and some almost seem to hope that these theological revisions of gender and family will go away of their own accord, a few people in positions of power have begun to accept the tenacity and merits of these ideas.

Womanist and mujerista theologians, entering the discussion most recently from within their respective religious bodies as African American and Hispanic women, have especially changed the tide and terms.

Their voices open up new possibilities. Religion has played a central role in the lives of many of these women. While most African American women distrusted a largely white, middle-class movement that failed to address their concerns, and even relied on their domestic service, many still supported the primary goal of women's worth as women long before the white mainstream.

But instead of identifying the church or men or motherhood as the problem, many womanists and mujeristas have linked sexism with racism and have centered the cause of women in the church, in motherhood, and in the family. It is not motherhood that is the obstacle to freedom, but racism, lack of jobs, skills, education, and a number of other issues. Work within the family confirms the identity and humanity of African American women.[25] Womanists and mujeristas have spoken with authority of social systems predicated on the independence and self-reliance of women, and on the economic interdependence of men and women. They have spoken about their experiences of families and churches guided by community Mothers and an "ethic of 'family-hood.' "[26]

In American feminist theory more broadly, there has been a notable shift away from what Iris Marion Young calls a "humanist feminism," which was the predominant force until the late 1970s. In contrast to a humanist feminism that rejects femininity and motherhood as sources of women's oppression and also rejects differential treatment of women based on purportedly inherent gender differences, a gynocentric feminism retrieves values within traditionally female experience for a more radical critique of dominant social spheres.

More exactly, for some earlier twentieth-century feminists, female reproductive biology was a curse, pregnancy an ordeal, and children a hindrance to the development of woman's full potential.[27] For some more recent feminists, female reproductive consciousness is at the heart of the women's revolution, pregnancy a worthy human endeavor, and children a complex source of new thought and experience.[28] A gynocentric trend is most evident in the renewed attention to motherhood. As Mary O'Brian observes, "Feminist scholarship is now honing in on the problems of reproduction, of birth, of the historical significance as well as the emotional trauma of motherhood.[29]

Others, like Karen Offen, have characterized the realignments in feminism geographically, in terms of a "relational feminism" in Europe and France over against the "individualist feminism" of America. In this scenario, American feminists have tended to strive for personal autonomy, self-realization, and entrance into male-dominated institutions, while European feminists were more likely to celebrate woman's maternal role as a way to mount a wide-ranging critique of these institutions. Offen believes that by attacking gender roles, physiological difference, familial institutions, and motherhood, American feminists "simply placed the sociopolitical context, as well as the relational aspects, of most women's lives outside discussion and left this terrain to be effectively claimed by opponents who succeeded in moblilizing public fears."[30] The claim that women's equal rights include a right to mother, which escaped many American feminists who tended to bracket it, functioned in some European countries to insure better family leave and child-care policies. We would do well, in Offen's opinion, to listen to our sisters across the Atlantic, as well as to the strains of relational feminism on our own shores.

While both currents have been evident to certain degrees throughout the history of American feminism, gynocentric, or relational, feminism has received heightened attention in recent years for many reasons. Young names three factors: "antifeminist reaction to feminism, the emergence of black feminism, and the development of women's history and feminist anthropology."[31] In particular, African American feminism made clear that domesticated images of women as dependent and frail grew from a class and race bias. Women of color knew what it meant to have to be strong and to work, and questioned a women's liberation that prevails by replacing maternal, domestic labor with the labor of "somebody's nice black grandmother."[32] Whatever the ultimate cause, there has been a shift. The movement of humanist feminism, which works for inclusion of women, needed to take place before gynocentric, or relational, feminism, which celebrates difference, could seriously entertain itself. The second development assumes the achievements of the first and may be almost inevitable.

The resurgence of new currents in feminism, however, is not unambiguous. Offen's position, for example, is hotly contested in a later issue of *Signs*, the journal in which Offen's article appeared. Nancy Cott thinks Offen's advocacy of relational feminism is not much different from the "standard, conservative, status quo view of women's position." Why, she protests, call this "entire approach 'feminist'—even with the 'relational' modifier?" Women who claim motherhood as politically empowering should find some other rubric to classify their position.[33] And Faludi is quick to point out that European governments were enacting family leave and child-care measures because of concern over falling birthrates and war-devastated populations, reasons that had little to do with relational feminist causes.

The ambiguity is particularly evident as feminists such as Faludi, Stacey, Stephanie Coontz, and others dispute the contributions and dangers of conservative, profamily feminist voices, including Betty Friedan's *Second Stage*, a somewhat tainted attempt to reclaim gender differences and the family as a new feminist frontier. The shift has come as major feminist spokespeople like Friedan grayed, and women in general began to rethink their values and past choices. The power of feminism's influence began not with the judicious extension of theories, but in response to cries of rage and anguish, to testimonies of exploitation by the mothers, sisters, wives, and daughters of many nations, colors, classes, and religious traditions. Now, the unanticipated trials of having children, of raising children alone on limited resources, of infertility and miscarriage, of living without an intimate other, have unpredictably fueled, and will continue to fuel the passions behind the new, more conservative trends with which relational or gynocentric feminism has some obvious affinities.

Much of conservative profamily feminism gathers its energies precisely from tragedies related to marriage and children in the personal lives of its major spokespeople. This is certainly true in Hewlett's case. A miscarriage, a premature birth, her attempt to juggle teaching and child care, the denial of tenure early in her career—all combine to produce an abundance of ill-directed rage. According to Stacey, feminists who refused marriage, delayed childbearing, experimented with sexuality and collective households, now face three sorts of trauma with little or no recourse: " 'involuntary' singlehood, involuntary childlessness, and single parenthood."[34] Although these traumas threaten to undo the feminist humanist political struggle against the subordination of women as a social category, conservative backlash feminists have at least responded to genuine social and personal problems.

Of crucial import is the question of how gynocentric, or relational, feminism will be used. Some justifiably fear the hazards of its positions and its misuse and abuse by those less sympathetic to the feminist cause.

Will it mean a regression to Victorian values of sexual dualism, a rejection of feminism's political critique of the dynamics of sexist family systems? Or will it open up new avenues for achieving women's place as full human beings? The critical question, as Stacey frames it, is whether it is "possible to devise a personal politics that respects the . . . anxieties and exhaustion of women contending with the destabilized family and work conditions of the postindustrial era . . . without succumbing to conservative nostalgia for patriarchal familial and religious forms."[35]

In a word, the second wave tamed, but then set loose, a whitecap endemic to the greater history of women and human rights, the tension between women's claims as mothers and their claims for equality as individuals in the public sphere. The key question for postsuffrage feminists, according to historian Nancy Cott, is still our fundamental question. Can we, and should we, sustain the movement's "double aims"—the concept of women's equality with men and the concept of women's sexual difference?[36] The crisis of confidence in feminism today turns upon our ability to make a way through the fresh, cloudy undulations of this old tension.

Women in the Trenches: Treading Water Between Waves

Between the warring ideological fronts stand women in the trenches, who must combine work and love in the midst of life's daily demands. Succeeding generations of women have had to find ways to make the equality sought by earlier generations livable, ways to manage the conflicts left unresolved. In the case of those living in the aftermath of first- and second-wave feminism, a primary task has been to figure out how to realize women's equality alongside the ability to bear children, whether understood as an essential difference or not.

Few issues are of graver concern, discovers Ruth Sidel in 150 interviews with young women across the country, women of diverse class, race, ethnic, and educational backgrounds, than "the question of how to combine work and child rearing."[37] Perceiving sex discrimination as a relatively settled problem, these women assume the advances gained by political consciousness, but fail to appreciate the costs of those gains or to anticipate the remaining battles. Many have the complicated hope of combining "marriage to a communicative, egalitarian man with motherhood and a successful, engaging career."[38] Under the current inequalities and the realities of work and family, this refashioned vision of the American dream will become an unattainable mirage for those women who lack realistic means and supports.

Many women mistakenly thought the struggle for women's self-worth would be won quickly and easily, and women would earn a place in esteemed professions. As one colleague put it, "Fifteen years ago I foolishly believed that it would just be a matter of time before suddenly, everywhere, I would find female colleagues who were raising children and having fulfilling professional lives too. Where are these women?" she asks. "I do have *one* female colleague with two children, but she has practically dropped out of the profession."

Many women today sail past some of the political battles over equal rights that faced the first feminist wave. But they face squalls on progressively more obscure seas. When women secured the vote, it cost men next to nothing, in terms of what they might have to give up beyond the promise of liberty. The second wave forecast untold economic, psychological, and social storms, as women demanded a fair share of the nation's resources, improved access to employment, property rights, credit, education, and a more equal distribution of the workload at home.

These material demands brought with them significant emotional and social costs. As people committed themselves to new, psychologically dissonant roles, they encountered intrapsychic strife, interrelational and familial conflicts, intergenerational discord, and role proliferation. Conventional networks essential to the common good, and previously largely sustained by the unpaid labors of women in families and communities, have undergone subtle but significant and troubling changes. Without women, many of these largely voluntary support structures cannot function well or at all. When women recognize the limits of their caring and have less energy and time for caring, who cares?

Turmoil over the term *feminist* is very illustrative. When asked, "Are you a feminist?" many women may say no. When asked, "Do you believe that women deserve equality of opportunity, without respect to gender, and have unique insights and experiences to contribute to the dominant culture?" most say yes. Many women espouse the core ideas of the feminist agenda, some enact them without second thought, but many hesitate to call themselves "feminist"—the all-too-familiar, "I'm not a feminist but . . . . "

On the one hand, some people give this phenomenon a hopeful cast. Feminist action has simply changed from marches, consciousness raising, and pressure-group activity to "unobtrusive mobilization" inside male-governed institutions of higher education, the foundations, the professions, the churches, the media, the armed forces, thus assuring the "continuation of feminism as a vital force for change into the 1990s."[39] Despite active resistance to feminism, a general critique of gender discrimination continues to spread not only across social categories of age, marital status, educational level, and geographical locale, but also across the traditional barriers of the liberal/conservative axis.

From this perspective, discomfort with the nomenclature represents less a retreat than an adaptive transmutation, the "incorporation, revision, and depoliticization" of many of feminism's central goals.[40] Women who distance themselves from feminist identity do so in order to resist the burdens that feminism seems to impose, while incorporating feminist principles into their expectations and strategies for families and work. Davis concludes her history of the women's movement since 1960 on this positive note:

> Feminists had raised the consciousness of the nation and that was probably their most significant achievement. Many of the ideas introduced by the second wave had diffused into every corner of society, leaving no one untouched, and had been so thoroughly absorbed that they now shaped most people's beliefs about what women were like and what they could expect to do with their lives. Much of the time, those ideas were so commonly accepted that they were no longer even labeled "feminist."[41]

Feminism may no longer provide the solace or support that it once did. But the movement has broadened and continues to encourage self-assertion and to instigate for social change. Other dynamics, however, give cause for concern.

Many women selectively blend and adapt certain feminist ideas to conventional strategies of work and family. They recognize the stultifying effects of female domesticity but still have children. The end result: They improvise, sometimes to their advantage, but often to their demise. Some women, especially the white and upper-class, have found ways to care for children and also pursue a livelihood. But their success rests on the backs of their sisters.[42] And most improvise to such an extent that men and the government have been free to continue on as if nothing has changed. A heavy portion of the burden for change in private and public life still falls upon women. The disinclination to claim the name *feminist* does signify at least a partial alienation of women, precisely in terms of those concerns of which second-wave feminism strove to address and resolve—home and family.

What's a Feminist Mother to Do? Stir Up the Next Wave!

Are women equal to men? Are women different? The answer to both questions, confirmed by a careful riding of the feminist waves in America itself, is yes. Insistence upon a yes to both questions creates strong resistance in a culture which insists that one is *either* equal *or* different. Under current definitions, equality requires a uniform sameness. Difference in kind means exclusion and inferiority. Feminist mothers make the seemingly contradictory demand for equality *and* difference in their work and in their families. Given the current cultural and social climate, this is bound to bring harsh consequences.

Feminists have served nicely as a lightning rod for the problems that have emerged as American society tries to realign boundaries of accountability to home, children, and community, in more just and inclusive terms. At times, men also have. The accusations of each party are partly valid. But the problems lie more in a general failure to reconstruct and implement adequate ideals of human fulfillment. Although feminists and mothers often feel the blame and suffer the guilt, disregard for children and the family is not their fault. Feminists and working mothers merely join the general populace in the acute failure to envision adequate models of loving and working—that is, of caring for those *whom* we produce while we are so busy worrying about *what* we produce and consume.

To return to an earlier question: If women have gained, why are mothers and children worse off? In a society that esteems a generativity centered around productivity, while it denigrates the less tangible generativity centered around care, we should not be surprised that mothers and children have neither been factored in nor fared well. Nor should we be surprised that when women sought liberation, securing the needs of mothers and children was not the first order of business.

Feminists have had good reason to feel reluctant about speaking up for the values of rearing children and motherhood. For too long, men left to women the relentlessly repetitive chores of "world-repair," the "million tiny stitches," the "cleaning up of soil and waste left behind by men and children."[43] Creating public policies to allow more time for women to perform these activities is a dubious accomplishment at best; at worst, it is a reinstitution of restrictive definitions of gender complementarity and circumstances of injustice. Retrieving anything related to the institutions of motherhood, family, and children has its inherent dangers.[44] Women have paid, and continue to pay dearly for nurturing children, costs that men have not known. The constraints of nurturing children are real. Reproductive difference, a potential source of power, is at the same time the source of women's greatest vulnerability. Initially, throwing the baby out with the bath water may have been the only viable option.

Yet to disavow children is not, I believe, what truly thoughtful feminists ultimately had in mind in their struggle for equality. Unlike Hewlett, I cannot think of a feminist who hates children, and I know several whose personal lives reveal embattled commitment to them. In response to such portrayals of the most extreme voices in the movement, Friedan declares, "That's not what we meant, not at all." Equality never meant "destruction of the family, repudiation of marriage and motherhood."[45] Rather, it meant the destruction of certain familial, marital, and maternal forms and ideals.

Although the current period has been typified as being one of erosion of the gains made by feminism, and clear evidence of certain setbacks abound, this is also a period of reorientation. The wave analogy is apt. The stream of women's participation in the waters of cultural formation is steadfast. It will not dry up. The unresolved tensions crest, the public absorbs as much as it can stand until reaction sets in, then the waters pour over and abate. But the next surge comes. If motherhood and children received criticism and little theoretical attention hitherto, it was more a matter of emphasis, priority, and self-protection than hostility and rejection. The questioning of the inherent biological and psychological differences of motherhood, and of the essential place of children in women's lives, was a means, not a foregone conclusion. Children and mothering are an issue whose time had to come, and it has come. In a word, notices of feminism's demise are significantly premature.

CHAPTER FOUR

Orpah's Untold Story

GENERATIVITY AND FEMINIST THEOLOGY

---

*But Naomi said to her two daughters-in-law, "Go back
each of you to your mother's house. May the LORD deal
kindly with you, as you have dealt with the dead and
with me."*

Ruth 1:8

I am a student of theology; I am also a woman.
Valerie Saiving, "The Human Situation:
A Feminine View"

With the words, "I am a student of theology; I am also a
woman," the first sentence of Valerie Saiving's pivotal 1960s
article, "The Human Situation: A Feminine View," which
appeared in the April 1960 *Journal of Religion,* begins an important
period of revision and revolution in theology. However, few have added
and embellished a sentence implicit in Saiving's essay itself: "I am also a
mother." Failure to do so is a mistake, particularly during a time when
the term *family values* has become a distorted and sometimes politically
dangerous code word for reinstituting male dominance and female
self-sacrifice. With what, beyond criticism, denunciation, and silence,

have feminist theologians proposed to replace our failing family structures and ideals?

Most feminist theologians have agreed with the general feminist view that the patriarchal family no longer has a place. For too long it has been a primary nucleus for the construction of oppressive, unjust relations, enculturating its members into stereotypical gender roles. Beyond this critical stance, some have advanced alternatives to the conventional theological definitions of work and love. Much of this reflection, however, has not received the kind of attention or codification it needs. Few feminist theologians have actually identified alternative family models. The conversation is even more sparse when it comes to the role of motherhood.

After exploring the nature and implications of the silence that surrounds the phrase "also a mother," this chapter attempts to codify and assess some of what feminist theology has to offer to the discussion of generativity, before we turn to the second half of this book and the task of elaborating the missing conversation. The chapter begins with a few sketchy and troubling biblical passages from the first chapter of Ruth, passages that are in need of a new reading. At this point, I simply introduce the lost voice of Orpah, as an impetus for hearing the lost voices in the valuable work of Saiving and other theologians. In the last chapter, we will return to this story to elaborate the creative imaginings of the three women in the wilderness, with the hope of creating a new story by which to live.

What's a Feminist Christian Mother to Do?

Black women have found certain biblical stories central to comprehending the demands, complications, and injustices of their work and love. According to womanist theologian Delores S. Williams, the passages about Hagar, in Genesis 16:1-16 and 21:9-21, represent such a story.

While the black liberation theology of James Cone, James Deontis Roberts, and others has appropriated the Exodus story and its "tradition of liberation," liberation theology has not reflected on an equally central "tradition of survival/quality-of-life" found in Hagar.[1] Within African American churches, women have appropriated Hagar for more than a century. The realities of her life as slave mother, cast into the wilderness, disenfranchised and exiled, yet strong in her God-inspired survival and rebellion, models the history of black collective life and infuses a life of faith in God. Among other repercussions, the example of Hagar has encouraged mothers to support one another in order to foster self-esteem, self-love, and self-survival; it has affirmed the irreplaceable value of children and their care; it has motivated people to perceive the nurturing of children as a task of the entire community.

I cannot name a comparable biblical story for white women as mothers, much less a religious tradition of biblical appropriation. The distinctiveness white women might have as a group is more nebulous, our struggles more ill-defined. This complicates the task of finding a scriptural tradition that might inspire and sustain us, as Hagar has done for many black women. Methodologically, it is necessary to go beyond the limits of the canon to name and elaborate the unnamed, undeveloped narratives within the narrative. Inadvertently, as I sought fresh stories, I found myself drawn anew to that intricately woven Hebrew story of Ruth and Naomi, which for centuries has provided a compelling image of women caught between cultures. This particular biblical tale came to mind and would not let me go.

My peculiar attraction, however, was not to Ruth and her radical alliance with Naomi, or to the end of the story, which positions Ruth securely within the lineage of King David. I was drawn to the image of the three women in the wilderness. Ultimately, I was engrossed by the little known, little discussed character Orpah, whose destiny is etched in only a few brief passages. This woman, silenced and lost, rose up as a soul-mate. Her story—my story and the story of many women caught between clearly defined ideals of womanhood—is oddly untold. Most people do not even recognize her name.

Recently, a few feminist biblical scholars have lifted up the book of Ruth as a potentially liberating paradigm for female loyalty and unconventional claims to divine action. In Ruth and Naomi, notes Phyllis Trible, we find "women working out their own salvation with fear and trembling," with Naomi bridging tradition and innovation, and Ruth an exemplar of "radicality."[2] Others, like Renita Weems and Denise Lardner Carmody, praise Ruth and Naomi for their remarkable friendship. They offer a model of religious bonding, remarks Carmody, that ought to give "feminists of all persuasions a valuable lesson" in putting love first and differences second.[3]

So what becomes of Orpah? Theological tradition, the church, and now feminist theology, have admired and idealized Ruth's decision to follow her late husband's mother, while virtually ignoring the courage and conflicts of Orpah, the forgotten daughter, sister, and friend who chooses to return to her "mother's house" (Ruth 1:8). Granted, she "dies to the story," as Trible says, because she takes a course that does not follow the "dynamic of the tale."[4] She simply chooses "another path."[5]

But this does not suffice. As long as we continue to see Orpah as merely a "paradigm of the sane and reasonable," acting in accordance with custom and "common sense," Orpah is as good as dead.[6] As long as we see her way as a negative foil to highlight Ruth's choice, the power of her story as a liberating vision remains limited. In the silence that surrounds Orpah, I recognize the silence that surrounds many women today who follow different paths, choose a different god/dess, and otherwise fail to meet certain expectations. Rethinking her position, even in stretching the dyad of Ruth and Naomi to a threesome, might allow us to reconsider the struggles of many contemporary women, overlooked both by mainline churches and by feminist theology, because their choices do not fit the given types. To include "feminists of all persuasions," as Carmody desires, we must pay Orpah and the Orpahs of today their due.

Orpahs of Today

White feminist women who choose the path of motherhood can, in one sense, be understood as Orpahs who choose not to renounce the "mother's house." I will discuss the literary meanings of the term "mother's house" in chapter 8. Here, I use it metaphorically to point to a return to one's desires, including, but going beyond, the desires for motherhood. Many women who take up motherhood alongside other ambitions today pay the price of a namelessness and subtle condemnation similar to that which clouds the history of Orpah.

Again and again, I read autobiographical notes in the prefaces of books by professional women that confess a certain shock upon becoming a mother. The tale is largely the same: "Until my children were born, I went along quite nicely," writes Amy Rossiter in *From Private to Public: A Feminist Exploration of Early Mothering*. Sara Ruddick, in *Maternal Thinking*, writes that she developed a commitment to equality between the sexes and particular ways of reasoning and "then I had children." Sylvia Ann Hewlett, in *A Lesser Life: The Myth of Women's Liberation in America,* says, "Up until the time I had children, I was profoundly confident of my ability to find fulfillment in both love and work." In *Feminist Mothers,* Tuula Gordon quotes a mother who describes her bind: "I have enjoyed motherhood; but sometimes I feel that I should not talk about it . . . . There is a sense that in order to develop yourself, you should not enjoy motherhood."[7] "I was 'liberated,' " remarks another preschool mother as we drop our boys off at the door, "until I had children."

These mothers raise compelling questions. On one hand, must women who have children give up their lives and aspirations beyond their children? On the other hand, must the birthing and upbringing of children be something that women hide, or simply do on the side?

The category of Orpah stretches beyond the white middle-class woman who struggles to integrate feminist theories of liberation into the "private" and deprecated values of home and family. What about the few men who actually share the chores of the home and otherwise make children and family a top priority? What about the growing number of young single mothers who bear full economic and emotional responsibilities for work and home? What about the older divorced or widowed woman who lived for years in a traditional marriage in which her needs were secondary to husband and children, and her skills unrewarded, and now, while released from some of these restrictions, still has little real power in terms of financial support or social and political status? What about the Central American woman who wants to claim her motherhood as a resource to save herself, her family, and her community? And the Ghanaian woman who embraces mothering as a religious duty, but faces economic hardship in a world where Western materialist definitions of work fail to include her immense unpaid labor as a legitimate category?

These people raise concerns beyond the scope of this book. I mention them because of a few Orpah-like qualities they share. All these people, in different ways, find themselves caught in the clash of the conflicting social values assigned to motherhood, nurture, independence, achievement, and work. They claim desires and values that contradict the dominant values that surround them. They recognize the value of children and of care for them. They choose a less acclaimed, less honored path.

"I Am Also a Mother": Reading Between the Lines

Feminist theology has invited the voices of these various Orpahs, even as it sometimes has failed to listen seriously to them. At times, the language of mothering is like a foreign language which the academic world cannot understand. This is certainly true in the very earliest essay in feminist theology. In one sense, Saiving's own maternal thinking must be read between the lines. She writes about the mother who at once "rejoices in her maternal role" and "learns, too, that a woman can give too much."[8] Yet she never identifies herself as this mother. Without saying "I rejoiced" or "I despaired," she is this "I" upon whom academic standards at that time frowned. It is, I believe, her own maternal experience that furnishes the ground for a revelatory breakthrough in the nature of self-love and agape. In a more recent conversation, she tells us, "I wrote out of my own experience—my experience at the time I wrote and before," but only dared to do so through the guise of third person singular and the writings of other people.[9]

In its explorations of love and sin, "The Human Situation: A Feminine View" is a bold and classic essay. Although some observations no longer pertain, her insights into existential human experience still do. I returned to Saiving's remarks, partly out of a preconscious curiosity that new scrutiny would lead to unnoticed details, but also because her reflections on motherhood, per se, have gone largely unnoticed and deserve our attention. Not until, with children of my own, I reread her article more than a decade after my first reading, did I actually notice the maternal reasoning that had eluded my undergraduate and childless insights.

My intrigue with her theses about the nature of sin from a woman's perspective, and my own disinclination in the 1970s to think about childbearing in my twenties—looking back, I think I did not dare to—blinded me to the central place she gives to the experiences of mothering. It is Saiving's experiences and anthropological studies of those experiences that support her bold claims. The fact that I still gleaned profound insights into who we are and how the world works not only demonstrates the place of this work as a classic theological text. It indicates that observations built on female reproductive experiences, carefully and critically used, can have resonance with many women, regardless of whether they have given birth to children.

A critical rereading of the account of female experience in "The Human Situation" does reveal inevitable time-bound judgments. Drawing primarily on the work of Margaret Mead, she contends, for example, that though a boy must prove his manhood, a girl reaches womanhood "quite naturally—merely by the maturation of her body," an observation challenged by more recent developmental literature and contemporary female experience. Elsewhere, she argues that female participation in the processes of impregnation, pregnancy, childbirth, and lactation have a "certain passivity about them." Recent commentary on "passivity" questions this construction. And the conclusion of the essay explores the idea that American society in the 1960s seemed to be adopting a more "feminine orientation," which the intervening years have disconfirmed.

Saiving herself acknowledges the limits of the essay. She has drawn the distinctions between male and female experience as sharply as possible, she remarks, in order to accentuate their divergences. In a recent interview about this essay in the *Journal of Feminist Studies in Religion,* Saiving notes some of the problems in her attempt to portray woman's experience. Her intent was not to claim her observations as definitional or universal for womanhood, but to proclaim the centrality of "where you are when you do your theology." Theology from a female experience, "whatever female experience may be," must be written. For her, this came "out of not only the middle class, but the white middle class." What she observes may have wider validity, but it will be "said quite differently by people from other cultures."[10]

In my mind, there is still much truth to Saiving's original arguments, even those most suspect, such as the naturalness or passivity of womanhood. In the first place, these assertions are never proclaimed. They are suggested, and always with finely textured nuances about their meanings. For example, she qualifies her observation about the more passive quality of female sexuality by noting that the woman "*may* take an active role, but it is not necessary for her to do so, either to satisfy the man or to fulfill her reproductive function." Many of her observations put into words important hunches about sexual differences that ring so true to experience that it is hard to disagree with them entirely, despite their limitations.

Saiving's misreadings of female experience and of broader social phenomena do not undermine the nature of her argument and its central contributions. Although we are still trying to determine what it means to be female or male, the answer, she reiterates in 1988, will "not be found either in biology or in socialization, but in some dialectical relationship between the two." Biological givens function as "limits, rather than specificities," limits with which we must contend.[11] Her essay dares to contend with the limits of maternity.

The sentence "I am also a mother" in Saiving's article is not implicit as much as understated. In the later conversation about the essay, she makes this clear. Mary Gerhart asks Saiving how her "feminist consciousness was born," at a time in which such thought received little encouragement. While there are many motivating factors, such as six years in an all-girls school and the model of Mrs. Roosevelt, Saiving's experience as a mother is primary. She had first studied theology in Chicago during World War II, accepted as the only woman there for a doctorate, because "they were having trouble finding enough students [men] even for a ministerial degree." She left the degree unfinished to marry, but returned thirteen years later, divorced and with a child, convinced, over against cultural definitions of femininity, that she could indeed teach and still fit the "category *woman*." The paper itself was written in 1958 for a class, while she was, in her words,

> trying to take care of my daughter Emily who was very small then. She was three, or four, maybe. I was trying to be a responsible student and also a good mother, and *sometimes it just seemed impossible*, especially since I was living in the city, and I didn't have any relatives or anybody like that to call on. I don't know what else to say.[12]

This says enough. Fertile tensions between the creative and the procreative mother stand at the heart of her essay and her own altered consciousness.

It is not so surprising, then, that Saiving begins her discussion of human experience with the "central fact about sexual differences": "In every society it is women—and only women—who bear children" and remain "closest to the infant and young child," because of "the physiology of lactation." She struggles to understand the many meanings and implications of this statement. The power of female biological creativity challenges male creativity at this most immediate, fundamental level. That is, a man's "inability to bear children" becomes "a deficiency for which he must compensate."[13] Men must strive to achieve what women already have—a role in the powers of creation and the existential confirmation of childbearing. Hence the modern monuments erected to celebrate male achievements, the male temptation for pride and self-promotion, and its hidden underside, the male envy of maternal powers.

Mothers, on the other hand, participate in biological creation directly, immediately, and in a more prolonged and spontaneous fashion. They very often discover that the "one essential, indispensable relationship of a mother to her child *is* the I-Thou relationship." This special intimate relationship is an "irreplaceable school" for the essentialities of that illusive virtue, love, and an instance of moving past the alienation of life to stand momentarily in the "power of being."[14] However, at the very same time the religious sensibilities of a divine nature are tapped, a critical temptation arises. Hearing a child demands abandoning one's own point of view, or at least moving the self slightly off-center to meet acute needs. Hence the different temptation for many women, particularly mothers: the temptation to lose oneself. Feminist theologians, since that time, have been busy determining what we have lost of ourselves through female biology—certainly an important task—while bypassing an equally critical agenda—what we gain.

In the Interlude: A Pregnant Silence

For the past three decades feminist theologians have filled in the rest of Saiving's sentence, "I am a student; I am also a woman," with conclusions that have challenged the field of theology, the underpinnings of traditional religion, and the various institutions upheld by religion, including marriage and family. Building on the consciousness-raising model of the women's movement in the wider culture, early feminists in theology turned to their experiences as women to recast religion. They made it clear that, without the voices of women, theological and moral reflection cannot offer realistic standards of human fulfillment, nor can it understand the power of religious myth and symbol. These voices refuted the religious reinforcement of sexism on at least three fronts: male God language and ideology; the exclusion of women from religious vocation and reflection; and the religious sanction of subordination of women in the home. Religion, like so much else, will never be the same.

As essential as these challenges were in themselves, they also tended to leave some women, certainly women of color, but also women who became mothers, in the lurch. Many theologians are mothers, but few have investigated in any depth what is learned about theology from this pivotal life experience. Few have made the complex intersection of work and family a primary topic of research. Many advocate maternal God imagery and language, but say little about actual mothers and mothering. Some use the metaphor of mothering, but do not consider seriously the problems of modern models of parenthood, work, and family. The feminist movement in religion does not write a great deal out of these particular experiences. Consequently, observes Elisabeth Schüssler Fiorenza, it has not paid "sufficient attention to the needs of children and of women with children."[15]

The needs of children and of women with children raise pressing questions for feminist theology. Does motherhood, by definition, necessitate subservience? If women do not need to obey their husbands anymore or sacrifice their desires to "keep the peace," how are conflicts of interest to be arbitrated? If the control and use of women's procreative powers in the service of men's aims and desires has been systematically reinforced by the theological worldview of biblical faith, are there alternative symbols and formulas? If religious sanctions for the patriarchal family system are debunked, what kind of system and sanctions are endorsed instead?

As we have observed, religious ideology has played a powerful role in formulating ideas about the "right" and "wrong" ways to mother. The absence of the maternal voice in religion more recently has led to an impoverished choice in religious images of mothering. In the words of Julia Kristeva, most women face the choice of either a "total negation" of motherhood or "an acceptance . . . of its traditional representations." The latter is still the choice of a "great mass of people, women and men."[16] Without alternative religious ideologies, conservative values that encourage wives and mothers to subject their needs to those of their husbands and children continue to fill the vacuum.

Beside the practical consequences of silence, there are several theoretical problems: How can feminist theology endorse a method that begins with experience if it does not take into account the hours that many women spend birthing, tending, and mentoring? How can we envision human nature without working female procreativity into the picture in some positive way, despite the ambiguities and entrapments? How can we envision God as mother, when so much controversy and misunderstanding about the institution and experience of mothering abounds? Feminist theology is bound—by social context, by method, and by content—to incorporate the complicated yet positive aspects of a mother's discourse.

When a question about women and children arose in a Women and Religion session on "Living the Deepening Contradictions" at an American Academy of Religion meeting in 1989, only one woman on the otherwise colorful panel of white, Hispanic, Asian, and African American women had children. She attempted no response. The Hispanic woman observed that if this were a Hispanic meeting, the hall would sing with the voices of the many children present. Another panelist remarked candidly that she had made her choice: She could not accomplish what she wanted if she had chosen to have children. No one questioned professional accomplishment and mothering as seemingly mutually exclusive ideals. No one asked what it might mean to allow the halls of the academy to sing. Of the many apparent "contradictions" women live, feminist theologians have trouble naming and talking about the tensions between creativity and procreativity that exist for many feminist theologian mothers and for many mothers in general.

This phenomenon is not uncommon. The mother as speaking subject is also missing from literary, psychoanalytic, and ethical dramas. Literary scholar Carol Heilbrun, for instance, has written a fascinating book, *Writing a Woman's Life*, without so much as a chapter on mothering.[17] Her silence and the silence of women in religion is understandable. In some ways, silence was absolutely necessary as a protective device. Women have had a lot of catching up to do on a multitude of other fronts. Just as mothers who entered the male-dominated workplace in the 1970s remained silent about their maternal anxieties to avoid jeopardizing their jobs or giving the other side ammunition, women scholars actually needed to remain silent for a certain period on this very ambiguous subject. Patriarchal images of motherhood must be deconstructed, it seems, before new images can be constructed.

I will return later to the broader nature of maternal silence and its implications. At this point, it is important to observe that in the midst of the silence, mothers have had to continue to find ways to live and survive in worlds hostile to motherhood for opposite reasons. Not only is silence no longer necessary, it will now be more harmful than talking about motherhood, for the discussion will proceed by the sheer force of social history, whether feminist theologians participate or not. It is proceeding, not just among conservative parties, but on more politically diversified fronts. As I have discussed, the question of motherhood and the maternal is a topic of considerable debate among a growing number of feminists in other fields.

Whereas in the 1960s, feminists like Shulamith Firestone, Betty Friedan, and Kate Millet identified motherhood as the site of women's oppression, now sometimes even these same women see it as a site for renewed political praxis with transformative possibilities. The critical task will be to distinguish interpretations that play into the hands of societal backlash against women, in the name of "family values," from those that support women by fostering alternative values. It is at this point that the need for a feminist theological perspective increases.

Quickening

Just as there have been modifications in feminist theory, so also have important transitions begun to occur in feminist theology. These transitions do not reflect the same degree of concern over motherhood as does feminist theory more broadly. They do lay foundations for the expression of such concern, however. For the last few years, for instance, the call for papers from the Women and Religion section of the American Academy of Religion has asked for "reconsiderations of motherhood and mothering," even though few sessions have materialized.

Differences between two representative collections of essays, edited by Carol Christ and Judith Plaskow and published in 1979 and 1989 respectively, illustrate well some of the relevant transitions. Plaskow and Christ organized the essays in their initial volume, *Womanspirit Rising*, one of the first collections of essays in feminist theology, according to two distinct understandings of women's experiences: those who write about the *"feminist* experience" of liberation, and those who write from women's *"traditional* experience." The categories "reformist" and "revolutionary" are used also to structure the first book. In fact, almost the entire introduction to this volume is dedicated to organizing and classifying women in the feminist theological movement.[18] When Christ and Plaskow try to position Saiving's essay in *Womanspirit Rising*, however, it does not quite fit.

Ten years later, on the first page of the introduction to *Weaving the Visions*, not only must Christ and Plaskow acknowledge the "dramatic broadening and diversification of feminist theology and theology." They retract the original delineations and debate the pros and cons of classificatory systems themselves.[19] The delineations served to silence the enormous variety subsumed under each pole.

Most intriguing, in *Womanspirit Rising*, women's "body experience" was relegated to the category of "traditional experience." We can understand some of the reasons for this division in retrospect, but it still seems particularly odd and inadequate. This classification implies that there was little that initially was considered liberating about body experiences in themselves, including maternal body experiences. They provide clues to unraveling patriarchal culture, but little else. If these experiences were not suspect, they were certainly seen as less "feminist" and less able to transcend limiting patriarchal theologies. It is not yet thought that they might actually provoke particular kinds of constructive philosophical thinking. Body experiences primarily signify entrapments that many saw as alienating and too male-defined to be retrievable.

In *Womanspirit Rising*, Christ and Plaskow are aware that they had left the integration of "women's traditional experience of biologically defined roles," and "feminist experience" or "freedom from" these roles, to the future. Women were more intent on refusing to let biology determine destiny than allowing biology to inform and transform it. Few suggest that rootedness in nature might even give one freedom from male-defined life goals or this-worldly values. Even Saiving, who is more sympathetic to female biology, assumes the classical split between nature and spirit: A "woman's closeness to nature," she maintains, is a "measure of the distance she must travel to reach spirit"—an assumption no longer acceptable in the world of *Weaving the Visions*.[20]

Although Penelope Washbourn's essay in *Womanspirit Rising* retrieves menstruation as an essentially sacred event, few theologians refer to the bodily experiences of mothering. Christ's essay celebrates motherhood, according to the introduction, as a source of spiritual transformation. In her essay "Spiritual Quest and Women's Experience," she even argues that a "religious symbol system adequate to . . . experience must include, as possible models for achieving transcendence, motherhood." But she makes this claim from afar. Spiritual transcendence is the goal. The introduction stresses that she is not a mother, and in this essay itself, Christ chooses a character from a Doris Lessing novel who mothers children not her own. Mothering seems more a means to another end, self-development and spiritual quest. Distance from motherhood, as much as immersion in its exhausting day-to-day struggles, is emphasized: "Motherhood can provide opportunities for insight only when the mother has a sense of distance from her children that is hard to achieve when they are her own."[21]

Christ's second essay, "Why Women Need the Goddess," is more affirming of the actual bodily processes of the female life cycle, including giving birth. However, even here the emphasis is on the symbolic powers of giving birth, as representative of "all the creative, life-giving powers of the universe."[22] The physical demands of giving birth or nursing are a limit, not a resource.

This is like looking at a negative of the mother-child interaction, rather than at the developed photograph. Only by *not* becoming mothers, it seems, can "modern feminist women" reclaim their bodies without letting biology become destiny. But have they really reclaimed their bodies, refused biology as destiny, or integrated the limits that biology can impose on life choices? Only Saiving's article, which predates all the others in the volume by at least ten years, begins to answer this question. It is curious, then, that few, including the editors' own introduction, seem to notice her reliance on motherhood.

The promotion of embodied or erotic experiences as a source of knowledge may be one of the more outstanding differences between *Womanspirit Rising* and *Weaving the Visions*. This is most prominent in essays by women of color and lesbians, but it is not restricted to them. Alongside this, if there is a common thread that runs through *Weaving the Visions*, it is the disclaimer that white women can define a universal women's experience. If there is a single popular word, it is *diversity*. This volume suggests a "continuum model" as more appropriate than the models used in the first volume and opens up for investigation the distinct particularities of women's experience.

This still does not mean that many authors turn to maternal experience as one kind of particularity. An article on the maternal per se, or on work and family, is still missing from this volume. Several authors evoke related claims. Several explore the further implications and meanings of female, maternal, God imagery, including that found in Native American and African traditions and in goddess religion. Several invoke the centrality of bodily and erotic knowing, urging, with Adrienne Rich, that we "think through the body."[23] Almost all proclaim the importance of relationality in women's experience, in human existence, and as part of the nature of the sacred. The authors in the section on "self in relation," or human nature, admittedly the "most unwieldy part of this volume," are united in the claim that the self is "essentially *embodied, passionate, relational, and communal.*"[24]

While no one speaks out of her own maternal experience in *Weaving the Visions*, Sallie McFague talks at length about the virtues of maternal love and justice.[25] She does so in the service of amplifying a new metaphor of God as Mother. She thereby walks around important problems of modern models of parenthood, abstracting the value of maternal activities from their context. Portraying the love of God in terms of maternal love, without attending to the ambiguous realities of mothering, can easily lend itself to the perpetuation of unrealistic expectations—that mothers are, or somehow should be, exemplary models of a giving love that requires no return. This is not to say McFague's original project is not a worthy one. It is, and it does participate in the quickening movement of conversation about mothers in general, but it cannot stand alone without the work of others more attentive to the intersection of theology and culture.

Paula Gunn Allen and Delores Williams, both women of color, offer more graphic and more realistic conceptions of maternal experience in general. From her perspective as a Laguna Pueblo/Sioux Native American, Paula Gunn Allen asserts that at the "center of all is Woman," that "no thing is sacred . . . without her blessing." But to confine the "creative prowess of the Creatrix," commonly diminished and demeaned as a "fertility goddess," to maternal power limits the power inherent in femininity, which includes both the womb and the thought. "She Who Thinks" is every bit as important as "She Who Bears." Moreover, she who bears, "Hard Beings Woman," as the Hopi name her, "also destroys." The power to make life, to create, and to transform, including but never limited to the biological power to give birth, is seen as the source of all power, and "no other power can gainsay it." Hence the ability inherent in mothering to transform something from one state or condition to another is an ability "sought and treasured" among Native Americans.[26] Mothers are esteemed.

In a more pragmatic sense, this is true for other women of color, and womanists in particular. According to Delores Williams's depiction, "Womanist reality begins with mothers relating to their children."[27] What does womanist reality experience from this vantage point? The demand to make "a way out of no way," in Alice Walker's words of dedication to her mother. Mothers are honored for this gift: "Black mothers have passed on wisdom for survival . . . for as long as anyone can remember." But this demand to nurture great numbers of people, exemplified by Sojourner Truth, Harriet Tubman, and others, is never mutually exclusive of the demand for black women's self-love. Womanists, building on this history of strong mothers, seek survival and community building, but also are determined to love themselves —"Regardless." This means avoiding the "self-destruction of bearing a disproportionately large burden in the work of community building and maintenance."[28]

In contrast to *Weaving the Visions, Inheriting Our Mother's Gardens,* a volume that appeared about the same time, puts the term *mother* right in the title. But not without second thought. As the introduction attests, the term invokes rich examples of empowerment and innovation, *and* painful disappointments and rejections, especially when radically divergent life choices are made, as with the lesbian authors. Every essay in this collection of feminist theologies from the "third-world perspective" makes direct reference to gleanings from the mother's garden. While the writers talk about the "joys and problems of relationships with their mothers," not about their own pleasures and qualms about mothering, this volume moves maternal creation front and center. It goes one step further than *Weaving the Visions* in creating fertile ground for reclaiming maternal knowing.

We can hail one groundbreaking exception to the dearth of material on motherhood in theology, which appeared about the same time as *Weaving the Visions* and *Inheriting Our Mother's Gardens:* a *Concilium* issue, edited by Anne Carr and Elisabeth Schüssler Fiorenza, titled "Motherhood: Experience, Institution, Theology." The text reflects a certain novice state of affairs. Many of the essays remain at the level of critique of the institution and its ideologies. Fewer consistently draw upon or expound constructions derived from the intimate, immediate experiences of mothering. Christine Gudorf's essay, as one example, enumerates in a brief paragraph the rudiments of an ethic of motherhood that begs for further amplification.

Nonetheless, the editor's introduction is careful to list the unexplored topics: "children's rights, the rights of lesbian mothers . . . mothers under slavery, mothers as workers . . . ." Perhaps one of the more remarkable contributions of this volume is Ursula Pfäfflin's suggestion and promotion of the paradigm of motherhood as a starting point for dialogue across differences in sex, age, class, sexual orientation, ethnicity, and worldview. This has the capacity, the editor's introduction reiterates, "not only for overcoming the split between the worlds of women and men but also splits among different cultures, nations, races, classes, and religions."[29] The essays in *Inheriting Our Mother's Gardens*, authored by women from across the globe, seem to show that this is partially true.

The Birth of New Horizons: "I Am Also a Mother"

Saiving's nuanced interpretation of what she has learned about theology, both as a woman and as a mother, resists classification along the lines imposed later by Christ and Plaskow in *Womanspirit Rising*. Saiving falls right in the middle between the two poles that those authors believed divided feminist attempts to rewrite religious tradition. Saiving draws on both the "feminist experience" of liberation *and* the so-called "traditional experience" of women. Occupying a position somewhere between these two camps, she interweaves a critique of sexist views of selfless love with a reevaluation of women's unique experiences as mothers. She finds the latter liberating and the former limited, unless it encompasses childbearing. She talks about women who wish to be both mothers "*and* full human beings." A mother who "rejoices in her maternal role . . . knows the profound experience" of a unique I-Thou love. She also knows that total devotion to endless housewifely tasks and a deadening self-giving can become a woman's gravest temptation and sin, a sin traditional theology has mistakenly upheld as a virtue.[30]

A handful of recent feminist theologians join Saiving in balancing these two commitments, some speaking directly out of their maternal experiences. A very few—Christine Gudorf, Sally Purvis, Pamela Couture, and McFague—have drawn upon their experiences as mothers, Gudorf and Purvis more explicitly, but not as extensively as Couture and McFague. Some, like Beverly Harrison, Margaret A. Farley, and Catherine Keller, draw less explicitly upon so-called traditional experience, but retain immense respect for mothering and link its meanings to the cause of human liberation. Instead of mothering per se, they rely upon related motifs of the power of female connection and personal commitment. A few, like Mary E. Hunt, Carter Heyward, and Kathryn Rabuzzi, ground theologies in related metaphors of women's friendship, erotic love, or even housework and childbirth.[31]

Two texts, those of Gudorf and Purvis, draw particularly on maternal knowledge and demonstrate the reflective power of this kind of thinking for theology and ethics. The best example is Gudorf's sage essay, which critically correlates scriptural, theological readings of Jesus' sacrifice on the cross with her own experiences in mothering two children with handicaps. Foremost, she challenges the oppressive idealization of heroic self-sacrifice as the primary model of Christian agape and suggests, instead, the give and take of mutuality as the ultimate Christian ideal. I will explore her observations in greater detail later, when we discuss children and generativity. Her article "Parenting, Mutual Love, and Sacrifice" appeared in 1985. Not surprisingly, perhaps, it has only slowly received the kind of attention it deserves. It is not easy for many religious scholars to admit that children and parenting could be the source of important ethical theological reflection.

Another rendition of this argument, "Mothers, Neighbors, and Strangers: Another Look at Agape," by Sally Purvis, points out why this might be so. Although it seems odd from the perspective of thirty years of feminist theology, Christian theological and philosophical ethics has always been deeply suspicious of the implications of "special relations" in understanding the imperative of agape. No one has articulated a specifically positive role for special relationships in the understanding of agape because of the sense that the mere power of special relations with loved ones will "swamp universal human dignity," in Gene Outka's words.[32] In cautious defiance of this skepticism, Purvis writes, "It may be a biographic accident that my richest and most powerful experience of agape, of unqualified, unconditional love for another, has come with my experience of being a mother."[33]

I do not think it is accidental. But we can understand her reluctance to introduce her claim more boldly. For she must defy a model of agapic love proposed by Søren Kierkegaard and upheld by a long tradition of theological ethics. In Kierkegaard's words, the highest model of love is found in "The Work of Love in Remembering One Who Is Dead," because it is the most "disinterested, the freest, the most faithful."[34] But Purvis's experiences as a mother force her to question this imperative. The ideal of true agapic love is neither radically impartial nor "utterly disinterested," Purvis implies, and I would argue that the work of love is in *remembering the one who is just born*—the child. Love requires the "caring intensity" witnessed in mother love. This love, which society has grossly romanticized in order *not* to take it and the mothers who attempt it seriously, occurs sporadically, at best, as only a small part of the more ambiguous, chaotic practice of mothering. It is distinctive in its revelatory powers, nonetheless.

Unfortunately, Purvis herself cannot escape the need to universalize, or at least generalize, from the sporadic particularities of this love. The weakest section of her article is that which attempts to isolate the features of this mother love from its fragmentary, and even impossible, actualization: It is "inclusive," "intensely involved and other-regard-ing"—"unconditional." She unhelpfully brackets the question of whether "the distortions, the evils" of contemporary society, "racism, classism, sexism, heterosexism, poverty, isolation," have nearly eradi-cated the possibility of such love.[35] She leaves some of the more intrigu-ing heuristic values of mother love for agapic love to our imagination and to the footnotes.

In a footnote, Purvis identifies a problem central to any adequate reconsideration of traditional doctrines of agape, the "problem mothers have balancing their own needs and the needs of their children, particu-larly small children." This "has not received the professional attention I hope it will," she adds.[36] I agree. A mother's needs themselves challenge her own contention that mother love can be "unconditional." No won-der Purvis must qualify her list of the "features" of mother love by reiterating that it is only occasional. Her account has not dealt with the interaction between maternal and child needs, and with the occasional quality of all maternal love. A reconsideration of maternal needs, which the next three chapters explore here, forces a reading of love different from the one she gives, a reading that incorporates love's ambiguities and failures as part of its necessary actualization.

Love must fail—something the recent school of self-psychology has called "optimal frustration"—in order for life and growth to occur. Gudorf, arguing more forcefully in favor of a kind of balancing of needs, asserts that "agape is valuable in the service of eros and does not exist otherwise." Doctrines of agape must recognize the needs of the mother, or, ironically, the mother will become "less able to give." That is, a mother cannot genuinely recognize the needs of the other unless her own subjectivity is recognized. Recognition of the needs of others is "best done by those who recognize their own."[37] Purvis implies this when she acknowledges the erratic appearance of mother love in the midst of the "inevitable chorus" of the "other feelings, immense distractions, deadening trivia" that surround it. Her mistake is to see this ambiguous chorus as somehow separate from the actualization of the qualities of mother love, rather than as an integral part of its possibilities.

Pamela Couture makes an even stronger case for an ethic, not simply of mutual love, but indeed of "shared responsibility." She moves the discussion of agape into the midst of the distortions and evils of public policy. Although the stories of her maternal experiences remain implicit to the text itself, *Blessed Are the Poor?* presents one of the best examples of research motivated and shaped by an author's own experiences as a divorced mother of two young daughters. The divorce made apparent the ways in which American rhetoric about equality, embodied in the legal adversary system and public policy, totally ignores the needs of mothers and their children, promoting an ethic of self-sufficiency that bypasses the necessary connections of life. Her experiences of the "mercy of the church," those who "not only helped, but *cared*," mentioned in passing in her acknowledgments, also make apparent the underrated, ignored nets of interdependence that hold American society together, the "frequently invisible supports which anchor the flourishing of both children and adults."[38]

But it is Couture's examination of motherhood in America, and as seen in Luther and Wesley, which leads her to conclude that, embedded in all three, are the seeds for an ethic of care upon which American society must capitalize now or risk the increasing poverty of its mothers and children, and even its own eventual demise. By "shared responsibility," Couture refers to a position grounded in Christian claims for the worth of individuals, the equal value of domestic and public work, the importance of economic and relational reciprocity in families and society, and the imperative to care for the vulnerable.[39] This ethic of care rests upon a theological criterion of care for the vulnerable understood by both Luther and Wesley, which includes the maternal vulnerability necessitated by the act of reproducing the human race.

A Feminist Maternal Theology

As Gudorf, Purvis, and Couture demonstrate so well, the phrase, "I am a student of theology; I am also a mother," opens a new horizon of theological possibilities. Feminist theology and feminist maternal theology provide an important foundation for the evaluation of doctrines of love and responsibility. While Saiving draws implicitly upon her experience as a mother, she did not or could not make the source of her inspiration explicit until more recently. Others, including myself, are more free to do so, partly because women like Saiving opened the doors of theological inquiry and vocational opportunity.

A feminist maternal theology necessarily builds on, and extends several core premises of, feminist theology. First, theological and moral reflection begins with a thick description of human experience that gives privileged voice to the underside, the oppressed, the outcast, who often struggle to hear their own voices. This critical commitment has played back on the voices of feminists themselves. In this case, it is mothers and children who have been silenced and need to be heard.

Second, contrary to twenty centuries of misogyny deeply embedded in cultural symbols, myths, philosophy, and religion, feminist theology stresses the self-worth of women as human beings created by God/dess in the image of God/dess. It refutes the equation of women and evil. Few degradations ever devised or permitted, in Bernard Shaw's opinion, are "as disastrous as this degradation."[40] Although I would contend that many degradations, including those of race, class, and sexual abuse are equally or more devastating, the emphasis of Shaw's point is important. In particular, women's sexual and maternal bodies have been either demonized or perversely idealized. The human worth of the one who bears, the pregnant body, the mothering woman, must be de-idealized and revalued in turn. There are no inequalities between men and women as they stand before God's grace.

Third, feminist theology has dramatically shifted the discussion of theological doctrines and cultural ideals of love and sin. The doctrine of agape as exhaustive self-sacrifice, and of sin as prideful self-assertion, has ignored and betrayed the experiences of women. It also has betrayed the experiences of mothers. A closer reading of maternal knowing helps to correct these interpretations. If so-called "mere mutuality" is in actuality "love in its deepest radicality . . . so *radical* that many of us have yet to learn to bear it," in Beverly Harrison's words, and if "relationality is at the heart of all things," then many mothers hover near the heart of things and bear much that merits learning.[41]

Finally, feminist theology has argued for justice, equality, and liberation of the oppressed. Liberation, based upon sameness as the standard for equality, flounders once the pregnant body and the child announce themselves as potential differences. Motherhood and children complicate and then reorient the question of life, liberty, and the pursuit of happiness. We need a richer conception of equality in work and love, and a richer depiction of liberation. Can feminist theology help articulate and enact more adequate ideals of human equality, generativity, and fulfillment that can make the flourishing of mothers and children a possibility, even a priority? This question comprises the next frontier of liberation. Part Two of this book will attend to this and the other three premises identified above.

In short, as we will see in the following chapters, feminist theologians have a great deal at stake and much to contribute in addressing constructions of work, love, home, and family, and in identifying the voices of mothers and children as being essential to the work of theology and ethics. If feminist theologians and mothers begin to attend to the hours spent nursing and rearing children, we will bring about, I believe, a fundamental reevaluation of definitions of work and value, and a revaluing of the essentiality of caring labor. We must not underestimate the vitality of a feminist theological evolution of the private realm based upon a reconceptualization of generative processes, including the processes of birth and child rearing.

First, women established within the American Academy of Religion a section for women and religion. Now we can ask forbidden questions that challenge the limitations of "male-stream thought." As Mary O'Brien formulates it, "What, if all labor creates value, is the value produced by reproductive labor?"[42] If patriarchal religion has appropriated women's procreative powers, what happens when feminist theologians reclaim and unleash it? What if the halls of the academy begin to sing?

❦ ❦ ❦

Part Two

The Mother's Voice

New Visions of Work and Family

❦ ❦ ❦

CHAPTER FIVE

Generativity Crises of My Own

THE STORY BEHIND
THE LIFE

What matters is that lives do not serve as models; only stories do that. And it is hard to make up stories to live by . . . .
. . . I have read many moving lives of women, but they are painful, the price is high, the anxiety is intense, because there is no script to follow, no story portraying how one is to act, let alone any alternative stories. . . .
Male power has made certain stories unthinkable.
Carolyn G. Heilbrun, *Writing a Woman's Life*

Then they lifted up their voices and wept again; and Orpah kissed her mother-in-law [and returned to her mother's house].

Ruth 1:14*a* RSV

Τhe story of Naomi, Ruth, and Orpah is paradigmatic. These three women suddenly find themselves cast adrift, outside the classical social mores that defined the position of men and women. Today many such social norms no longer hold, but if the book of Ruth is to function as the "theological interpretation of feminism" that Phyllis Trible claims, then it must be read with its full cast of characters.

Part one of this book has confirmed that stories of work and family in American society, likewise, have not been read with their full cast of characters. Stories of mothers, in particular, remain partially untold. When they are not woven into the fabric of society, ideals and practices of generativity become threadbare and shabby. Under the shadow of outmoded religious narratives and a life cycle defined primarily from the perspective of men, representative psychologies and theologies have become enamored of a generativity understood as material productivity, relegating the virtue of care to later stages of development, or demoting it as secondary and peripheral. To its detriment, much of modern psychology and theology ignores the experiences of many women and mothers. Part two furthers the task of reconstructing stories and interpretations of generativity that include the mother's voice.

This chapter emerges as a hesitant, wary response to the challenge of a friend who observed that my own story was buried in, but missing from, my observations about Orpah and Ruth. He knew the nature of a part of my reluctance. "The level of appropriate self-disclosure in an academic book is always tricky to determine," he wrote. He may not have suspected, however, my additional reluctance to use myself as illustration, when many women's gifts remain thwarted and silenced because they are "washing the dishes and looking after the children." My response is limited by comparison. But my friend was convinced that "persons crave stories" about the merging of family and career in order to make sense of their lives, even if it is hard to make up stories to live by. So "share some more of your own." This chapter does so by weaving in with the stories of other women some threads from stories behind the life that lies at the wellspring of this book.

A Double Plot

The study of the conflicts of *Women of Academe* by Nadya Aisenberg and Mona Harrington is the first book I have seen that captures adequately the alienation of women academics, *Outsiders in the Sacred Grove,* its appropriate subtitle. While the observations are based upon interviews with a limited population of sixty-four tenured and displaced academic women, some of their conclusions and generalizations about the processes of women's work lives and vocational development apply also to the plight of women who are outsiders in the sacred workplaces of society more generally.

Contrary to the perception of sweeping changes, women have not made significant progress in those sacred pastures. They have not attained the positions of prestige and power that some predicted, particularly in the professions. The perception of change is greater than the actual changes themselves. Why?

The answers are manifold. A few significant ones pertain here. First and most significantly, women are barred by the remaining force of old social norms. Despite the powerful challenge to perceptions of adult generativity discussed in part one, two basic life plans persist: (1) the "marriage plot" that defines a woman's primary sphere as private and domestic; and (2) the "quest" or "adventure plot" that reserves an assertive public life for men only.[1] Although marriage, home, and children may no longer be a viable profession for women, old social scripts of these jobs as a woman's primary responsibility linger. Even though the time and energy these tasks consume has diminished in one sense, the responsibilities have proliferated in other respects. Although U.S. women have taken two-thirds of the millions of newly created jobs in the recent information era and will continue to do so, the expectation that women will continue to perform domestic services remains.[2] New rules do not easily displace the old ones. Deep-set beliefs endure. People who deviate from these gender-differentiated plots still know the stigma. They have somehow defied nature.

As a result, many women who pursue a job or higher education have a double agenda, even before they take their first job. They face not one, but two significant hurdles. Adulthood for men and women alike involves the developmental task of determining the place of work in their life and then learning the trade or acquiring the credentials, degrees, recommendations, and other proofs of accomplishment. Many women have an additional hurdle: They not only enter upon the external process of vocational change from lay person to trained person, they enter upon an internal process of transformation of their core identity from private to public worker.

For some women, this entails a "great internal drama" in which they must radically reenvision themselves and who they have understood themselves to be. Many must repeatedly break the restricting chains of all the old "can'ts" and "don'ts" of bygone norms. Some of the character virtues of the marriage plot—patience, receptivity, accommodation, unselfishness, modesty, passivity—must be challenged and transformed. Many women must build, not simply reclaim, a radically new identity and assume forbidden virtues of assertiveness, initiative, competence, public visibility, and leadership. In contrast to the more formulaic career patterns of most men, women often "veer and tack" from project to project in the attempt to create new norms.[3] They appear indecisive, unsure, hesitant, nonserious, and even frivolous. Many drift into their accomplishments rather than pursue them. In the end, they must do something that goes against the grain of their socialization: They must learn to use educational knowledge as a tool for personal advancement and power.

Because the internal drama is quite compelling as well as energy and time consuming, many women become so absorbed in it that they forsake the requisite process of acquiring external credentials for a job. Equally disorienting, many prefer to define success in more personal and less detached and ambitious terms than do men. Reluctance to recognize and play by the "rules of the game," as defined by men, repeatedly puts women at a disadvantage. Aisenberg and Harrington also notice that certain events such as marriage and childbirth can reignite the internal drama and cause formerly resolved issues to resurface. The energy this drama consumes is "particularly great where religious values prevail," because they tend to reinforce the conventional plots.[4]

According to Aisenberg and Harrington, the number of women who successfully integrate their home and work lives is "minuscule." Unforeseen troubles such as a divorce, a sick child, a husband's illness or move, an elderly parent, or, more often, less grave problems become major roadblocks.[5] Compromises of all sorts—accepting less demanding work, losing work or scaling down, opting for a slow track, subordinating work to other chosen priorities, even failed marriages—are almost inevitable. Possible successes occur primarily when some extra measure has intervened—financial resources that buy time and services, a partner's or husband's willingness to step off the fast track, the virtual inversion of traditional scripts, and the absence of major or minor disasters.

In most cases, the working woman fits neither the marriage nor the adventure mold. This is precisely where many women are stymied.

Trying to fit partially into both molds requires a very complicated coordination between the timing of family and the timing of work, and women become caught in plotting the "logistical and chronological intricacies of a double generativity," while most men do not.[6] A battle rages within themselves as well as with the external world. Many blame themselves. But the real locus of the conflict lies in the structures of the work site, the structures of the family, the structures of social policy, and the ideologies related to all three. In American society, few people, men or women, attain an integrated work and home life.

"Am I a Woman?": Writing a New Script

My own confrontation with established scripts assumed its formal beginning at a small liberal arts college in the Midwest in the mid-1970s. The most memorable academic paper from that time was written during my final year, to complete an assignment on my own "search for identity," for an anthropology course that included the study of Erikson's *Young Man Luther.* It is significant to note that this paper was written for one of the few courses at the college taught by a woman at that time. Her mere presence as a woman allowed for new thought and new stories. In self-effacingly titling my paper "Am I a Woman?" I did what women so often do, although I did not know it at the time: I personalized a social and political dilemma and blamed myself. The title should have read, "What Does It Mean to Be a White Middle-class Woman in a Postindustrial, and Possibly Postfeminist Society?" In both cases, the "Post" prefix does not refer to the demise of either, but to the realities of living in a transitional time, *after* the demise of certain work and family forms, but *before* what I did not know.

Undergraduate education in those transitional times had made my answer to the identity question only more muddled. The political movements of the sixties, particularly the women's movement, invariably had an impact. By my last year, the assumption with which I had entered college, one which went back as far as the late eighteenth century—that women lucky enough to receive advanced education would use it not for their own promotion but for the private realm of family and community—seemed antiquated. Expectations of what women could and should do with their lives had broadened immensely. Up to a certain point, I felt freed from restricting definitions of what a woman could think and do, freed from a limited view of body, mind, and self, and freed from limited views of men and relationships.

Yet as words appeared on paper for the anthropology class, this seemed less true. The relationship between my education and my future in the public sphere was fraught with contradiction and limitation. Encouraged to aspire to goals which the structures of society made it difficult, if not impossible, to fulfill, I felt confused, and even deceived by what Mirra Komzrovsky describes as the "scarcity of resources for role fulfillment" in combining work and family.[7] Neither the family nor the workplace, nor the larger social structure provided the means for this kind of integrated life. Disdaining conventional role play between the sexes, and convinced of the greater integrity of alternative possibilities, I saw even then that I had "torn down without rebuilding." I was "lost because I had no other model to substitute."[8] The image of myself as working or as single felt hazy, vacuous, and ill-defined. A mere four years of imagining its virtues could not undo at least sixteen of imagining otherwise, nor could it offset a culture that still provided limited avenues of satisfaction for women.

My life did not follow the "dynamic of the tale" told by my family. It did not completely follow the dynamic of the dawning tales of the women's movement, either. Over against men's "wonderful banquet of possible quests, conceivable stories, available narratives," women's storylessness felt stark.[9] The college essay testifies to the "restraints and values" that I "shed," and to the "void" that this left.[10] It symbolizes the beginning of a personal, as well as a broader ethical, religious, and ideological quest for new stories and new virtues.

I concluded the college paper on a tenuous note. A "seemingly endless period of youth" stretched before me, adulthood shimmering like a mirage "far beyond my reach." While society deems college an initiation into adulthood, its ritual processes which culminate in graduation fail in many ways. Colleges and universities can no longer carry the moral and religious load that is expected of them. I left with few of the tangible signs that society holds up as adult watersheds and unclear about the virtues of an adult woman. The search for identity had not ended as Erikson forecast, but had become only more complicated in a world he never explored, a world that gives few positive clues and plenty of negative ones to women with generative aspirations.

College education is ambiguous for many women. Whereas college is a high school girl's sufficient future if she puts it before marriage, once in college, the demands of adult life and the expectations of marriage are no longer a matter of the distant future. The college experience often serves to erode, rather than build up a woman's sense of herself as a worker and in general.[11]

Protected by the hallowed halls of learning, I could go through the motions of acquiring the credentials and sustain the demand for equality with my male peers. Once beyond those college walls, the realities were bleak. I did not see many relationships or work situations that embodied equality and a full life. I knew few stories that could serve as models for constructing a new identity as a working woman, or for determining alternative values. Few men seemed to feel the strain of value-laden questions about marriage and children. I did not hear many of them asking, How will I combine work and family, and which is more important now? Elite, isolated, age-restricted, child-free educational institutions could pretend to be nonsexist and gender-free. The rest of society was certainly not, and in more cases than I liked to admit, did not even bother pretending.

I joined the long history of "thousands of women" before me by beginning my adult life with the same question: Must I choose? Initially, according to Aisenberg and Harrington, most refuse to choose, or even refuse to believe that such a choice is necessary. Then they create a vast variety of strategies to prove it.[12] Aware of the paucity of cultural models, but naively distancing myself from the effort it would take, I held on to the two scripts: the picture of myself as a wife and mother and the relatively new picture of myself pursuing the kinds of achievements previously reserved for men. When I embarked upon graduate education a year after completing my college degree, my intent was clear: I wanted a Ph.D., and I wanted the sort of intimate, serious relationship that might eventuate in marriage. I carefully refrained from admitting either intention. Many who would have endorsed the one would not have liked the other.

Frogs, Snails, and Feminist Tales:
Pre-children Hassles

My path since, a relationship which did lead to marriage, and graduate work that led to a Ph.D., appears steady. This misrepresents the inner turmoil, the overt conflicts, and the insidious veering and tacking. Role reversal, or taking turns with chores or job moves proved to be shallow solutions. These strategies simply disguised the ways in which roles do not easily reverse, and taking turns seldom happens easily or fairly in complex lives. Even working out the petty details of an equal distribution of the domestic tasks proved to be a bigger challenge than either my husband Mark or I had anticipated. Dividing household chores, long before children complicated the workload, is an illustrative example of the unexpected cognitive dissonance and emotional discord we incurred because of our shared commitment to gender justice.

Living in the shadow of resilient rules about roles and tasks, I had to let go of an irrational but insidious guilt because I was not cleaning, cooking, and otherwise ordering the home, and suppress anger when friends and family praised Mark for his "extra" work and told *me* "how lucky" I was. (Imagine someone telling him how lucky *he* was!) He had his own share of grievances. He also worked in a world that continued to predicate its rewards upon the assumption that someone, a woman, was at home doing the wash, that resisted the idea that he, a man, might have such work to do. The strength of this discord, and the tenacity of conventional expectations within heterosexual marriage, is particularly apparent when set beside the contrasting strategies of same-sexed couples. Gay and lesbian couples often resist assigning either person the role of homemaker or economic provider.[13] Moreover, they have long known the difficulties of sustaining an enduring mutual partnership in a society which is even less supportive of them than of heterosexual couples. As biblical scholar L. William Countryman argues, "If there are useful models to be had [for egalitarian partnerships], they will probably be found among [gay and lesbian couples]."[14]

The cognitive dissonance and emotional discord in the household is not unrelated to the kind of discord experienced in the workplace. Despite good intentions and the changes that have occurred, people still feel uncomfortable when women assume positions of authority on par with men at work, when they assert divergent opinions in leadership roles and then ask for maternity leave, or, more to the point, when men ask for paternity leave, as my husband tried to do. How can we explain the resistance to changing these scripts and moving toward a model of shared opportunities for self-fulfillment and nurture of others, for both women and men?

Generativity Crises of My Own

The resistance to a democratic family and work order runs deep, both internally and socially. Bronwyn Davies' intriguing study, *Frogs and Snails and Feminist Tales*, uncovers some of the internal forces. Her book was inspired by a curiosity about the emotionally loaded reaction of preschool children to gender discrepancies. Five-year-olds, trying hard to figure out their place in the world, Davies observes, react with a sense of moral outrage when adults, concerned about the prevalence of sexism, read them feminist fairy tales. Children do not want to hear about the heroine in *The Paper Bag Princess*, who goes to great lengths to save a prince from a fierce dragon, only to skip off alone into the sunset when he criticizes her appearance. They find this terribly disconcerting. Why?

What Davies discovers in her three-year study of the gendered world of four- and five-year-olds is the "incorrigibility of the male-female dualism and its construction as a central element of human identity."[15] Children need categories in order to understand their worlds. Within current discursive practice, which reduces the complexities of gender to two mutually exclusive bipolar choices, children learn quickly: One is either a girl or a boy. This is the only comprehensible identity available. These categories are deeply embedded in human constructions of reality and of one's place in it. We are a long way from Davies' proposed solution: (1) imaging alternative discourses, in which people are neither male nor female first, but human; and (2) distinguishing between genital sex on the one hand and, on the other, the range of traits people are free to adopt.

In reading feminist fairy tales to children, people have not considered that children cannot be both required to understand themselves as male or female *and* deprived of the very means of signifying maleness and femaleness. No matter how much is done to dispel oppressive sex roles, if categorizing oneself as male or female remains so important, children inevitably will search for key signifiers of gender identity, however restricting and parochial. The same is true for adults with nonsexist agendas. Creating a reality in which identity and the social world is not constructed around being male or female is a formidable task. It is difficult, and sometimes impossible, to create new values and new signifiers not grounded in this dualism. The opposition of male/female, and the many related oppositions of active/passive, self-sufficient/dependent, provider/nurturer, husband/wife, breadwinner/homemaker, quickly acquire an incorrigibility which forbids that we consider them anything less than inevitable.

These characteriological oppositions are directly tied into and correlated with social oppositions between public and private, work and home. Judith Stacey concludes her ethnographic study of two-family systems in the Silicon Valley, *Brave New Families*, with a similar question: Why do many people recoil from the prospect of "a truly democratic gender and kinship order, one that does not favor male authority, heterosexuality, a particular division of labor, or a singular household or parenting arrangement"? Her book broadens Davies' analysis and suggests a number of social and cultural reasons. Along with their promise, new arrangements and a norm-less gender order bring the cost of conjugal, and thus parental, instability. Second, conflicts and insecurity are magnified under turbulent social conditions. Third, failure to replace the social protections provided by the traditional family structures places a vast majority of women at disproportionate risk. Finally, the "structural inequalities of postindustrial occupational structure" and the "individualist, fast-track culture" make it all too difficult to form stable, intimate relations on a democratic basis, or on any other basis.[16]

Gender distinctions, however distorted and unjust, remain a backbone of social order, undergirding not just society's reproductive arrangements, but more plainly, the way people see and understand the world. People and institutions have a heavy investment in perpetuating these distinctions. Ambiguity in gender identity, from mothers in the workplace to transsexuality, is amazingly "difficult to tolerate," observes Cynthia Fuchs Epstein in *Deceptive Distinctions*. As the movie *The Crying Game* proves so powerfully, people are terribly disturbed when known gender categories are disrupted. They are uncomfortable with the inconsistency, the lack of clarity, and the impossibilities of closure. Although adults learn far more sophisticated ways than do children to camouflage their uneasiness when a young father arrives at a preschool tea, and his wife comes and talks about her profession, they are just as uncomfortable. In the end, Epstein remarks, society tends to "punish those who deviate" from the general practice.[17]

Life in a Shoe

More complicated trials came when our children arrived. These trials test the boundaries of our imagination and stamina. They test our commitment to democratic values in our relationship and to the priority we place on family life in general. This particular part of our lives is so essential to my desire to reconstruct theological and ethical ideals of generativity that what I touch on in the remainder of this chapter will become a source for further reflection in the following chapters.

Caring for children consumes more energy than most people acknowledge. "Consider the facts," urges Virginia Woolf. "First there are nine months before the baby is born. Then the baby is born. Then there are three or four months spent in feeding the baby. After the baby is fed there are certainly five years spent in playing with the baby. You cannot, it seems, let children run about the streets." It is not a "pleasant" sight.[18] Woolf does not mention the unpleasant sights of the later years, such as weathering the adolescent storms or launching children into their adult lives. The tasks do not end as readily as some suppose.

Most people cannot fathom the facts about children until they happen. Cultural images, like the common picture in obstetrical offices of a mother dressed in white lace, beatifically cradling an acquiescent infant, do not help. The clutter of children's paraphernalia and their unscheduled interruptions in the home of my midwife turned out to be a far more realistic portrayal. A mother of two, Mary Guerrera Congo, a "feministically critical Catholic," recounts her saga:

> I also had not foreseen that, while becoming a parent would strengthen the trust and tie I shared with my husband, it would also erode our relationship as we both suffered exhaustion and frustration . . . within the bonds and responsibilities of parenthood. . . .
>
> I had not foreseen that my sacrifice of energy and time to parenting would result in a continually widening gap between my own ability to advance in a financially sustaining career and the comparable ability of my husband and some of our single women friends. . . .
>
> I was repeatedly frustrated in my attempts to "go back to work." I found it required constant reassessment of my priorities. The very ground beneath me seemed to shift and then shift again and again, as I tried to balance my work, my energy, my confidence, my own sense of purpose and direction, and of course the child-care needs of my children. What I finally have found is that trying to weave mothering together with work . . . is an ongoing and nagging and unresolved puzzle in my life. . . .
>
> I had not anticipated that grappling with how to parcel myself out among my new responsibilities would finally demand of me a total reassessment of my identity, my talents, my strengths and weaknesses,

and of all my relationships. I never dreamt that this reassessment would require of me nothing less than the clearest truth about my deepest and most protected feelings and hurts.[19]

As Guerrera Congo implies, becoming a parent requires nothing less than the clearest truth about one's deepest values. A person's self-concept and life commitments shift dramatically when children enter the picture. Robbie Davis-Floyd contends that pregnancy is perhaps the most "overlooked life-crisis rite of passage" in American society, thus denying people an informed awareness of its powerful transformative potential.[20] According to theologian Penelope Washbourn, this stage of life raises "fundamental religious questions" about the meaning of life and one's place within it, and about what is most important, valuable, and holy.[21]

Not only has the import of this stage been denied and often lost, the existential questions it raises have become more complex. As Guerrera Congo testifies, parenthood is a social construction under seige. With minimal institutional and ideological support to answer its complex, value-laden questions, people enter it at their own risk. For both my husband and I, childbirth pressed us to consider a generativity conflict that Erikson had not considered—how to integrate productivity in our work lives with procreativity in our family and community life. It was not a matter of "generativity vs. stagnation" and boredom. Far from it. It was a question of "generativity vs. fragmentation" and exhaustion.

Today the personal and the political is nowhere "experienced more powerfully than in the practice of mothering," Sally Purvis observes.[22] Before our first son, I could compartmentalize work and love, expecting equal treatment at work and establishing an egalitarian partnership in private life that seldom impinged directly upon the world of work. Upon becoming parents, a personal commitment to fairness in the home and to the valued priorities of the home could no longer remain private. Suddenly, our individual home-based commitments and egalitarian standards disrupted our work lives, at times taking both of us away from work and causing us to ask for certain allowances. Definitions of equality at work, based upon an undifferentiated similarity between men and women, and predicated on the contributions of a full-time housekeeper, had to expand to include the desires and diversities of child bearing and rearing, and the increased demands of domestic maintenance.

Historically, the labors of reproduction simply are not factored into American definitions of productivity. Reproductive labors go on behind the scenes, and those who engage in them pay the costs. We discovered, in a less acute way, what John Raines and Donna Day-Lower observe in their study of the tragic demise of working-class neighborhoods because of the socially unrestricted interests of capital accumulation: We keep two separate books in our society. What shows up as profit for capital in the public world of economics and politics, where power and greed hold sway, may register on the books of community as loss and injury. What registers as essential for families and the community never shows up in the books of economics. But "because there are two sets of books, no one seems to be responsible" for the destructive fallout. As a result, we "never get hold of our society as a whole—capital and community together."[23]

The question, "Who will move on behalf of the other's career?" exemplifies the fundamental contradiction between the division of labor as viewed by the family and the community, and as viewed by the market economy. The market economy assumes, as Ulrich Beck has observed, that the employee is a single individual, unhindered by personal, marital, familial, or community commitments.[24] The market demand for individual mobility ignores the requirements of familial and social bonds, demanding that they not interfere with the needs of the market. Until the contradiction between the two worlds is addressed, inequality between the sexes, or more precisely, inequality between those in market labor and those in domestic labor, of either sex, will persist.

"Daughters of Eve": Reaching to Love One's Neighbor as Oneself

Working mothers experience the contradictions forcefully. With an infant, at least, "uterus and breasts precluded equal attachment" of men and women to their children, as sociologist Amy Rossiter avows in the preface of a feminist book on early mothering. Her study itself is inspired by the contradiction between this experience and her desires for equality. Regardless of her intent to share the tasks of child care, when she denied her body and baby in favor of equal parenting, in her "gut" "it felt bad" for the baby and for herself.[25] Although Rossiter discovers in her interviews with five mothers that these feelings are all too often socially imposed and reinforced, her portrayal of the intensity of the bodily relationship with children confirms my own sense of the forceful lure of the "mother's house." Neither the world of men nor the women's movement, it seemed to me, had come to grips with the "reality of that painful, wonderful, destructive, liberating love that many of us feel for our children," as another mother puts it.[26]

Almost immediately, between Mark and me, the physiological disparities of bearing and nursing children necessitated a reappraisal of the mutuality internal to our relationship. However, these differences did not lessen our commitment to a mutuality and partnership. Nor did the differences lessen my desire or need for "a work of one's own."[27] Rather, it intensified the pursuit and began to teach us the complicated lessons of the arduous practice of a mutuality that embodies more fully the tension inherent in the biblical commandment to "love your neighbor as yourself" (Mark 12:31). In retrospect, the period of acute physical difference was relatively brief and gave way to the trickier problems of socialized gender differences. This phase did prove a worthy testing ground for the breadth and depth of our commitment to a joint participation in parenting.

It is important to name, rather than ignore these difficulties of achieving equality in child bearing by a simple act of will—not to excuse or rationalize the conflicts, but to ameliorate and work through them. As Mary Becker observes, it is silence that perpetuates inequality, not the recognition of the intensity of maternal involvement in the pains and pleasures of their children. "Failing to discuss how difficult it is to equalize the emotional attachment of mothers and fathers to their children will inevitably cause continuing inequality."[28] Only by recognizing this can we move toward equalizing paternal involvement.

We discovered that the mutuality we wanted to maintain could not be spelled out as easily as kitchen duty, but required a measured and steady response to the continually emerging, evolving needs of our children for love, and our needs to love ourselves as parents and otherwise. Actualizing this mutuality amidst the flux and disparities between us required compensation for the person who had given too much. It required flexibility, improvisation, and support. Daily, we tried to find ways to balance the inequities of the demands that my physical proximity created for both of us, and to build avenues for common participation, often with little outside encouragement or support. This sometimes meant intentionally inverting and overriding what seemed our natural impulses. When it seemed right and necessary, it even meant overriding the real physical inclinations of the "gut" with an affirmation of the deeper realities which our socialization had denied us—Mark's physical experience of the lure of our children and my experience of a desire for creative work.

Achieving parental mutuality also required better knowledge of the evolution of mutuality between adult and child. It required learning and adjudicating the fine balance between less pressing parental needs and the more urgent needs of a child. The painting "Out of Reach, Daughters of Eve" on the front cover captures this balance. As she pulls down the limb with the apple that is "out of reach" of the child, there is a sense in which she is also reaching for a "work of her own." She leans back, self-absorbed and thinking, partly to help, but partly to keep unto herself what is hers and balance or offset the demand of the child, which she recognizes as sometimes no more urgent than her own. Only as she reaches for what is hers will the child, who has dropped her own doll to wet her lips on the delight of the apple, learn to reach for life herself. Only by loving herself can the mother fully love her child.

Yet this self-love has a timeliness. It must wait until the child can reach. The mother knows that some of her desires are "out of reach" because her child's needs often are more immediate and essential, and some lie forever "out of reach" in this life. In this artist's portrayal, the mother needs support—in this case the strength of the table—but in general, the support of a community of others standing by. Creative work involves self-absorption and sometimes extensive self-concern, and it rests on the support of someone else's nurture. Nurturing work involves a certain self-giving and sometimes self-sacrifice. Above all, Mark and I knew that at some level, each of us wanted and needed comparable measures of both to keep our mutuality honest. We improvised until we found ways to make this happen in a fair way, in response to the needs of our children and our own needs.

In other words, something more than a "revision of household rules and the alternation of household roles" is required for mutuality in contemporary families. William Countryman argues that complex moral and theological shifts also are necessary:

It involves new understandings of manliness and womanliness that can come about only with some pain and anxiety as well as some sense of liberation and joy. If the husband gives up the image of himself as sole ruler . . . he must also give up its spiritual equivalent—the image of himself as the family's unique sacrificial sustainer, isolated in his moral strength and grandeur. If the wife gives up being the servant of all . . . she must also give up the spiritual vision of herself as the one who gives all for others' good. . . . None of this will be easy.[29]

Learning new moral and religious values and virtues is never easy.

As the work of Carol Gilligan has suggested, for this familial rear-rangement to occur, it is critical that a woman recognize her love of self—that it is legitimate to consider the interests of the self and that each self must claim a certain measure of moral agency. For men, it is not recognition of rights or choice—concepts that many men take for granted—but intimacy or a significant personal relationship that moves them to higher levels of moral development.[30] We discovered that sometimes it was essential to put my desire for and commitment to creative work on a par with—heaven forbid—the needs of the infant. Recognizing that Mark had a need and obligation to engage in the moral practice of birth and attachment was equally important. Particularly when the larger public was not supportive, we depended heavily upon the support of each other and the reciprocal affirmation of our children.

Pregnancy and care of children present an opportunity to realize, perhaps for the first time, that sacrifice—responsiveness to others, and autonomy—responsiveness to oneself—are not mutually exclusive. To consider caring for a baby, or to choose between carrying or aborting a fetus within one's own body, forces women to differentiate and consider how they care for themselves. Like some of the women in Gilligan's study, I found that giving birth and considering Woolf's "facts" of child care moved me from a stage in which considering one's own needs and desires is equated with selfishness, to a stage in which to act responsibly toward myself and my needs was to further my ability to respond to the needs of others. We struggled to learn the difficult lessons of loving our children as we loved ourselves.

Through many battles, toils, and snares, we have haltingly come to a give-and-take that includes transitional moments of self-giving and self-fulfillment for both of us. Conflicts between us are characterized by an angry threat by one party that we should list how much we have done, and each of us is always sure we have done more than the other.

However, despite the strife and, optimally, the recognition that there is *too* much to do, we know this to be a more genuine mutuality than alternative models of woman's love of others and man's self-love. In the end, we have never followed through on our threat to list our labors, but some kind of mental list of checks and balances is actually necessary, as is overt, gracious recognition of how much these labors actually demand. And when my five-year-old brought *The Paper Bag Princess* home from the preschool library recently, both he and my three-year-old liked her immensely.

A Patchwork Story:
The "Pitch in" Family

So what are the rudimentary contours of the life that my husband and I have resurrected in what often has felt like a vacuum? The experience of becoming a parent has had a transformative impact upon our thinking and acting. Traditional solutions that others have used, such as prioritizing work over family, or family over work, or making a sharp separation between work and family, simply did not work. Motherhood heightened my resentment of women's lack of real power in a male-defined work force, at the same time that it heightened my awareness of the low status of mothers and children.

Neither of us has simply moved in some straightforward, chronological fashion from one identity to another, from youth to adult, unmarried to married, spouse to parent. Rather, we experience what one study calls "role proliferation," a coterminous, continuous, and additive combination of multiple but disparate roles (domestic, occupational, marital, parental), to each of which one has equally high commitments.[31] In addition, I feel what Celia Gilbert describes, in her own experiences as a working mother—the cultural "taboo on work as powerful as the proscription against incest"—which forbids her to admit that she loves her work as much as she loves her husband and children.[32] Conversely, there are equally powerful taboos which forbid my husband to love his children as much as his work, or to spend comparable time with them.

But we asked for it: We entered reproductive and child-care decisions with a high regard for the priority of a relational partnership, and with different standards for ourselves within that partnership. While traditional women's work brings little recognition, much of it is integrally valuable, particularly that which pertains to attending to the development of a child or another person, and to securing networks of community support. Putting this value into words that are not saccharine or superficial is a more difficult task.

Contrary to a public world, where the model male adult labors at work but spends little time with children, we find ourselves more child-centered than the work world usually expects or assumes. During many weeks, we fall short of the standard "forty hours" and add hours with our children. We miss meetings, decline responsibilities, forsake job opportunities, forfeit certain promotions; we leave work for parent-teacher conferences, special programs, field trips. On the other hand, we find ourselves less child-centered than the cookies-and-milk images of child rearing and, on another level, more demanding of our children and their resilient resources, which social mores also underestimate. Cookies are store-bought, baked at odd hours, or more likely, our kids drag their own stools over to the stove and "pitch in," to borrow one of my friend's favorite family phrases, to make them, or even the main course.

Is not the narrative of the "pitch in" family more wholesome than the cookies-and-milk narrative, even if it conjures up images of overt conflicts, rather than temporary tranquility? Embodied in this pithy phrase is the idea that given love, children also need daily exercise at the practice of loving others as they love themselves, and this means a family system in which their pitching in is also essential to the family's functioning. With a certain kind of help and support, the young daughter in the "Daughters of Eve" picture can pick her own apple.

While not alone in our struggle over the values that guide our work and child rearing, we often feel like strangers in a strange land. Perhaps this is partly because we live in the midst of a more conservative community in the Chicago suburbs. Many of our neighbors—mostly the men—work in the corporate sector with its higher incomes, while both of us work in the service sector with lower clerical incomes. From a position on the outer peripheries of a white upper-middle-class suburb, I observe a struggle to retain the status quo that has been forfeited by the working and underclass. Mothers who have chosen not to work juggle school programs, extracurricular activities, and car pools. Even if only 8 percent of U.S. mothers and fathers maintain the 1950s arrangement of breadwinner-homemaker, most school and work schedules still assume such a division, and many enclaves of convention, like the one in which we live, would like to preserve it.

Alternative models of shared responsibility are still very fresh. Their failure is predicted by conventional society, and their success lacks careful articulation. Although religious congregations offer potential, there are few forums to consider the changes. In the words of one of my colleagues, when time and energy are at a premium, "friendships are the first to go." So are genuine public conversations. According to Shreve's interviews with sixty-five women who had once belonged to consciousness raising groups, working women and mothers have become so overloaded that they have lost the support that once came in the 1960s and 1970s, with the collective phenomenon of talking together.[33]

The lack of support goes still further. It is hard to sustain equal regard between us in a society that does not recognize the importance of equal regard, the values of domestic labor, or the necessary dependencies and demands of family life, whether raising children, caring for the impaired, or providing for the aging. People involved in these acts cannot sustain the necessary self-giving without the help of supportive public structures.

These reflections raise a more important question for me. If I am finding it hard to adjudicate the demands of work and family life, what about those with less flexible steady jobs, fewer and poorer day-care options, lower irregular incomes, or abusive, destructive family situations, and minimal support systems? All people face pressures in a society that provides little support for the intricacies of combining the generative activities of family with the demands of work. But the penalties weigh most heavily upon those who do not have the means to survive. The greatest costs may indeed be for the children of this generation and generations to come, who grow up in a world that allows little time or place for them.

Religious Narratives:
Crèche Scene with Kings, Shepherds, and Father

Our choices have assumed a basic responsiveness on the part of our respective employing institutions, the church in Mark's case and the seminary in mine, that does not prevail in most working institutions. While seldom articulated, this responsiveness has something to do with their identities as religious institutions. As has been discussed, while valuing family and work, Protestantism recognizes the limits of earthly devotions and the dangers of idolatry, whether of material wealth, excessive workaholism, or even excessive familism. Church teachings juxtapose the "treasures of earth" that moth and rust consume and thieves break in and steal with the "treasures in heaven" (Matt. 6:19-20). One cannot "serve God and mammon" (Matt. 6:24b). One ought not to be solely loyal, or even heavily committed to the limited, albeit worthy values of one's own work or one's family. In this vein, religiously committed people with whom we have worked have understood our mutual commitment to the less tangible, less material rewards of family life.

At the same time, there have been limits to this understanding. There have been times when the institutions did not want to budge, as with certain requests for paternity leave or reduced time, and we simply had to live with our frustrations. More profoundly, I have found the practices of mainline churches in general peculiarly less receptive to the struggles of the people in their midst, and more resistant to challenging the status quo. While national denominational meetings may use inclusive language and elect women officials, when women arrive at the communion table as elders in local congregations, they often still pray to a "Father God." When my first son reached the age of three, he insisted that God is male. Who could blame him for claiming what he had inevitably heard and seen? David Heller's study of The Children's God reveals that my son is not unique.[34]

These examples just skim the surface. Gendered attitudes toward care giving and gender roles endure. The caring demands of the institutional church, from nursery duty to funeral meals, assume a woman's active participation. Most women under the age of fifty now work. In the next decade, 80 percent of these working women will be of childbearing age, and 90 percent of those will become pregnant. Most continue to take on major responsibilities with their families. Yet the churches' traditional expectations of women have not adapted to the changes in women's lives. Women still usually fix the funeral meals, staff the nursery, cook the potlucks, clean up, teach Sunday school, run rummage sales, and now, in addition, take on new roles of leadership.

A male minister, who identifies the "changing role of women" as a "convenient" point of entry into his discussion of the major changes he has witnessed in a few decades of parish life, sees the problem from the other side. There are no bodies to run the programs. He is not particularly concerned about the fact that feminism has not had much impact on liturgical language or on women's groups in his congregation; what bothers him is the decline of "numerous, reliable, and ambitious" volunteers, and the difficulty of church attendance on Sundays when parents work.[35] A female minister captures the same phenomenon when she titles a recent article on women ministers and women's fellowship groups: "Serving Potlucks and Pulpits."[36] Unfortunately, she is not too concerned, either, about the implications of this double load for women.

Many ministers and white mainline congregations have lost touch with the women in their midst who have felt the impact of the gender revolutions of the past two decades. One woman describes her "gut wrenching" experience of the co-optation that "is nowhere more poignantly experienced than in the institutional churches." Is it "even worth it to attempt to work from the inside?" she asks. A gulf separates her raised consciousness from the typical Sunday morning service.[37]

Guerrera Congo connects her crisis of faith directly to her new powers and burdens as a laboring, caring mother:

> It would gradually become painful and then intolerable for me to sit in church and watch robed men, who had cooks and housekeepers running the rectory for them, playing out the supposedly sacred roles of giving "new life" to children in baptism, children they had never labored to birth, and feeding such children with sacred bread they had never labored to bake.[38]

This robbed her of any sense of her own essential place as a mother, either in the church or in religion.

Although on one level I knew that it is God who gives new life and new hope in baptism and communion, on another level I experienced a similar disenchantment when I looked upon a crèche scene of kings, shepherds, and a father, absent of women except for a Mary, who in Protestant sanctuaries fades away into the shadows. Carrying thirty extra pounds of baby, and later bearing the sticky weight of nursing told me that I knew something about the giving of one's body and blood that did not seem reflected in the way the rituals of communion and baptism are enacted. In its most powerful rituals and stories, it seemed as if a male church had forsaken women, and then wrongly appropriated the bounty of female bodily knowledge.

Many women come to church wanting nourishment and leave empty. They expect changes and find stagnation. Conservative churches clearly advocate a return to the "traditional" family. Mainline churches stand in the cross fire between the feminist revolution and conservative trends. When all is said and done, they pay little heed to the transformations of the former or the hazardous retrenchments of the latter. The so-called Moral Majority claims the image of Eden as home, while radical feminism claims the Exodus story. In this scenario, a woman must either return home to save the family from decline, observes Elisabeth Schüssler Fiorenza, or she must abandon the oppressive confines of home and church as hopelessly corrupt.[39] Most women and mainline congregations are caught somewhere in-between.

In the wasteland, there is much more that mainline churches could be offering. This book's final chapter returns to this subject, but I conclude this chapter with some suggestions. Mainline churches might simply provide a forum for listening to the strains of the women and men caught in these conflicts, then work to make church theology and practice reflect their lives and fresh experiences. A second, equally challenging step would be to confront the normative values of the materialistic "Protestant" work ethic, which puts profits (and men) before other people (primarily women and children), and thus affirm and uphold alternative values.

Churches are in a good position to assign value to what is contributed to society by parents, and all those who offer care in other forms. Churches can recognize and urge a stronger connection between the interests of communities and families, and the interests of economics and politics; based on biblical and theological principles, they can demand greater justice in the home and greater care in the workplace. This would mean disputing the distorted, genderized definitions of the "good woman" and traditional family, and determining more adequate virtues for "good enough" mothers, "good enough" families, and "good enough" communities, communities that do not exploit women, exclude men, or ignore the impact of social structures. This is no easy agenda.

CHAPTER SIX

Behold the Mother

GENERATIVE LESSONS UNKNOWN TO MEN AND ANGELS

Let a woman learn in silence with full submission. I permit no woman to teach or to have authority over a man; she is to keep silent. For Adam was formed first, then Eve; and Adam was not deceived, but the woman was deceived and became a transgressor. Yet she will be saved through childbearing.

First Timothy 2:11-15*a*

Mothers don't write, they are written. . . . *We know very little about the inner discourse of a mother; and as long as our own emphasis, encouraged by psychoanalytic theory and by the looming presence of (mostly male) mother-fixated writers, continues to be on the-mother-as-she-is-written rather than on the-mother-as-she-writes, we shall continue in our ignorance.*

Susan Rubin Suleiman,
"Writing and Motherhood"

Under patriarchy, pregnancy and childbirth are savage 'tests' of your ability to survive the wilderness alone. And to keep quiet about what you've seen. Whether you're accepted back depends on your ability, your

willingness to live without any confirmation that
you've undergone a rite of passage. . . . You must keep
quiet and pretend to return to life as usual.

Phyllis Chester, With Child

It was the strongest love she knew, this mother love, knit
up of blood.

Mary Gordon, *Men and Angels*

T he words of First Timothy reflect a view of women and female
generativity that has dominated Western consciousness for most
of the last twenty centuries. These verses condone, and even
sanction the silencing of women, at the same time they esteem the
physical act of bearing children. The other quotations above depict
some of the detrimental fallout from this juxtaposition. Female procreative generativity has received a certain weight and authority in human
history. But the implications of bearing children have almost always
been ambiguous for women. Under patriarchy, observes Phyllis Chesler,
pregnancy and childbirth are "savage 'tests' of your ability to survive the
wilderness alone. And to keep quiet about what you've seen." Women
have been silenced and have been particularly silent about the innuen-
dos of "mother love, knit up of blood," in Mary Gordon's phrase, as well
as about the possible salvific merits of the bodily experience of human
reproduction.[1]

This chapter disturbs such silence by claiming the initial physical acts
of childbearing as important revelatory moments. In the next chapter,
we will turn from the biocultural matrix of pregnancy and nursing to
some of the sociocultural insights of living with children, as a further
resource in rethinking the dominant views of generativity. Neither
chapter, however, pretends to undo the damage of centuries lived under
the rule of this letter to Timothy, or to avoid all the hazards. Nor do I
speak for all mothers, or about the exemplary implications of many
mothering situations. I would write a different book if I had adolescent
children or, as Sara Ruddick observes, if I "felt punished for my passion
and deprived of maternal love," like the heroine of Sue Miller's *The
Good Mother,* or "if I were a lesbian."[2] The voices of many mothers

whose conflicts occur on different social fronts have yet to be heard. I do hope to initiate a lively conversation in which mothers in congregations, mothers in the religious academy, and women in general are no longer compelled to keep silent about the truths they have seen while we continue in our ignorance.

Maternal Silence

What, Julia Kristeva asks, "do we know about the inner discourse of a mother?"[3] Not much. Silence reigns in most public realms. From literature to liturgy, the many Marys keep "all these things, pondering them" in their hearts (Luke 2:19). Hymns sing the thoughts of Father, Master, and Lord. But where do we hear about the ruminations of the Mother-God? Or, as Pauline Bart remarks, have you ever wondered about "Portnoy's *mother's* complaint"?[4]

Psychoanalytic theory gives censorship of maternal complaints a certain scientific validity. We do not hear much about the contributing circumstances of the anxious, withdrawn, and hostile mother said to breed a schizophrenic son, in the family systems theories of Gregory Bateson; about the needs of the depressed mothers credited with depriving their children of adequate mirroring, in the records of psychoanalyst Heinz Kohut. The mother—tellingly labeled a "self-object"—is seen as the chief cause of her child's pathology, but only the child's point of view finds representation. Likewise, there is a taboo in the legal academy, claims law expert Mary Becker, against realistically exploring "either the intense pleasures or the difficulties and the pains of women's relationships with their children."[5] And the rational or mathematical law-and-principle language of most Western moral theory has been that of the father. "The mother's voice," says Nel Noddings, "has been silent."[6]

For the most part, women and minorities have remained only consumers in the production of knowledge. Among women, mothers, regardless of race, class, and worldview, have had less opportunity to participate as subjects, or as critics of the products of knowledge. When women with children do write, observes Tillie Olsen in a book that explores the *Silences,* few use the "material open to them out of motherhood" as a central source for their work.[7] The work of motherhood and other creative work still seem mutually exclusive endeavors.

The final irony is this: Deliberation about generativity and, more specifically, about how to provide for children, is done by those who do not tend to children's daily care. Reflection in subjects as far afield as the psychological sciences, and theology upon human development and nature of human fulfillment, is done by those who leave the care of children to others and have little or no idea how that care is a critical factor in understanding the healthy person and the full moral and religious life.

Her Waters Have Broken:
Birth as Catalyst to Seeing

In a much discussed book, *Women's Ways of Knowing*, Mary Field Belenky, Blythe McVicker Clinchy, Nancy Rule Goldberger, and Jill Mattuck Tarule document just how far that sentence to silence has reached in the lives of most women.[8] Confident at age eleven, confused by sixteen, girls "go underground." In Carol Gilligan's words, "They start saying, 'I don't know. I don't know. I don't know.'" They begin not knowing what they formerly had known, in response to a culture which sends the message, "keep quiet and notice the absence of women."[9] Even more critically, women learn to doubt not only what they know, but even *how they go about knowing*.

At the same time, several women interviewed in *Women's Ways of Knowing* point to a particular life experience that dramatically transformed their sense of knowing: The process of becoming a mother.[10] And Gilligan's *In a Different Voice* makes a similar observation. A few mothers in theology, philosophy, and literature also have begun to name the experience, as did Mary Guerrera Congo, a startling "catalyst" that launches new worlds, possibly new schools of thought.[11]

In response to the felt obligation of her unborn child, for example, theologian Marilyn Chapin Massey decides to accept what she experienced as the "mandate of motherhood" to speak with the father on equal terms and to bring together, in a new, unanticipated conjunction, "maternity and mastery of intellectual discourse." Although she admits to keeping this impulse quiet for a decade, it is ultimately her reading of Kristeva's depiction of pregnancy that motivates her to speak in the realm of public discourse, out of the "unquestionably physical act of giving birth."[12]

Massey is not alone in finding in the scholarly reflections of another woman the requisite permission to speak about what she has seen from within the pregnant body. With the writings of Kristeva and others, a ripple effect has stirred across the seemingly dormant pools of childbearing, and the waters have broken. Sara Ruddick has been among the first to claim the "chattering" about their children's lives, in which she engaged with a few close friends, as a reasoned "thinking," deserving of philosophical and ethical recognition. These mothers were not just chattering. They sought immediate answers to the small questions that actually involved the much larger question—how to become, "during these hard times, 'good enough' mothers."[13]

From this perspective, childbearing need not function as a biological trap, any more or less than the need to eat, the need for sex, and the inevitability of death. The need to eat, which requires work, informs Marxism; the need for sex, Freudianism; and the limit of death, existential philosophies. Whereas Western philosophical history has honored these explanatory theories as comprehensive and adequate portrayals of human behavior and ideals (for example, according to existentialism, the essence of being human is that we do not just die; we know we die), the necessity for pregnant females to give birth has not been so honored. To the contrary, it often has been maligned.

A comprehensive philosophy that rests upon the necessity that impregnated females give birth raises important questions.[14] What does it mean that we do not just give birth; we know we give birth? Or, as Riane Eisler asks, what if the central image of Christianity were a woman giving birth, rather than a man dying?[15] More specifically for my purposes, what might it mean to claim "maternal thinking," to use Ruddick's term, as a significant source of knowledge about human generativity?[16]

Am I suggesting that women, as mothers, have some kind of authoritative philosophical and religious standpoint on matters of generativity? Women's embodiment, specifically the bodily and still painful experience of birth, as well as pregnancy and lactation, represents a distinct perspective and may evoke particular ways of perceiving and thinking.

I say "may evoke" because I am not trying to depict a universal or essential characteristic of all women and mothers. Not all birthing, nursing women inherently share one distinct mode of knowing. Nor should this common female experience dictate limited social roles which, given human freedom, remain extremely malleable. I say "evoke" because, although men do not have the physical equipment per se to experience maternal knowing per se, the embodied moments of nonmothers have comparable evocative power to shape and inform our understandings of generativity. Becoming a parent, both biologically and through adoption, elicits changes—sometimes strikingly unexpected changes. What is learned from biological motherhood has parallels in other persons, in form, if not in exact content. It is with the desire that reflection on such analogues be triggered that I claim we have something to learn from birthing, lactating women. In this way, the richness of our knowledge about generativity is deepened.

Biological Motherhood:
Epitome of Disorder

At times, motherhood is the epitome of disorder and messiness. As noted already, retrieving anything related to motherhood has inherent dangers. Feminist theologians have worked hard to counter the damaging consequences of equating women and their religious salvation or condemnation with the biological roles they fill. For too long, society and Christian culture have defined women almost exclusively in terms of their sexual function as wives and mothers, seeing sociological structures as biological and psychological givens or as religious imperatives. Difference, particularly reproductive difference, has been exaggerated and manipulated in the past to deny equality to women. I do not want to perpetuate those self-restricting definitions of gender complementarity and oppressive circumstances of injustice.

Nor do I want to equate a biological process—the capacity to bear children—with full normative humanity.[17] I turn to the biological processes of birthing and bearing children and the social labors of mothering as a particular, and in some ways unique resource, without claiming its superiority or exclusivity in the pursuit of genuine human generativity. I say "unique" in the sense of "remarkable," not in the sense of "unmatched" or "unequaled." Just as we cannot reduce the complexities of motherhood to a singular voice, or a natural or " 'essential' source of anything," neither should we reduce the complexities of human fulfillment to a single mode.[18] My remarks, then, are not inclusive in an immediate sense, drawing as they do upon the singular experience of bearing children, but are intended as illustrative and provocative of new ways of conceiving generative possibilities. Specifically, they are not a judgment upon the childless, or upon those with divergent experiences of generativity or mothering. They are an invitation to a more inclusive conversation about generativity.

As a third related problem, under the sway of patriarchy and particular religious tenets about love, people have romanticized motherhood, creating the "fantasy of the perfect mother," never failing in her sacrifice and responsibility for her children's needs.[19] The joint idealization of disinterested love and self-sacrificing motherhood creates virtues impossible to achieve. Worse, it distorts the relationships between parent and child and between mother and father as they relate to each other and to their children. We would do well to remain wary of reflections on mothering that fail to question the omnipotence and unconditionality of maternal love. We must also be careful about the misappropriation of the recent work of some feminists, such as Carol Gilligan, to reinforce stereotyped views of women as more giving and nurturing. Capturing the complex dimensions of the "strongest love . . . knit up of blood," as Mary Gordon does in her fiction, without trivializing or romanticizing its revelational powers, is difficult indeed.

It is important to counter these misunderstandings by offering a fuller view of the demands of mothering, and a more complex definition of love, mutuality, self-giving, and human development, as demonstrated in the last chapter. If we do this, we will uncover an experience of motherhood that lies somewhere between the extremes of oppressive traditional discourse and the avant-garde feminist protest which totally rejects the traditional, but offers nothing in its place. Although perhaps impossible as a white woman who experiences motherhood in a Western capitalistic, patriarchal, racist society, I want to stand in the "no-man's land" between this either/or to grapple with the potential "power of a woman close to a child, riding our tides into the sand dunes of the public spaces," as in Alicia Suskin Ostriker's "Propaganda Poem." For I agree with Kristeva that while a certain brooding feminism protests the fact of motherhood itself, "genuine feminine innovation . . . will not be possible until we have elucidated motherhood, feminine creation, and the relationship between them."[20]

A Bedrock for Breaking the Silence: Behold, the Mother

Western theology and society have yet to recover from the likes of the author of First Timothy, and the damage perpetuated in Paul's name. Echoing the words of Paul's letter to Corinth (I Cor. 14:34-35), the second chapter shames women to silence in the congregation and confirms that men have headship over women, based upon the very order of creation and the fall. As if this were not penance enough, in an ambiguous and contested final passage on the subject, the pseudo-Pauline author proclaims a woman's reproductive capacities as her road to salvation. This idea has done its share of damage also, as has the inverse claim that a woman's childbearing signifies her divine punishment. It is no wonder that some have seen fit to do away altogether with religious notions of family values.

Women's reproductive labor does have redemptive, life-giving dimensions of a certain kind. Mother love may be among the greatest sources of spiritual and moral insight. Nonetheless, under the heavy weight of religious claims about woman's lesser place in creation and fall that have permeated Western consciousness over the centuries, the ethical and redemptive features of women's procreative powers have collapsed into patronizing sentiments of a Mother's Day sort. Recovering mothers' voices in the rites of passage of pregnancy and childbirth is a formidable task at best, and at worst, a hazardous, volatile venture.

Alternative theological values and interpretations themselves lay the groundwork for taking the risk. Despite the sexual subordination in both New Testament and Hebrew Scriptures, despite the patriarchal character of ancient Israel and the Roman and Hellenistic cultures in which Christianity arose, and despite the ways in which the Christian tradition has perpetuated ideals of male dominance in the centuries since, current scholarship continues to confirm important streams of thought at variance with these assumptions.

Foremost among such proponents, Elisabeth Schüssler Fiorenza claims that in Mark's Gospel, it is women who emerge as the "true Christian ministers and witnesses" and are the most courageous of all the disciples.[21] Others join her in confirming the prominent role of women in Jesus' ministry to the downtrodden and the outcast.[22] Against social convention, Jesus kept egalitarian premises at the core of the breaking in of the kingdom.

Motherhood did not exclude women from participating. To the contrary, the significance of motherhood, familial ties, and the role of sexuality are assumed, and then subsumed within the greater cause of Jesus' mission. In stories like those of the woman with a flow of blood (Mark 6:26), the Canaanite woman who begs for the healing of her daughter (Matt. 15:22), and the Samaritan woman at the well (John 4:7), women's physical, sexual, and maternal needs are recognized. And they are affirmed, even from the height of the cross, when Jesus commands a new kind of maternal bond between the "disciple he loved" and his mother. "Woman, behold, your son." "Behold, your mother" (John 19:26-27). The focus here and elsewhere in Jesus' teachings is not on childbearing or familial ties per se, but on a personal relationship and discipleship that is analogous but transcending. What is learned in the bonded love of motherhood can be exemplary, and it should be transferable to other relationships.

Paul follows suit, even as he struggles and sometimes fails to realize the ideal of equality and discipleship in some of his words to the actual communities he was founding. His absolute insistence on the silence of women in the church in some passages contradicts the radical inclusivity of his message elsewhere. The First Corinthians passage (14:34-35) has been explained as a concession to the prevailing values of his time, or even as the imposition and addition of someone else's words. In either case, it is a compromise undercut by his other claims. Authoritative moral norms about women, divorce, and other concerns are reinterpreted by Paul in light of a greater moral criterion—the existence and preservation of community in the midst of the proclamation of the reign of God. He puts at the center of a life in Christ a revolutionary creed: "As many of you as were baptized into Christ have clothed yourselves with Christ. There is no longer Jew or Greek, there is no longer slave or free, there is no longer male and female; for all of you are one in Christ Jesus" (Gal. 3:27-28).

Schüssler Fiorenza believes that this creed represents a pre-Pauline baptismal confession which Paul boldly endorses as a new self-understanding of the early Christian movement, and which departs radically from the self-understanding of the surrounding culture.[23] Women and mothers recognized the Christ, discovered the empty tomb, witnessed the resurrection, received the Holy Spirit, prophesied, taught, were persecuted and jailed. Then, as the authors of the deutero-Pauline letters (Timothy, Titus, Ephesians, Colossians, and Peter) surpassed Paul in accommodating to pressures of the hierarchical customs of antiquity, women were selectively written out of religious leadership and out of history.

Nevertheless, remnants of egalitarian themes run even further back in scriptural traditions. The same creation stories (Gen. 1–3) that the author of First Timothy uses to justify women's subordination can serve instead as evidence of the equality of women and men. New readings demonstrate that women have no lesser place in creation and no greater culpability than men in perpetuating human corruption. Female and maternal subjugation and silence is not divinely ordained and revealed in the Hebrew Scriptures any more than it is in the New Testament. To the contrary, sexual inequality, rather than divine decree, perpetuates sin.

The creation stories portray as normative the equal partnership of women and men in dominion and in fruitful propagation of the species. The order of creation in chapters one and two of Genesis is not first man, then woman, with an implied sexual hierarchy. Rather, as Phyllis Trible observes, Yahweh creates humanity, then sexuality, with the implied worth of all creation.[24] This observation is not based only on narrative interpretation, but is a matter of translation. According to Trible and others, there are more suitable translations of the Hebrew term 'adam than "man."[25] When 'adam is created (Gen. 1:26, 2:7), Yahweh creates not "man," but "humanity," or "earth creature." Humanity—male and female—is created in the divine image, and the Creator embodies the character of both sexes. When Yahweh creates man and woman in Genesis 2:18, the new being is depicted as *ezer k'negdo,* commonly translated as "a helper fit for him." But this also is a poor translation. Elsewhere in Hebrew writings, the word *k'negdo* actually means "equal to," or even "greater than." *Ezer,* or "helper," is not a word that connotes inferiority; in other biblical contexts, it is a word commonly used for "God."

In both Genesis accounts, sexual distinctions are not incidental or accidental. Human existence as created is essentially embodied existence, molded from dust and breathed into life. Human essence cannot be abstracted from its embodied forms, nor can physical forms and differences be dualistically divorced from a correspondence with divergent cognitive or affective attributes.[26] From the vantage point of creation, however, the advent of sexual characteristics does not imply inequality and subordination, but evolves out of the goodness of creation (Gen. 1:31) and the necessity for human relationality at the core of human existence. It is not good to "be alone" (Gen. 2:18). While in the first chapter of Genesis, sexual differences serve the purpose of fruitful procreation for all created animal life, this is neither primary nor essential in the second chapter. In Genesis 2, the intent is companionship and social cooperation. Coming to terms with the potential and the limitations of physical forms and related differences becomes one of the tests and temptations of human freedom.

According to Genesis 3, this is a test that humans eventually fail. With the creation of embodied human potential and human freedom in the realization of that dignified potential, come human limits, frailty, and disobedience. With the entrance of human trespass and evil, human partnership degenerates into gender hierarchy, and sexual differences lead to discord and tyranny. Ironically, in Genesis 3:16-17, Yahweh condemns to the sweat of hard labor the "more passive sinner, the man, who took and ate," and the "more active sinner, the woman, who debated with the serpent and led her husband," was condemned to an intense longing for him who will now "rule over" her, and to the pain of childbearing.[27] The shared dominion for which humans were created becomes domination, usually male. The mutual companionship becomes social enmeshment, usually female.[28] Sexuality becomes a source of shame and pain, and sexual differentiation collapses into stereotypes and oppression. In an understandable act of defiance of human limitation—the "tree *was* good for food . . . it *was* a delight to the eye" (Gen. 3:6, emphasis added)—the world is changed into one marked by the knowledge of good and evil, the protection and concealment of clothing, and sexual status.

Restoring the goodness of creation and, ultimately, the essence of the gospel itself, warrants writing women back into history and allowing mothers to speak. As Lisa Sowle Cahill argues, the sexual subordination endorsed elsewhere in the Bible, such as in First Timothy, can be criticized by the "cumulative criterion of Genesis 1–3."[29] The silencing of women can be criticized also by the egalitarian principle at the heart of the message of Jesus and Paul. Not only should mothers speak, but the hidden truths of the labors of childbearing are multiple.

Generative Lessons Unknown to Men and Angels

Mothers know something essential about generativity, in a negative sense, from the constrictions that prevent careful articulation of what is known and thus impede certain kinds of generativity. Second, mothers have accessibility to certain invaluable ways of knowing, particularly bodily knowing, that are avenues for learning about what it takes to nurture and create personhood. In other words, a certain wealth of knowledge of human nature and nurture rests upon bodily labors, historically defined as inferior to the more "valuable" or "productive" cerebral labors of men.

Over the past few years, as birth itself has become a more public concern, whether the topic was premature birth, abortion, or procreative technologies, the medical, ethical, and religious journals have featured articles by men about the generative struggles of women in relation to having children. In each case I have wondered, where are the women, and what do they think? Why don't women have a "public" voice on these "private" issues so very close to their hearts? Now, after three children of my own, I have some idea of one answer.

This whole exercise of mine ultimately rests on the back of my sitter and, in part, as it should, on my husband, both of whom practice the knowing and generativity that I preach. I am still unsure about the trade-offs. I cannot begin to describe the multiple costs of putting these words on paper. I lost many precious moments playing with my three sons. At the same time, I gained a great deal. The waste of a mother's creative energies in this daily conflict between work and love, Susan Rubin Suleiman argues, "cannot be overestimated."[30] Would many men weigh these generative tensions? I am not so sure. At least, they have not done so overtly, or not until recently.

Thinking critically about generativity from a maternal perspective reveals the secondary nature of all such deliberation. I wonder if, in actual fact, a more authentic generativity is not that which responds to the immediacy of the cry of another human being, rather than that which creates products destined to wither and die. We are most generative when passionately engaged in life's struggle, not when reflectively detached. Conflicts between the desire to live fully now, and the need to distance oneself in order to create enduring ideas, have banished much of the world's greatest wisdom. The academy does not usually understand this creative, generative tension. A mother might.

One absolutely critical source of the mothers' silence on generativity, then, lies in what Ruddick describes as the "passions of maternity," which are "so sudden, intense, and confusing" that we remain ignorant of and fail to deepen the thoughts that develop from mothering.[31]

Putting aside a four-month-old to muse here upon the category of generativity is emotionally, even physically wrenching at times, the desire to hold the child blinding me to the desirability of pursuing the topic in the form of public discourse. As the children have grown, this becomes less wrenching, but no less time and energy consuming.

Serious involvement in child bearing and rearing involves a constraint, an internal and, in some ways, unrelenting tug of attachment, what Kristeva calls a pain that "comes from the inside" and "never remains apart": "You may close your eyes . . . teach courses, run errands . . . think about objects, subjects." But a mother is marked by a tenacious link to another that begins at conception and never quite goes away.[32] Some "deep encoded pattern," writes Gordon, draws the heroine in *Men and Angels* physically to her two children and makes her encircle them in a way that neither men nor angels seem to understand. As babies, they had "lived in the curves" of her body, and now as they enter the later years of childhood, her body itself is a "divide between them and the rest of the human world."[33]

Pregnancy epitomizes this constraint and divide. It is a publicly subversive state, "a continuous separation, a division of the very flesh," says Kristeva. In the pregnant body, the self and the other coexist. The other is both my self and not my self, hourly, daily becoming more separate, until that which was mine becomes irrevocably another. In the pregnant moment, I am one, but two. My self is multiple, divided between a part of me—"what was mine"—for which I care, but which my sons, little knowing, now carry forth into the world "henceforth irreparably alien." As long as the woman has the womb that bears the child, we cannot ignore an initial biological inclination behind heightened maternal investment. As long as the woman carries "this internal graft and fold" which divides, grows, and then is severed at the umbilical cord, we should talk only cautiously about an emotional and cognitive equity between mothers and fathers as "easily attainable."[34] And we should reconsider views of selfhood as an independent, singular, and separate state.

Children, particularly during the first few days, weeks, and months, call forth a sense of immediacy, a visceral response to the cry of the moment. Children need one *now*, not after one has read, researched, and postulated. Abstraction obscures what is indispensable—attentive answer to expressed need. President of the Children's Defense Fund,

Marian Wright Edelman, describes the tensions of writing a book about children. Granting that effective action requires analysis, she declares nonetheless: "I am less interested in formulating theoretical frameworks . . . than I am in feeding, clothing, healing, housing, and educating as many American children as soon as possible."[35] Anyone who wishes to reflect upon children, out of direct participation in their care, encounters a lively personal and ethical generative tension between practical, concrete commitments to offspring and the pursuit of theoretical work, or work of any kind.

"Holding up Half the Sky"

While motherhood heightens these generative tensions, by no means are they restricted to mothers. Theorizing about generativity and maternal knowing comes at the expense of moments with babies. More generally, to theorize about generativity in theology has its price in human relationships, and rests upon the backs of those others who practice the insights and carry on the tasks of living. It rests upon those on the front line. Which comes first and, when out of time, what gives? One's gender just may tip the scale.

As discussed before, a mother's physiological investments in her offspring should never be used to deny the attainability of an emotional and cognitive equity between women and men in the care of offspring. It suggests instead that if attachment is more attained than given for men, and if it is more given than attained for women, then men must make more efforts to learn the practice of caring for others, and women may need to make efforts to tip the scale the other way. The gravest difficulty in this arbitration of equity between the sexes, however, is remembering that it involves a third party, who is also human and not an acquisition or by-product. Men and women must recognize the equity of children as human beings, with needs for assertion and recognition of their own.

Failure to obtain equity between women and men on this score points to a second lesson of generativity that is especially understood by mothers: to engage in other kinds of creative generativity besides procreative generativity requires freedom and time for reflection. To "conceive," in both scholarly and familial ways at the same time, raises peculiar demands and has typically served to disempower women, particularly women with lesser means and social status. To think reflectively about generativity, then, is a kind of luxury previously granted only to those with power.

Bodily, monthly, women know life's limits. I have vivid memories of trying to concentrate on a project amidst the constant so-called morning sickness, the indescribable fatigue, and what one study called the "diminished cognitive acuity" in the first and third trimesters.[36] Conception furnishes new food for thought and yet takes its toll. These initial physical restrictions are trivial beside the heavier material, emotional, and spiritual demands of "reproducing the world," in Mary O'Brien's words, and, once reproduced, maintaining it. About children, women have much to say but little time, less energy, and almost no voice. Children rapidly consume these elements. Women are busy minding the fort. This book on generativity itself was hammered out in small pieces, between minor crises in tending my children. Writing it has been an arduous task that illustrates the nature and complexity of the silence.

Again, if this task is arduous under minimally conflictual circumstances, what happens in less fortunate or more crisis-ridden situations? Maternal voices are lost. The constraints of pregnancy and birth for women in industrialized countries, where the average woman spends three to five years of her adult life pregnant, are small compared to her counterpart in other countries, where a woman invests as many as eighteen to twenty years of her adult life.[37] In our own country, the general public is ill-informed about the struggles of the poorer mothers who persevere against sobering odds. My freedom to deliberate on generativity, and the freedom of many middle- and upper-middle-class women to perform alternative generative tasks, has simply shifted the weight of procreative generativity from one group of exploited, silenced women—mothers in general—to another group: lower-class mothers, the baby-sitter, housekeeper, cleaning woman, day-care staff, teacher, stay-at-home mother, volunteer Scout leader, and so forth.

Women know the strain of "holding up half the sky," or often, more than their share. In *A Room of One's Own*, Virginia Woolf fictitiously reprimands women for their so-called lesser accomplishments. Her women reply, "We have borne and bred and washed and taught perhaps to the age of six or seven years, the one thousand six hundred and twenty-three million human beings who are, according to statistics, at present in existence, and that, allowing that some had help, takes time."[38] Speculating about generativity in general demands what many women and most mothers lack: space, time, energy, money, permission, circumstances, choice, education, travel, varied experience, and two other critical ingredients indispensable to full creativity—unrestrained solitude and the *"essential angel"*—Olsen's term for the woman who is thanked on the dedication pages of men's books for assuring a "daily life made easy and noiseless . . . by a silent, watchful, tireless affection."[39]

Because most male workers and geniuses have had some kind of female housekeeper, most people simply have never noticed that these are elements without which another kind of generativity, human productivity, creativity, and genius would seldom occur. Reproductive patterns built upon the fantasy of an omnipotent mother and the reality of male absence perpetuate this myth. They erode women's health, exhaust their energies, fragment their time, and hinder mothers from contributing to the wider community's understandings of generativity what they have learned from reproductive labor.

So What Does It Mean to Lactate?

Despite, or partly because of, these maternal passions and demands, particular understandings of generativity do develop. Having children has forever changed my ways of knowing and thinking about generativity. Parting the passions in order to articulate those ways comes less easily. From quickening to birth, to giving suck, to today's daily throes, I have come to appreciate the integrity of bodily generativity. Holding an infant at the intersection of nature and the symbolic order, I, as mother, have access to the power of nurture and to the integral processes whereby the order of culture and language emerges in the life of a child.

How might we systematically conceptualize this maternal knowing, which, in Gordon's words, is more physical, and certainly more erotic "than anybody admits"?[40] By no sheer coincidence, the scriptural use of the verb "to know" refers to the intimate act of sexual intercourse. Yet even in our supposedly sexually liberated era, Western theology and philosophy still speak "like a Greek man," inserting a wedge between sex and maternity, ignoring the differences that arise from different kinds of sexual experiences and bodies.[41] Disembodied, dispassionate reason still seems more trustworthy and valid.

As a pregnant, and then nursing mother, however, I found that this simply was not true at some very crucial points. Similar to Beverly Harrison's remark about Christian ethics, a maternal feminist theology is "profoundly worldly, a spirituality of sensuality."[42] It reminds us that all knowledge is body-mediated. As point of proof, what does it mean to lactate, to have a body that, sensing another's thirst, "lets-down," drenching me with sweet-smelling milk?[43] Does it alter knowing?

I know physically through a muscular ache. Apart from the ache, I can scarcely know. In this knowing, few abstractions come between myself and the other, mouth to nipple—no bottle, no instrument to measure birth size or fetal movement. As with pregnancy, lactation subverts artificial boundaries between self and other, inside and outside. Both undermine the integrity of my body and my self, and root me fluidly, solidly, to the depths of my body's capacities. I know by knowing physically the feelings of the other, because they are paradoxically both mine and not mine. It is important to observe that this experience is one of a continuity in difference, not one of polar opposition of feelings or the enmeshed symbiosis between mother and child described by some psychologists. I know by an affective connection that moves toward differentiation, not by comparison, contrast, and critique or by some idealized oneness or union with the child. I know immediately, tactilely, erotically, the supposedly "lowest and least worthy of all human senses," according to Aquinas.[44]

To a great degree, however untrustworthy or dangerous, at least in the Western history of sexuality, I must rely upon a bodily passion, a knowing driven by a welcomed lust or need that seeks satisfaction. In this state of awareness, I have actually left a train car in which a child cried, because of the stir it created in me. In general, just the sight of a baby can evoke a milk let-down response in lactating mothers. In this state, I learn, change, and develop; if I don't, the child won't. Yet most theories of development falsely see the process toward individuation as involving only the child.

As many mothers learn, authentic reflective praxis requires a generative knowing, in which "what one learns cannot be applied exactly, often not even by analogy, to a new situation."[45] Very few abstracted rules hold. In the movement between the knowing and the acting of nursing and tending an infant, I use a mode of circular bodily reasoning, interweaving physical sensation, momentary cognition, behavioral reaction, and a physical sensing and intellectual reading of the results—a trial and error, hit-and-miss strategy, which, in its bodily ethos, surpasses that described under the rubric of Catholic moral casuistry. When the circular bodily reasoning works, I relax; when it fails, I repeat it ceaselessly because I must, unless someone else adopts the burden; when it fails one too many times and no one else is there to relieve or distract me, I must master a physical desire to retaliate in stormy, mindless abuse.

Fleshly maternal generativity, then, has inherent value, as well as immense power for misuse. I believe, however, that it is better to try to understand fleshly knowing than to repress it and suffer the negative consequences of abuse that our society has begun to recognize. Partially justified fears of the dangers of bodily sensuality have turned us away from distinguishing its possible resources and understandable dangers. In contrast to the hierarchy of knowledge that ranks rational knowledge above other forms, we know much in and through our bodies that is intrinsically valuable and precious.

Let me dare to go one step further: Female anatomy in general provides its own ground for metaphor, which theories of generativity have preferred to ignore. All generativity is not phallic. That is, if men think and create phallicly, to borrow Freud's compelling and sometimes ill-used analogy, women think and create vaginally. Or, in actuality, it is not a matter of naming a replacement organ, as I discover when I explain female genitalia to my young sons. Women's organs have an intrinsic multiplicity that cannot be easily explained.

What might this greater multiplicity in sexual form and function mean for women's knowing in general? The hymen and the "two-lipped vulva," as noted by Jacques Derrida and Luce Irigaray, suggest fluid, diffuse, multiple, embracing language, in place of the linear, unified, and visible language of the phallus.[46] Not surprisingly, we find Noddings and the women interviewed in *Women's Ways of Knowing* describing a caring and a knowing that involves not projection, but a receiving into oneself.[47] Note, however, that this is not necessarily a passive receptive generativity, but an active engagement, on a different basis than we have thus far understood. For the receptive vagina is also the "birth-pushing womb"; the nurturing breast, an industrious milk-making organ.[48] Nor, might I add, is the penis always assertively erect. And behind it lies the much ignored, more vulnerable scrotum. If nothing else, a serious exploration of bodily knowing calls into question the previously self-evident categories and judgments about generativity and human knowledge.

Maternal generativity begins to suggest a better way to understand the problem of integrating praxis and theory than almost anything I have seen in the current literature of practical theology. It challenges false dichotomies: Theory does not involve simply verbalizable knowledge and insight, as much as many have wished. Practice does not mean unmediated action. Both involve qualities more nebulous, fleeting, relative, and momentary. Theory involves the passing recognition of empathic attunement; practice, movement within the realm of attuned theory. Noddings describes a similar relational casuistry between mother and infant. Maternal care and ethical reasoning, she argues, must begin with a "feeling with" the other which cannot be exhaustively characterized as emotional feeling, and which involves a suspension of judgment and structure. This embodied reasoned feeling is not all that is involved, but it is "essentially involved."[49]

Undoing the Rule of Timothy:
A Caveat About Biology

With child at breast, women have particular knowledge rooted in their bodies. To lactate when another thirsts teaches a certain empathic, connected knowing. Harrison claims that this knowledge of nurture and the arts of human survival, grounded in the biological constant of childbearing and nursing, far surpasses any technological power in its ability not only to create solid bonds between people but, in essence, to create or thwart life itself.[50] In this regard, the physical acts of creation and nurturance of biological motherhood carry revelatory potential. They reveal the burdens of creating life and offer opportunities for the light of grace and new life to break through in the birth of personhood and community. This is not privileged knowledge. This is knowledge that must be shared.

Several decades ago, John MacMurray argued that personhood is grounded in the "covenant of caring" evident in the physical relationship between child and adult:

[The child's] expression of satisfaction . . . associated with being cared for, with being nursed, with the physical presence of the mother, and particularly with physical contact . . . would seem to be, from a biological point of view, unnecessary. There is no obvious utilitarian purpose in it. . . . It seems impossible to account for it except as an expression of satisfaction in the relation itself. . . . The infant has a need which is not simply biological but personal, a need to be in touch with the mother and in conscious perceptual relation with her. . . . If nobody intends [the child's] survival and acts with intention to secure it, he cannot survive. . . . He can live only through other people and in dynamic relation with them.[51]

The biological activities of birthing, giving suck, and rearing hones this distinctly human ability to create personhood and community. Giving birth and suck, however, are not exhaustive of what one needs in order to learn and perform caring labor. As MacMurray infers, we cannot confine what happens in the creation of personhood to strictly biological categories: "Even the term 'mother' in this connection is not a biological term. It means simply the adult who cares for the baby. . . . A man can do all the mothering that is necessary, if he is provided with a feeding-bottle, and learns how to do it in precisely the same fashion that a woman must learn."[52]

If we are to take MacMurray seriously, this activity must not be called "mothering," as MacMurray still presumes, but must be conceived in new, more inclusive terms. The initial primacy of a mother's embodiment in parenting does not mean that women or mothers are "inherently life-affirming nurturers." As bell hooks asserts, the equation of the biological experiences of motherhood with an inherent superiority in parenting misleads us.[53] None of the passions of mothering that I have described guarantees the actualization of mother love.

As the most forthright character in Gordon's *Men and Angels* remarks, "Mother love. I haven't the vaguest idea what it means. All these children claiming their mothers didn't love them, and all these mothers saying they'd die for their cihldren. Even women who beat their children say they love them." There are mothers of all kinds, mothers "who loved their children in a way that cut the children's breath and stopped their hearts," and mothers "for whom the sight of their children meant nothing."[54] The actualization of mother love is a complex phenomenon that depends on forces far greater than the mother's bodily knowing itself. As long as we continue to equate these two distinct functions— biological mothering and parenting—we perpetuate a system which says that only mothers can have significant bonds with children, while it avoids looking at what it actually takes to love a child and lead a generative life.

To come full circle and return to First Timothy, motherhood is not a woman's truest generative vocation or final salvation. Women who do not have children are not doomed to less fulfilling lives. Gordon concludes her novel by noting that there is "the other part of mother love: it was not all of life." The mercy of biological generativity is to "turn from [children] to something else."[55] In the life of mothering, pregnancy, birth, and lactation are crucial but relatively fleeting moments. In the lives of women, mothering is important, but not necessarily more rewarding than other labors. We must be particularly cautious about sending such a message in a world where women continue to assume the heavy burdens of parenting, and where the poverty of mothers is rising.

I close this chapter, then, with a caveat that points us toward the chapters that follow. Biology is not destiny, but it does shape our means and our understandings of generativity. Yet biology should never be allowed to determine modes of generativity and the division of its labors, much less one's salvation or condemnation. To the contrary, the intensity and vulnerabilities of a mother's bodily generativity that I have noted call for, and even demand the wider participation and support of others besides the biological mother, in the physical, material activities that are involved in reproducing the world. Biology has an important, but secondary and relative place in the construction of the ideals of family and work, and in the realization of the kingdom. Although the body does have much to tell us about the values of life, contrary to First Timothy, women's salvation does not rest on motherhood, but on the divine promise of grace. With grace, we may discover justice and love in the execution of human generativity.

CHAPTER SEVEN

According to the Pace
of the Children

GENERATIVE ACTS OF FAITH, DISCIPLINE, AND PARENTAL INCLINATION

But Jacob said to [Esau], "My lord knows that the children are frail and that the flocks and herds, which are nursing, are a care to me; and if they are overdriven for one day, all the flocks will die. Let my lord pass on ahead of his servant, and I will lead on slowly, according to the pace of the cattle that are before me and according to the pace of the children."

Genesis 33:13-14

Then little children were being brought to him in order that he might lay his hands on them and pray. The disciples spoke sternly to those who brought them; but Jesus said, "Let the little children come to me, and do not stop them; for it is to such as these that the kingdom of heaven belongs."

Matthew 19:13-14

Children are not just the responsibility of mothers, not even just the responsibility of both parents. Their rights

are given into the care of all of us, not because we are women but because they are our future.
　　　　　Elisabeth Schüssler Fiorenza, *In Memory of Her*

Without children, there would be no procreative generativity. As obvious as this sounds, children, it seems, are often the missing denominator in equations of adult generativity. Reigning visions of adulthood for men, and even for women in the workplace, picture the model adult laboring at work but spending little time with children. Children are seldom factored in. They do not count for much in notions of human fulfillment that esteem material productivity. Frail children move too slowly.

Biblical and theological reflection challenges this view. Even Jacob, who grows exceedingly rich through trickery and deceit, comes to learn this. He takes into account the frailness of the flocks for which he cares and adjusts his pace. The adjustment for children is part and parcel of his reconciliation with his brother Esau, when he recognizes late in life that "I have enough [of what life promises]" (Gen. 33:11*b* RSV).[1] He has no need to hurry. Nothing of real value is lost.

Children are given an even greater place in the Gospel accounts of Matthew, Mark, and Luke. Jesus indignantly intercedes when his followers reprimand the people, probably mothers, for bringing children for his blessing. He invites the children in. Indeed, Mark 10:16 tells us that he "took them up in his arms." He conveys the message to those who would hurry along elsewhere, in search of something deemed more important, that something revelational lies within the child. Children are identified as the "ideal members" of a new religious movement defined by lack of worldly power.[2] This is a message, however, that is frequently lost in many churches, in some theologies, and in society's market economy.

We have much to learn from children. As I concluded at the end of the last chapter, it is simply not true that only mothers can have significant bonds with them. Not only does this perpetuate a myth that isolates women and children in the home, in the classroom, and in the Sunday school, but it also deprives us of many of the moral and religious lessons

153

of children. If more people knew the necessities of living according to the pace of children, it might reshape all our views of love and work.

According to the Pace of the Children

Few men who teach and write in theology and ethics live according to the pace of children. Yet the voices of children are central to such work. Theological and moral reflection cannot offer realistic standards of human fulfillment without making way for the young. In defining generativity, they count for a great deal more than many people have conceded.

I return to the question with which I concluded chapter 4: What *is* the value produced by reproductive labor? I am sure that when Mary O'Brien raised this question, she did not envision a simple answer. But one of the values, or at least one of the results of reproductive labor is children. Yet we now ask what seemed obvious only a few years ago: Why do we want to become mothers or fathers in the first place? Why do we want children? The rest of this chapter will identify the value of children. However, it is important to be clear at the outset that I am not identifying reasons to have children as if children are a means to the end of obtaining these particular goods. My thesis is, in fact, the very opposite. I am identifying what children in themselves offer to the world, not because they need to, but because children are good gifts to the world. Throughout the discussion, my assumption is that children are valuable in themselves, for their own sake, simply because they are.

As human beings in their own right, not yet tainted by adult worries, children undercut assumptions about the American Dream. The slower, unconcerned pace with which almost all children move along fosters a reassessment of normative definitions of what it means to work and to love. They have no reason to hurry. In fact, as my three-year-old convinces me daily, they resist being hurried. If attended to with care, they shake up our limited definitions of adult success and priorities. In the best of circumstances, children possess an inexplicable *joie de vivre*, however short its duration, that emerges from living fully in the present. Giving themselves unto their activities, they do not hedge their bets with a thousand worries.

When with my children, I exert an effort to practice an altered mode of being—walking and playing with, not ahead of them, "according to the pace of the cattle and . . . the children." They evoke questions that undercut my anxieties and reveal them for the irrelevant and inconsequential frets they are. Does it really matter that I start my "work" late to "play" with them, or that the floor is clean? As adults with broader responsibilities, we cannot live at this pace all the time. In fact, trying to do so exhaustively, in the midst of realistic pressures and commitments, can lead only to frustrations and tension. It is important, however, that all of us, men and women alike, experience a child's altered perspective on life's meaning and values.

Children can touch us and teach us; we don't let them. Several factors make this matter difficult to handle: the risk of romanticizing children and the harsh realities of child care; the dangers of moralizing; the threat of falling back upon ideologies that subordinate women and children; the liabilities of speaking for children; and the peril of discounting situations in which children do not yield revelatory insights, but bring tedium, stress, exhaustion, and anger. Can we unpack the liveliness and challenge of children without falsifying the havoc?

Cognizant of the risks, I proceed cautiously here to tease out a few suggestive lessons. My efforts to identify some of what goes on in the minds and lives of children falls short of actually including their voices firsthand, as someone like Robert Coles has done so well.[3] We need more work like his. My attention is primarily to what happens in the intersubjective field *between* adult and child. Something of value there for our understandings of human generativity deserves careful retrieval and recognition. My experience, alongside recent writings of other women, confirms this. Nothing has ever subverted my peace of mind as has living according to the pace of my small sons, and yet nothing has ever taught me as much about myself and my location in the world.

Seeing the Face of God

Although children sometimes can set a burdensome pace of life, they also can bring a vitality and a generativity all their own. Sara Ruddick talks about this when she identifies a peculiar new energy she gained from the experience of pregnancy, which, despite its burdens, freed her from an "incapacitating work paralysis." There is something invigorating about the conjunction of work and mothering. She wonders, why should this "new parenthood, which subtracts enormously from the time available for work, nonetheless make work more likely"?[4]

There is no easy answer. In her own reply, Ruddick cautiously admits to the "pleasures of maternity" and the "inspiriting" nature of infant care. But she hesitates to credit the children themselves. As a secular philosopher, she refrains from making explicit theological claims about the divine gifts of children. Yet many people join Ruddick in underestimating what children evoke, contribute, and demand. Ruddick at least deserves ample credit for advancing the case for the significance of mothering and children far more than any other one person in theology. Perhaps, again, it takes the more sensual inclinations of someone like fiction author Mary Gordon to come closer to the heart of the matter. Noting the difficulties of putting it into words, she observes that having children "just ties you into life in an entirely new way. . . . You have a new stake in the world. You look at it differently. . . . Because of them I feel that I know something about life that's both profound and joyous, as well as frightening. And this affects my writing."[5]

Children cast a new light on life, love, and work. In *Women's Ways of Knowing*, several women name "attending to children" as a practice that provides fresh categories of meaning. The very presence of children, overflowing with expressed and unexpressed human needs and proficiencies, provokes elemental questions about one's philosophy of life. Children see what adults have long since failed to note. They ask questions, thousands of questions, that challenge the way life is lived. They attend religiously to the world's creations; moon, water, sand, fireflies, thunderstorms, are greeted with a certain respect and intrigue.

And they have little patience for those times when so-called religious life turns dull and monotonous, as do some worship services in mainline churches. In a word, it is the child who keeps alive the sense of religious awe before life itself. As Hans Jonas notes, the "young . . . ever renew and thus keep alive the sense of wonder, of relevance, of the unconditional, of ultimate commitment, which (let us be frank) goes to sleep in us as we grow older and tired."[6] This is at least partly what Jesus meant when he said we must "become like children" to enter the kingdom (Matt. 18:3).

Having children, then, is not just a natural event, but, as Stanley Hauerwas claims, "one of the most highly charged moral," and, I would add, spiritual events of our lives.[7] It is an act of faith and discipline. It is a privilege granted unto us in an always amazing spectacle of creation. Apart from the often hackneyed phrases about the miracle of life repeated by new parents and their visitors, having children is seldom thus identified. In a recent article on the spirituality of family, Wendy M. Wright observes that in the spiritual traditions of the Roman Catholic Church, spirituality has been located in the silence and solitude of a hermit's cell, in the transcendence of the body and material needs, and in a dispassionate love connected to no one in particular.

These are all near impossibilities for most parents. "Where is the language of God met in the midst of . . . world-maintaining? . . . in intimacy and embodiment? . . . Where can I hear of the sanctity of providing, nurturing, and tending, of stewarding possessions? Finally, where was the language of home-making, of *dwelling*?"⁸ Yet the sacred appears powerfully, precisely in the midst of stewardship of the home, in embodied nurture, and in holding up the world. Parenting is the "ascetic opportunity *par excellence*," according to Elizabeth Dreyer. Similar to, but distinct from, strict rituals of the religious in seclusion, a parent encounters unexpected opportunities to practice the disciplined religiosity that lies at the heart of asceticism's loving self-denial: "A full night's sleep, time to oneself, the freedom to come and go as one pleases—all this must be given up. . . . Huge chunks of life are laid down at the behest of infants. And then, later, parents must let go."⁹

Through long hours of arduous practice, mothers actually begin to acquire what Ruddick identifies as an entire metaphysical "discipline of thought," to assure at least three goals: the preservation, the growth, and the acceptability of their children. The discipline of maternal thought she describes, however, also has close affinity with those theological doctrines of creation and care which she does not note from her perspective as a philosopher. Genuine care of a small being demands finely tuned "metaphysical attitudes," which I would identify as the same significant moral and religious virtues long upheld by biblical and religious traditions: the priority of holding over acquiring; humility and a profound sense of one's limits; humor and resilient cheerfulness amid the realities of life; respect for persons; responsiveness to growth; and ultimately, the capacity for what Ruddick calls "attentive love." By this term, she refers to the exercise of "keeping over acquiring, of conserving the fragile, of maintaining whatever is at hand and necessary to the child's life," a loving without seizing or using that is akin to a divine love for human creation.[10]

This does not mean that all mothers succeed at realizing a kind of god-like attentive love or that any one mother succeeds all the time. It does imply, however, that living with children can teach a mode of ethical reasoning that will construct standards by which one can judge one's own errors and temptations. It can foster a religious practice of carefully reading the other, oneself, and human nature. It can lead to a deeper grasp of self and, at the same time, to a sort of self-transcendence that allows renewed consideration for those in need of care. A Nicaraguan revolutionary wrote to her young daughter shortly before she was killed, "A mother isn't just someone who gives birth and cares for her child. A mother feels the pain of all children, of all peoples, as if they had been born from her womb."[11] While this may exaggerate the expanse of empathy a child stirs up in most people, it still speaks of the potential engendered in the practice of attentive love with children.

Of course, there is nothing automatic or natural about any of this. Caring for children requires deep reserves of energy, extended periods of patience, and a heightened intellectual activity that seldom has been recognized as such. Moreover, the spiritual potential of living with children comes only when the spirituality of everyday life is recognized, affirmed, and attended to as being equally worthy with fasting and praying. Then, the sometimes tedious, sometimes wondrous intricacies of "caring labor" for another—dressing, nursing, feeding, cleaning, wiping, brushing, guarding, protecting, reprimanding, teaching, watching, following, listening, mediating, responding, and anointing the head of a child—teaches something nameless that is nonetheless essential to life and living. In caring for a child, as in caring intimately for any human being, one may glimpse the divine within creation. Seeing God in the face of the child opens the eyes to the face of God in those around us. Somehow, through the mutual understanding practiced over and over in the minute moments of attachment with a dependent, developing person, one who has struggled to care for a vulnerable, yet resilient child gains new empathy for other children, for one's spouse, for parents, for the oppressed. One begins to behold the vulnerable, yet resilient child in all people.

Seeing the Face of Death

Living with children is a moral and spiritual exercise also in another way: Human generativity is essentially linked to human finitude and to what people do in the face of limitation and death. Most people generally do not think about this connection. Most would agree with Erikson that, due to their extreme preoccupation with "taking care of actual births," adults possess "a supremely sanctioned disregard of death."[12] But this is not quite accurate. Penelope Washbourn's theological explorations of the stages of female development challenge Erikson's interpretation. She observes that the theme of death fills the daily contemplations of the pregnant woman. Preparing for, and then giving birth comes "as close to dying as any other human experience."[13] Pregnancy involves a double, or even triple death: (1) the symbolic death of an old, childless self; (2) the death of an internal relationship to a moving fetus; and (3) the fear of real death of the fetus in utero or upon birth, and of herself during the birth.

Generating adults intuit the shadow of nonbeing in every act of creativity, whether verbalized or not. The human wish to generate, whether children, works of art, or empires, indirectly acknowledges the presence of finitude. The fulfillment of the wish appeases death's threat to life. The failure to produce can come as death, whether literally with the cramping flow of menstrual blood that tells a woman in an instant that a potential life has not come to be, or more generally, with the experienced loss of repeated failures to live creatively. Where generation fails, "stagnation," to use Erikson's word, and regression to previous developmental stages result. So important is generativity of all kinds, he asserts, that its denial has as severe repercussions as the "denial of sexuality"; it is "as severe a source of inner tension." While persons take sexual frustration seriously, they tend to overlook the pathology caused by "generative frustration."[14]

Some have talked about this in more positive terms, claiming, in particular, the fruits of procreative generativity. In *Models of God*, Sallie McFague contends that becoming a biological parent is the closest most people come to "an experience of creation, that is, of bringing into existence" and passing on life. The act of giving birth inspires a sense of having glimpsed the very heart of things. Hauerwas describes children as a "sign that hope is stronger than despair," while he carefully avoids the "sinful pretension" that children ensure our immortality.[15] Robert Lifton, a psychologist intrigued by the human desire for immortality, identifies biological propagation as one of several "modes" that can satisfy what he sees as an innate and universal urge to maintain a sense of connectedness to life. Satisfaction of the desire for continuity and immortality can come through children—that is, through human perpetuation and regeneration.[16]

Few have explored in any depth, however, the complexities of this kind of generativity. As Hilary Rose points out, the production of people is "qualitatively different from the production of things." With children, one literally must give something of oneself to the other, an emotionally demanding labor that we have depicted with the "ideologically loaded term love."[17] This giving costs a person in ways that other forms of generativity seldom do, and the results can often be far more ambiguous.

Although generativity encompasses not only procreation, but the creation of new products and new ideas, failures of caring labor, such as problems of infertility and unplanned fertility, can present unique spiritual crises. One can choose not to write a book or not to pursue promotions in a particular career, and then turn to other creative outlets. But infertility most often comes unbidden, unexpected, undesired, and carries a particularly poignant sense of inner failure and physical, emotional, moral, and spiritual inadequacy. An unwanted pregnancy, an autistic preschooler, or a rebellious adolescent can have even more troubling effects. These moments raise radical choices, not between vying projects, but about human life and death—a loss and death intimately connected to the vitality of one's own life. If, as Erikson argues, only those who have "taken care of things and people" can bear the fruit of integrity and wisdom in life's later stage of old age, then those who do not or cannot conceive, or who cannot care for those they have conceived, for whatever reason, must find other ways to affirm themselves and their place in the life cycle.[18] They must find ways to justify life and to answer questions of its meaning.

It is ultimately children, however, who reinforce a message that theology has tried to convey: In the end, all generative adults must contend with human limits. The potential and realities of children make it readily apparent that people must choose among life's many possibilities, and then live "well enough" within the fixed parameters of these choices. Working out a life with or without children demands that people consider their limits and the limits of life, letting some aspirations go while claiming others instead. These may be among the hardest decisions of rightful living. But as Jacob's response to Esau reminds us, no one can "have it all" in any genuine sense; at some important point, we must recognize that we have enough of what life promises. Jesus himself seemed to think that children are just what people need to nudge them toward an understanding of the relativity of all human power. All of us are finite and, in the end, take with us nothing tangible of what we have produced. Children are often the best reminder of our ultimate vulnerability before life's whims.

Seeing the Truths of Love and Work

The difficult choices of children teach additional lessons about love and work which I have already touched upon and which will consume the remainder of this chapter. In a nutshell, children prompt a fuller definition of generativity: Human fulfillment rests upon some combination of two elements—productivity in work *and* realization in love. The demands and rewards of each, for both men and women, deserve respect, status, and reward. More specifically, to be deprived of the moral practice of attunement to an infant, T. Berry Brazelton says, leaves men with "an unfulfilled longing," "an unconscious anger," and a driven need to acquire, "compete, win, be first."[19] To be deprived of satisfying work of one's own leaves women with an inverse longing, anger, and self-dispersion. Nature never intended childbearing as a trade-off for neglecting all other forms of satisfaction and achievement. Nor were men in the public work world intended to neglect the lessons of human relationality.

None of the lessons of living with children that I have explored thus far can be seen or heard when life is too burdened by poverty and abuse, when it entails monotonous, unrewarding work, or when it revolves solely around work or solely around a child. Mary Guerrera Congo titles an essay on the truths of parent-child relationships, "The Truth Will Set You Free, But First It Will Make You Crazy." The lessons of children come with the advantage of a life that permits both satisfying work of one's own and the care of children. Guerrera Congo drinks deeply from a well that surprisingly "gushed forth love" for each child with each birth. At the same time, she admits that she desperately needs others to take care of the kids, because she cannot be with them day after day "without risking the limit of tolerance that might cause me to lash out uncontrollably in anger and do something I might regret."[20] For many people, poverty and lack of generative opportunities further distort the chances for both engaging parenting and meaningful work lives.

Children can inspire awe, teach curiosity, compassion, and the wonder of the commonplace, and awaken a recognition of our place in the world. But the "well of affection" can suddenly and unavoidably run dry. As we have seen, today we have fathers who sacrifice their families for their work, abandoning the liveliness of the institution of fatherhood, and mothers who sacrifice themselves for their children, endangering the vitality of the institution of motherhood. Biblical images of motherhood and fatherhood that have infiltrated the collective subconscious have often simply bolstered these practices. The mother in the story of Solomon, for example, has become the epitome of the self-sacrificing mother who forfeits her own rights so that the child might live, while father Abraham moves to sacrifice his child Isaac out of loyalty to his God. Either image, valuable in itself, has contributed to the impoverishment of the values of many modern families, when taken to its extreme and instituted into rigid gender roles and divisive structures of work and family.

Sacrificing Love: Children Require Less

Living with children teaches new lessons about the caring labor of love. Children require both more and less than the "ideal" modeled in "Father Knows Best." Most children do not need or benefit from the kind of unconditional self-sacrificial love that Christianity often esteems as the ideal, the one that adults (including psychologists) have fantasized and projected onto mothers. This argument is forcefully made in Christine Gudorf's article, "Parenting: Mutual Love and Sacrifice." Much revision, she claims, needs to be made in the way we as a society view children and child-rearing. And much revision needs to be made in Christian views of agape. She writes:

> After years of grappling with a severe personal uncomfortableness and periodic anger toward the way my decision to parent [two adopted

children with medical handicaps] was universally perceived—as heroic, self-sacrificing, Christian love . . . I believe this interpretation is very faulty, and results from a radical misunderstanding of parenting, personal relationships in general, and the ethic of Jesus.[21]

Contrary to everyone's immediate perception that selfless love must have motivated her to adopt a two-year-old who could not walk, talk, or eat, and a five-year-old who could barely walk, dress, or wash himself, selfless love was not a primary factor. The "most revealing lesson the children taught us" is that love can never be disinterested. Although initially she and her husband gave considerably of themselves, Gudorf recognizes that this giving was never unconditional or self-disregarding. Their love involved a necessary self-interest that actually enhanced their capacity to give. As parents, "our efforts for them rebounded to our credit. Failure to provide for them would have discredited us. And we had expectations that the giving would become more mutual."[22]

In general, "every achievement of the child is both a source of pride and a freeing of the parent from responsibility for the child." This is what Gudorf wanted and sought. In contrast to conventional views of children, their children controlled the relationship at least as much as they did. Because of the handicap of the two-year-old, they had to force-feed liquids, but "he kept down only as much as he wanted—never enough to gain weight, barely enough to stay alive." The children determined "where we went . . . what we ate, all home activities, who we saw, even how much sleep we got."[23] More than anything, the children gave to them. They gave them new hope about making the world a better place, fresh loyalty to the plight of Hispanics, African Americans, and those with medical handicaps and chronic illness. The children forever altered their lives and identities.

As Gudorf's observations reveal, the ethical dynamics of love are more complicated than the theories of men and nonmothers have ever known or understood. She questions the universal presumption that genuine parenting entails heroic sacrifice. This in turn leads her to question the idealization of agape in Christian ethics. Love, particularly the love between parent and child, involves ample self-giving, certainly, but self-giving must never become the ideal. As Gudorf discovers, "all love both involves sacrifice and aims at mutuality." Moments of self-diminishment, even the moment of sacrifice in the crucifixion of Jesus, are "just that—moments in a process designed to end in mutual love."[24] While no honest mother would ever want to deny the inevitable necessity of self-demise, even in the earliest moments of nurture the nurturer receives something in return, and hopes to continue to do so. While Jesus did urge sacrificial action, he always connected this demand with the promise of reward in the kingdom to come, of which the present rewards of mutual love are already a partial taste.

While critical moments call for self-giving love, therefore, this should not be the ideal that is hung over the heads of parents struggling to love their children. The ideal of sacrifice creates virtues impossible to emulate, distorting relationships between parent and child, and between mother and father. It exaggerates the amount of energy a single person can or should bestow upon children, and it misjudges the possible damage done by the absence of a father's matching self-giving love. Not only is loving sacrifice impossible as a goal, it denies women the complex realities of maternal labor—that a good mother can sometimes hate her children, that a mother may love her children, but hate mothering, that vesting one person with full responsibility for mothering may not be wise, or even possible. The ideal harms persons, particularly women, who already are overprogrammed to give endlessly, leaving them ashamed of the self-interest that naturally accompanies their love.

The distorted ideal of sacrificial love also harms the recipient, when these natural needs are disguised as gifts for which others should feel grateful. Undue maternal sacrifice deprives men of opportunities to learn the labor of "attentive love" and misleads them into expecting the impossible of the mother. Myths about innate maternal love convey the message that men are somehow ill-equiped to share the responsibility of child rearing, lacking some physiological love that only mothers have. Parents, and mothers in particular, do better to admit, and even affirm, their limits and the hopes and needs they harbor, both in relationship to their children and in regard to their own work.

As in the "Daughters of Eve" we have discussed, some mothers know the intricate dance around self-denial and self-survival that is a powerful and necessary dynamic of all real care. If women, mothers in particular, are to have creative work, they must be allowed self-absorption, uninterrupted by nagging thoughts and guilt about caring for others. The mother who says, "I'm a better mother because I work," or vice versa, is not trying to deny the demands of caring for her children or to dismiss the problems that working and mothering create. She names the importance of reciprocity between self-giving and self-gratification, both in her love and in her work. Empowerment of children necessarily means a "power with" rather than a "power over," which must empower the giver if it is to empower the recipient.

Although Gudorf does not rely on it, much recent social scientific theory upholds these theological reflections about empowerment and reciprocity. In *Mother Love*, Elisabeth Badinter attacks the social, religious lore that has led us to take for granted an innate maternal love. It has been assumed that all mothers naturally love their children and naturally know how to care for them. However, this has not been the case throughout history, according to Badinter's study of the last several centuries.[25] Human love is far more mutable, shaped by varying cultural mores and practices. In the past few decades, equally powerful notions have arisen around the phenomenon of bonding between mother and infant in the first few moments of birth. Scientific claims about the reality of this bond, and of its utter necessity for a child's normal development, also have come under more critical scrutiny, and although this bonding has now been dismissed by most of the scientific community, it still holds a firm grip on women's psyches.[26]

One of the strongest cases for reconsidering the old ideas about love and bonding is made by Jessica Benjamin in *The Bonds of Love*. Based on a psychoanalytic analysis of human development that refines the theories of Freud, Winnicott, and Chodorow, she advocates an ideal that thus far has been "scarcely put forward": balancing the recognition of the child's needs with the assertion of the mother's subjective needs.[27] Although Benjamin remains oblivious of the obvious ethical implications of her work, she has done a good job in unpacking a fundamental psychological tension in human development between the need to recognize the other and the desire to be recognized oneself. This essential tension collapses into the two poles typically occupied by men and women, of domination and submission, or of destructive rulership and self-annihilating self-sacrifice. Optimistically, from Benjamin's psychological perspective, this dynamic is not inevitable. Its subversion rests essentially on reclaiming the subjectivity of the mother.

From a theological perspective, however, it will take a great deal more than the power of individual human will to absolve this failure to love, given our fallen human nature. It will take assertion of female and maternal desire, surely, but it also will take recognition of ambiguities, failures, guilt, and the perpetual need of forgiveness. It will take a more refined understanding of the temporary necessities of self-giving and a postponement of the pursuit of maternal subjectivity, something Benjamin, in her psychoanalytic mode, does not comprehend. Finally, subversion of the dynamics of domination in love will require broader social and religious structures, rituals, and beliefs that can reinforce mutual regard. It would be better if Benjamin would admit that, at some point, her psychological discoveries about human nature and growth lead her to particular hopes and ideals for human relationality. Benjamin needs scholars in ethics and theology, like Gudorf, to take this next step.

Nonetheless, as a psychological and religious ideal, responsiveness to others and responsiveness to oneself need not be mutually exclusive of each other. When Erikson coined the term *generativity,* this is partly what he had in mind. A "mutuality" and "an ecology of mutual activation" between child and adult, youth and grandparent, young and old, governs each stage of growth. The adult both gives *and* gets, and the child both gives *and* gets. Children, albeit less adept and seasoned in the practice of mutuality, operate as partners in its temporal dimension and development. This generativity allows the child to continue to grow; the adult is expected to do likewise. Theories of development, including Erikson's own theory, which focus so essentially upon the child's progress, fail to consider adequately the adult's needs and the necessary coinciding changes in the adult, developments absolutely necessary for adequate care. If the mother and father do not balance their own interests with the work of parenting, if they do not grow with their children, the children will not prosper and flourish.

Gudorf, as well as Benjamin and Erikson, hint at but fail to develop an essential point here: Mutual regard and self-giving belong within a more comprehensive context of familial, social, and cultural support. Mutual love is the ideal. But particularly with children, mutual love does not begin mutually, and their care involves a certain measure of parental self-loss and self-renunciation. In the interlude, in the larger network of care, many hands must rock the cradle and share the burdens of self-giving and dependence, a central point I will expand upon shortly. When the less adept and dependent child cannot give back, the necessity to give, in response to the needs of a child, depends upon a broader context of give-and-take.

This context must be endorsed and supported by theological doctrines of love. Self-giving love never rests on its own, alone, unaided, uninterrupted. It must be alleviated and countered by contrasting moments of self-gratification, within the broader network of dependencies that make up human community. A parent cannot give to a child unless that giving is refreshed by the supportive attentions of another, whether spouse, neighbor, friend, or relative. In other words, the self-diminishment necessary for care of others is healthy and good, but only in a social context in which caring is neither a compulsory nor an exploitative experience. With a child who cannot give too much early on, self-giving needs others standing by until a later time of reciprocity.

Caring Labor: Children Require More

Children need less of the self-sacrificing labor that has gone by the name of love. But they need more caring labor than many people have recently acknowledged. In rearranging the family and dislodging women from the home, many subtly dismiss the amount of energy, time, empathy, and moral and religious guidance that children need. Children are immensely more valuable, more vulnerable, and, as we saw in the last chapter, a lot more work than our cultural imagination has conceded, and than our economic and political policies would like to acknowledge. In Dorothy Dinnerstein's frequently cited *Mermaid and the Minotaur,* she declares six months a "generous" estimate of the amount of time each child should remove a woman from her normal sphere of activity. To be "physically a mother," she concludes, should require only a minor percentage of one's mature adult life span.[28] Others suggest that the acute needs end after preschool.

Unfortunately, mothering is not merely physical, cannot be turned on and off to suit adult needs, and does not come quickly to a defined end. Estimates, like Dinnerstein's, of the demands of children, tend to assume a social and economic hierarchy in which someone else, usually another woman, and usually from a different class or race, picks up the slack of the remaining months and years. These estimates assume a school system capable of instilling values and responding to personal emergencies. They reflect a covert tendency to commodify children as objects, or private property, and to think of women as simply producers on a reproductive assembly line.

From a theological perspective, however, children are not products or private property; children are gifts. About this, Jesus is clear. Nowhere else in scripture or in mythic literature are children invited in, affectionately embraced, and blessed. As Gordon observes, "Nowhere . . . is there concern for the education, the upbringing of children, the inner lives of children, the idea that they exist not as possessions, as markers, as earthly immortality, but in themselves." Jesus "seems genuinely to want the physical presence of children, their company."[29] Caring for children is lifted up as a privilege which God entrusted to adults. Adults are temporary, but essential intermediaries of divine care, and recipients of an invaluable, irreplaceable charge.

This charge is not a piece of private property that can be disposed of as an individual parent desires, without accountability and responsibility to human personhood, to the larger human community, and to God. As this implies, the gift and promise of children is not just to a parent, but to the larger community. As I will develop below, the larger community is equally responsible, albeit in distinct ways, because, as Schüssler Fiorenza argues, they are "our future": "Children are not just the responsibility of mothers, not even just the responsibility of both parents. Their rights are given into the care of all of us." Part of this responsibility involves teaching the children, in turn, even at an early age, advises Delores Williams, that they too bear responsibility for "tending the soil beyond our own little vineyards," first pitching in around the house and, later, participating in the betterment of the wider community.[30]

The human family is unique in its complex construction of community and in its extended responsibilities for its members. Unlike animals who give birth to several offspring of identical age, whose development proceeds in a unified, linear fashion and whose periods of dependency are relatively brief, most parents stand in a complicated nexus of interrelations, with two or more offspring, sometimes at widely divergent stages of development, with lengthy periods of dependency. Practically speaking, children themselves refuse to be something that one does on the side, as an extracurricular activity, when convenient. The work of children is a wholesale, everyday, and, in some ways, lifelong commitment.

Certainly, in other ways, child rearing is a time-restricted obligation of a fairly definite number of years, requiring more than Dinnerstein proposes, but not one's whole life exclusive of other interests and vocational pursuits. It is distributed unevenly over the lifespan and must have some daily limits. As I argued, no one can sustain constant requests, and no one should avoid living one's own life. Everyone needs work of one's own.

In the last analysis, however, children question the highly prized place of paid work in American life-styles. In the refrain of Harry Chapin's "Cat's in the Cradle," the son asks again and again, "When you comin' home, Dad?" The father answers, "I don't know when, but we'll get together then; you know we'll have a good time then."

As described before, industrial and postindustrial occupational structures have been particularly unsympathetic to the different pace of children. Definitions of success based on market rewards, long hours, an uninterrupted career sequence, competitive concern for advancement, unquestioning devotion to job or employer, and predicated on the assumption of a male worker with a homemaker spouse, preclude children and children's time. Economic definitions of generativity in the public world stand at odds with the needs of children and parents in their private lives.

Children also need more in another direction, as I said at the end of the last section. They literally clamor for a wider range of social relationships than this problematic division of private and public generativity allows: A one-year-old instantly recognizes a peer and inspects the other with single-minded curiosity; a young child eagerly awaits the admiring attention of other adults; a three-year-old develops a special attachment to a caring ten-year-old; a ten-year-old befriends the dad across the street to learn how to pitch. Even small children, I am convinced, who live within a relatively limited sphere of intimate bonds, need many caring "parents," rather than just one, or even two.

Only in industrial and urban society has the job gone to the mother alone, the "most unusual pattern of parenting in the world."[31] Our competitive, individualistic society has been quick to delimit and isolate the tasks of rearing children. Many from beyond theological circles, like Nancy Chodorow, Alice Rossi, Susan Moller Okin, and others, have lifted up the "devastating" consequences, in Amelie Oksenberg Rorty's words, when children, during their early formative experiences, are "intimately exposed to only one person," an "unacknowledged and essentially unrewarded servant."[32] According to Chodorow, Dorothy

Dinnerstein, and others, mother as sole nurturer distorts a child's psychological capacities for attachment and separation along gender lines, pushing the son out of the family's intimate relationships and drawing the daughter inexorably in.[33]

Moreover, the isolated household reproduces a false sense of self-reliance and individualism that actually rests on the sacrifice of a few. It deprives children of the example of the real interdependency of all human living and, according to Rossi, deprives them of the support system that in the past helped reduce the weight upon parents and gave children ready access to peers and other adults, as guides, mentors, and regenerators of their world.[34] Children lack a variety of adult role models of both sexes and have little or no exposure to the occupational world of paid work. Finally, the unjust division of domestic labor, witnessed firsthand by a growing child, skews a child's development of an adequate sense of social and civic justice beyond the confines of the home.

When mothers today ask for public-supported child care, part of their motivation is not a desire to hand off the duties. Mothers do not seek child care out of a desire to lessen their own commitments or out of a selfish desire for their own gratification. Women cannot do it all, and they are urging a renewed communal commitment and shared responsibility for children, to supplement their own energies and obligations as parents. Granted, bearing a child takes individual parents, and the early attachments of the first few years are vital. However, the care of children, at its heart, is also a social and communal enterprise, involving a broader nexus of kin, neighbors, other parents, friends, and other unrelated adults.

Here, other periods and traditions correct the common practices of much of contemporary American society. In the course of human history, singular adults did not raise children; villages did. Today, mothers in almost all nonindustrial societies combine child care with important economic tasks. They do so by sharing responsibility for children with others, within the context of a wider social group. In this context, according to Ghanaian theologian Mercy Amba Oduyoye, mothering is not so much a physical act as a religious duty. As Oduyoye herself proclaims, "I have no biological children. . . . I am not a mother," but "I have children." In a mother-centered Akan culture, the entire community has children and, in this sense, a mother's responsibilities. Mothering is "what a good sociopolitical and economic system should be about if the human beings entrusted to the state are to be fully human, nurtured to care for, and take care of themselves, one another, and of their environments."[35]

Many Western European countries have public policies of paid parental leave, job and benefits protection, child-care facilities, and child-support funds; this reflects the greater value these countries place upon care of the child as a communal and social responsibility. One reason our country resists providing day care is that it is seen as simply an aid for women, who are ultimately responsible for children. In France and other countries, the provision of day care is not seen as a service for women as much as it is a help for children, because children are everyone's concern.[36]

We need not look beyond our shores, however, to see evidence of alternative attitudes toward children. In African American communities, "fluid and changing boundaries" mark the parameters of care for children, according to Patricia Hill Collins. Blood-mothers are assisted by "othermothers"—grandmothers, sisters, aunts, cousins, neighbors—who share the mothering responsibilities. The special status attributed to biological motherhood does not rule out the importance of "fictive kin," who adopt children to whom they are not biologically related. The esteem of biological mothering does not prevent the unique recognition accorded nonparents, who establish special relationships with the young in other ways. Nor does the value of cooperative care and the centrality of women-centered networks rest on male powerlessness, as many outside the African American community have feared or presupposed.[37]

This approach toward children reflects both "a continuation of West African cultural values and functional adaptations to race and gender oppression." Although life in the inner city tears apart the very fabric of the cooperative networks of care, African American valuation of children still challenges "one fundamental assumption underlying the capitalist system itself: that children are 'private property' and can be disposed of as such." Othermothers share the right and responsibility to discipline and to secure the betterment of the children.[38] As it turns out, the practice of othermothering has often served to stimulate a generalized ethic of care and accountability for the survival and enhancement of all the children in the community. For some community othermothers, the experience provides a foundational stepping stone into political activism.

Many Americans may not realize how unique are the privatistic, genderized values that characterize many social settings where several children are present. At the playground, a restaurant, or during church coffee hour, many mothers usually see themselves as exclusively responsible for their own children and no one else's, unless explicitly asked or given permission. Few would discipline another child, even if they found the behavior wrong or inappropriate. Adult men, more often than women, see their duties to the children present as a great deal secondary to their own conversation, food, and work. To do otherwise oversteps certain customary bounds. Many an Asian, African, or African American mother would see these boundaries as rather reckless and absurd. In many ways, they are.

Recovering Parental Inclinations

Maternal knowing may refer to thinking, particularly for women who have known another inhabiting themselves and have suckled, carried, and, finally, let go to live. But the caring labor that is required has general ramifications for others besides biological mothers, even in a culture like ours that has increasingly moved away from communal responsibility for children. While the term *mother* rests on physiological processes of conception and birth, the term is not just biological. As John MacMurray says, *mother* is a term for "the adult who cares." Others can and must learn to care. Care of children is far too important to be left to mothers alone, as are the thoughts and values that such care evokes.

Procreative generativity is an evocative moral and religious metaphor, with important ethical and theological implications that point beyond itself. In *Models of God,* McFague believes that the model of God as mother is a rich and neglected metaphor for rethinking Christian understandings of God's love, creation, and justice. Physical acts, such as giving birth and feeding the young, provide new ways to think about creation as bodied forth from the "womb" of the divine, and about love as the desire to nurture the most basic needs of the other and seek its flourishing.[39] However, to proclaim biological parenthood is not McFague's operating intent, any more than it is mine. Actual parenthood is not for everyone. As Janet Fishburn asserts in *Confronting the Idolatry of Family*, "Freedom in Christ means freedom from uncritical allegiance to [this] social convention."[40] We must no longer assume that all women will or must become mothers.

At the same time, biological parenthood still carries important symbolic meanings. McFague asserts, from the outset of her chapter on God as mother, a central thesis that runs throughout her book: Not only are there "other ways of being parental besides being a biological parent . . . but even more important for our purposes . . . all human beings have parental inclinations. All human beings have the potential for passing life along."[41] An "ethic of God the mother-creator as justice" rests upon a crucial presupposition:

> [There is a] will deep within all of us which could be called the parental instinct, the will not to save ourselves but to bring others into existence. Most broadly, whether or not one is a biological or adoptive parent, the parental instinct says to others, "It is good that you exist!" even if this involves a diminishment and in some cases, the demise of the self. . . . Therefore, to suggest universal parenthood as a model to help bring about justice through care calls upon our deepest instincts, where life and death mingle and where the preservation of life for others takes precedence over concern for the self.[42]

In essence, she asks us to use the metaphor of biological parenthood as a foundational model, from which flows a more general imperative to "parent the world."

McFague forgets a terribly important point: The current cultural climate that surrounds models of parenting leaves most people with less than adequate ideas of exactly what it would mean to universalize parental sentiments and practices. By and large, as I contend throughout this book, much of American society not only has failed to cultivate the broader "parental instincts" to give and secure life, of which McFague speaks, but struggles to determine the concrete definitions of good parenting. Most people must determine what it means to be a good parent in the immediate context, before they can extend the instinct of life preservation beyond themselves to the next generation, and beyond the human species to other species.

The simple willingness to pick up a sleeping, waking child, to look in its face and see that it is both human and divine—a heart that yearns for the child, as the heart of the mother who stands before Solomon in First Kings 3:26—is a key first step. Living according to the pace of children is a great training ground for an ethic of justice and care. Sometimes, only hands-on involvement in parental exercises and its teachings can ignite the instinct of which McFague speaks into its necessary life-preserving activities. More specifically, as Chodorow, Dinnerstein, and others have argued, until men become more involved in child rearing, the psychic dynamics that subtly subvert current efforts to preserve and care will go unchallenged and unchanged. Just as we must no longer take for granted that all women must become mothers, we must no longer take for granted that parenthood is a lesser, secondary vocation for men. Men have been heralded as family providers for too long. The demands of economic sustenance, apart from emotional intimacy, have gradually eroded their desire and capacity to care.

To excuse men, fathers, and nonparents from the regime of tending life, or to deprive them of their own versions of parental practice, is to lose a precious resource and negate a viable avenue of full humanhood. This is not to say that all men and women must replicate the bodily knowing involved in an act such as lactating. Nor can everyone participate in the primary cognitive and emotional activities of maternity. This is to urge that people begin, in their own lives, to listen to and sharpen the analogues to the daily attending required of caring labor, analogues that carry a kindred spirit of perception, connection, and insight into themselves and into the processes of sustaining another. Only then will the power to reproduce the species, biologically unique to women and historically a chief source of female oppression, reclaim its rightful place as a significant source of ethical and theological teaching and discovery.

CHAPTER EIGHT

Returning to the Mother's House and Mending the Web

A GOOD ENOUGH VISION OF THE GENERATIVE LIFE

Every line I write shrieks there are no easy solutions.
Audre Lorde, *Sister Outsider*

While he was still speaking to the crowds. . . . Someone told him, "Look, your mother and your brothers are standing outside, wanting to speak to you." But to the one who had told him this, Jesus replied, "Who is my mother, and who are my brothers?" And pointing to his disciples, he said, "Here are my mother and my brothers! For whoever does the will of my Father in heaven is my brother and sister and mother."
Matthew 12:46-50

Every line I write shrieks," says Audre Lorde, "there are no easy solutions." In this book, it is much the same. Lorde is talking about what it means to live a life that integrates complex identities and commitments as an African American, lesbian, feminist, mother of a son. There are no easy solutions when lesbian demands for separatism—"no boys allowed"—come face to face with her awareness

175

that her son embodies as much hope for the future as her daughter. Ten years as an interracial lesbian couple has taught them the "dangers of an oversimplified approach to the nature and solutions of any oppression, as well as the danger inherent in an incomplete vision."[1]

The clash of commitments in this book is of a different sort, but intimately related. With children in tow and with ideals of mutuality and equality as mainstays, I know afresh the water in which I navigate—a society driven by a marketplace that devalues the taking care of children, elevates material productivity, places in jeopardy those in significant care-taking roles, primarily women, and forbids men serious concern over friends, children, family, and domicile. Oversimplified responses to family and work dilemmas, while tempting for some in the field of religion, are dangerous. Lifting the oppressions of gender-based divisions of labor, attempting to raise children in nonsexist relationships that challenge society's power dynamics, crossing previously untrespassed boundaries, seeking new concepts of the good life and the good mother—these are desires that meet with the very deepest resistance. There are no simple solutions. At the very same time, there are the dangers of living with an incomplete vision. This book, and this final chapter, try to walk the narrow line between the two perils that Lorde enumerates.

This is not a how-to book with techniques and solutions, and this last chapter will be no exception. When it comes to shaping visions, however, there is much that can and must be said by those in theology and in religious congregations. The visions of theologians and faithful congregants can go a long way toward wearing down the resistance to what is good and right and just. Feminist theologians must support new concepts of what it means to be a generative person in this tumultuous time. We especially need to help mainline congregations break their silence on the family, revisiting scriptures that have shaped familial relationships and creating new visions and new strategies. With Lorde's warning in mind, it is to these penultimate tasks that I turn one last time: (1) revisiting Orpah; (2) generative selfhood; and (3) congregational possibilities, to conclude a book that, in one sense, remains necessarily unfinished.

Lorde's warning itself loses sight of a perspective known to theology, a perspective that theologians and congregational members tend to forget. In the Protestant principle that Paul Tillich traces back to

Luther, Paul, and Christ, *no* human vision can count itself complete. I can attempt to debunk the ideals of disinterested love and sacrifice, holding up mutual responsibility as a better ethical imperative. But there is an inevitable and necessary eschatological, soteriological bent to everything dreamed of in this book. It seeks a promised land about which we have only half-baked human inclinations. Remembering this keeps human endeavors honest and gives sustenance during the times of trial, temptation, and failure.

Jesus' own extremism—right next to the imperative to let the children come is his imperative to let all biological familial relationships go—points toward a kingdom that, at this point, we can only "see in a mirror dimly." Yes, the biological family is a source of essential lessons about life and relationships. Yes, one must honor and provide for both father and mother, love the neighbor as oneself, and let the children come. In the end, however, all human relationships are subordinated to loyalty to Jesus, and all human ideals of love and work are recast in a kingdom that has yet to come. In the meanwhile, all that is asked is that we find ways to live well enough within the parameters we believe to be divine will, and to seek grace and forgiveness when our vision fails—that is, a "good enough" vision.

Orpah Revisited

While the surface of the narrative of Ruth is "reticent," its "gaps" and "silences" are invitations to enter the world behind the text, Danna Nolan Fewell and David M. Gunn argue. The choices of today and the choices of the text of the first chapter of Ruth are not as different or as simple as they seem. Ruth and Naomi, as faultless exemplars of selflessness and devotion (wrongly used as a handy text at wedding services) deserve a less generous reading, and Orpah a more generous one.[2] All three function as realistic examples of complicated responses to cultural upheaval. If Ruth and Naomi are the "women in culture, women against culture, and women transforming culture" that Phyllis Trible dubs them, Orpah represents the woman caught between cultures.[3]

Living outside the classical social mores that defined the position of men and women, Ruth, Orpah, and Naomi are no man's property. On the one hand, they are bereft of husband and children in a male-dominated culture that promises very little to a woman without either. On the other hand, bereaved but not dead, adrift but not alone, they turn to one another. Recognizing their bonds and their momentary capacity to redefine self and society, they come to know a deeper joy, but still, given the patriarchal context, a deeper loss. Twice in this crucible of decision, they join arms, lift up their voices, and "weep" at the recognition of what they have *in one another,* a value that society seldom sees or sanctions, and at the knowledge of what more they have yet to lose in choosing.

The three women practice a particular approach to moral and religious agency. They play option against option, reasoning in intimate conversational petition, decision, indecision, appeal, and re-decision. Naomi petitions Orpah twice, Ruth thrice. Significantly, Orpah chooses both paths—first one, then the other. She makes known her desire for the impossible—to go both ways. Aware of the good that lies either way, she is unwilling to accept the compromises that conventional social structures impose upon her. These are *not* choices she designed. Only with Naomi's second urging does Orpah decide, perhaps with reluctance and acknowledgment of her loss, to return to her mother's house.

Naomi refashions the choice in unique terms: She beseeches each of them to return to the "mother's house." The use of *mother's* house is strikingly unconventional. Elsewhere in scripture (Gen. 38:11; Lev. 22:13; Num. 30:16; Deut. 22:21; Judg. 19:2-3), the conventional advice to the widowed and displaced woman is to return to the *father's* house. Trible believes this unusual reference emphasizes the opposition between mother and mother-in-law.[4]

Trible's reading skirts an important point. Naomi's words point beyond opposition to the unifying, solidifying power of the mother, whether mother or mother-in-law. Adrift in the wilderness, somewhere between Moab and Judah, these women envision a world in which paternity is not the central social relationship. Paternity constructs households and marital arrangements, but not the whole of reality. Maternal ties, albeit repressed, are never wholly lost. According to Amy-Jill Levine, when "mother's house" appears elsewhere in scripture (Gen. 24:28; Song 3:4, 8:2), it is in the context of "women who determine both their own destiny and that of others."[5] Naomi's petition discloses the value and lure of the "mother's house." Her request protests a system in which men control motherhood in order to maintain patriarchy. It points to what Barbara Katz Rothman, in *Recreating Motherhood,* calls a "mother-based system" of kinship. In this transformed world, they are no longer "men's children, coming through the bodies of women," but the "children of women," turning to the "mother's house."[6]

The Hebrew verb, *sub*, translated as both "return" and "turn back," appears twelve times in the first seventeen verses of Ruth and, as commentator Edward F. Campbell observes, "carries the whole movement and tension of the episode."[7] The text stresses particular questions: What in one's past does one reclaim? To what does one turn or return? And how does one return to the "mother's house" without losing the power of redefinition of self and society one has discovered in the wilderness?

No two women in the Ruth narrative answer in the same way. Nor is judgment about the adequacy and rightness of either choice proclaimed. Naomi "said no more" to Ruth (1:18). Her silence signifies anguish, resentment and, ultimately, a forced tolerance for the immense moral and religious ambiguity of the situation. Perhaps the significant moment comes with the blessing in the wilderness—the embrace between Orpah, her mother-in-law, and Ruth, and the affirmation of all three. To "care passionately about the quality of another woman's life . . . and to allow for each other's differences," these are ultimately the lessons embedded in the Book of Ruth, according to Renita J. Weems.[8]

Over the years, readers have clung to Ruth as the right way, even misusing the text, "whither thou go," to signify in wedding services the loyal spouse who follows *her husband* wherever *he* goes. More accurately, Ruth follows Naomi and the call of a new God; apparently Orpah does not. Even Weems, for example, commends Ruth at Orpah's expense: "Unlike her sister-in-law Orpah, Ruth elected to build upon the bonds she had already established."[9] However, Orpah also builds upon prior bonds, although she chooses different ones. Orpah is not merely the opposite of Ruth, her foil and shadow. She has her own story to tell. She makes a most difficult decision, to reclaim something of her maternal past, returning to "the mother's house." While we do not know the rest of her story, Orpah has not chosen wrongly; she has chosen *differently*. The silence of God throughout this episode allows us to ponder whether this God does not also go along with Orpah. She has encountered God and "turned back." God does bless Orpah: Naomi says to *both* daughter-in-laws—"May the Lord deal kindly with you, as you have dealt with the dead and with me" (1:8*b*). The paths of righteousness are manifold.

A Second Reading of Generativity

People today are caught in a struggle to redefine "family," "people," "God," and "home" in a foreign land. Finding images of support and validation that do not feel like betrayals of either the original nurturance of the "mother's house" or the aspirations of following the new Naomis of feminist theology and otherwise, is painfully difficult. The lives of women whose unspoken desires fail to follow the "dynamic of the tale" prescribed by the dominant visions of culture, women like Lorde, myself, and others, may find company in Orpah.

This book has called for a recognition of alternative paths for both women and men, and for a second reading of generativity. To its detriment, much of modern psychology and theology ignores the experience of many women and many mothers—that is, it ignores the earlier psychological emphasis on caring for others and the moral development of an ethic of connectedness and mutuality that occurs in early adulthood, well before any "mid-life crisis" later in life.

In coining the term *generativity*, Erikson embraces a moral notion that has affinities with maternal knowledge, but he fails to provide an adequate understanding of its development in women, or in a society geared toward productivity in a more intrusive, materialistic sense. In contrast to Erikson's portrayal and the tendencies in the lives of many men, generativity does not belong to a singular stage, the second to the last, and cannot arise in the relational vacuum of growth aimed solely toward independence, individuation, and self-reliant autonomy.

The "nonproductive" care-oriented activities of preserving, guarding, cultivating, nourishing, nursing, and relating must be seen as integral earlier in development, appearing as central values more explicitly in early adulthood, and emerging as profound virtues at the climax of adulthood. For an ethic of care and generativity to await the second to last stage in life, as in the lives and theories of many men and in today's society, is simply too late. Indeed, in this light, it seems especially odd that Erikson could even confine care to a singular stage and age.

For girls, the beginnings of generativity arise in early initiatives to care for others. Proud is the mother whose daughter demonstrates signs of generative impulses—who will, as one mother puts it, "care for her toys, watch out for her brothers, and . . . breastfeed her dolls."[10] Girls tend to develop an empathy to processes beyond themselves in childhood and continue this process as they grow. Openness to the needs of others and self, balanced by experience and knowledge, takes root early in a girl's development. As we saw in the last chapter, many women use the experience of motherhood as a moral and religious exercise to perfect the discipline of thought necessary to assure the preservation, growth, and acceptability of their children. In short, the fruition of generativity and care does not appear suddenly out of a vacuum, in a mid-life crisis, but appears after a long and steady process of concern about the practice of care-giving.

Through her well-known *In a Different Voice*, Carol Gilligan has been instrumental in drawing attention to the evolution of an ethic of care in women's lives. She believes, however, that men and women follow inverse paths to reach maturity. In her view, women who deny themselves in the enactment of care, defined initially as not hurting others, eventually learn the importance of justice; men who deny others, in pursuit of truth and a fairness defined by equality, ultimately recognize the importance of connection. But her presupposition of symmetry and complementarity in male and female moral development betrays and suppresses the power of her research. The creation of a second developmental grid for women subtly reinstitutes a dualistic reading of moral and psychological experience, in which activities of care, labeled "feminine," are still devalued.[11]

Gilligan can retain her optimism about the final reunion of the "two disparate modes of experience"—care and justice—only because she tends to neglect oppressive historical, political, and social realities. Society has fed off women's caring, women have suffered under the injunction to give of themselves, and social and political obstructions stand in the way of a fuller enactment of caring by both sexes. If we take these problems seriously, we must question the appropriateness of men postponing generative concerns, as she implies; we must demand more active participation by men in learning aspects of care, long before some visionary joining of the ways later in life; and we must demand requisite changes in society's values and the institutions of family and work.

As we look at the range of lively debates over equal opportunity and job management, new reproductive technologies, abortion, parenting, parental leaves, child care, care for the elderly, and so forth, we cannot, as Gilligan advises, passively wait for men to "catch up" in their moral development to correct the "potential indifference of a morality" of logic and a "conception of justice blinded to the differences in human life." We must attend to the development of the capacity to care, in both men and women, long before midlife, and we must learn to nurture the seeds of a fuller generativity and its attributes in both. We must begin to value, Gilligan herself says, the "importance *throughout life* of the connection between self and other," and, I would stress, for men as well as women.[12]

A "bedrock modicum of cooperativeness," says Jean Baker Miller, is absolutely essential for society to exist at all. In the most literal sense, humans must shelter, protect, and nurture their offspring, not for just the one or two years characteristic of other large mammals, but for at least ten to fifteen years, and sometimes longer. The capacity to do so depends upon a set of human qualities essential for survival. Baker Miller suggests that the "male-led society" has made women and mothers the "carriers" of certain qualities of the total human experience. It has "delegated to women not humanity's 'lowest needs' but its 'highest necessities'—that is, the intense, emotionally connected cooperation and creativity necessary for human life and growth."[13] Retrieval of the fuller meaning of generativity, and the way it develops, may help to mend the web of connection broken by those who depend upon it, yet ignore its care.

Mending the Web:
Generative Versus Separative Selfhood

This book has explored the many reasons women have acted as carriers of some of the most essential human traits and virtues, both to their demise and to their blessing. I have not yet explicitly named, however, an additional issue that underlies the problems we have studied: a profound fear of merger and self-dispersion that is fundamentally related to a fear of, and animosity toward, women and mothers. According to Catherine Keller in *From a Broken Web*, this fear of connection has permeated society for centuries, pervading our deepest mythic and religious images of human and divine nature. She unearths a number of intriguing examples in the history of philosophy, religion, and psychology, such as Aristotle's disdainful views of women's role in reproduction, the conquering of the "deep" in Genesis, and Freud's desire to oust the oceanic. In each instance, terror of maternal powers of birthing and binding turns into matricidal aggression to vanquish the mother and the "monstrous" connections she embodies.[14] Civilization has feared and hated the chaotic interconnections that women embody, and, I would emphasize, that mothers, in particular, embody. In various ways, it has proceeded to slay, repress, and tear apart the web that women weave.

It is this fear of the maternal and feminine web that motivates an insistence on the ideal of a purely separate, independent self. In this view, "selfhood requires separation," as Keller remarks, or, as Daniel Levinson believes, separation "fosters individual growth," while attachments hinder it.[15] By extension, this fear leads to the insistence on a limited public ideal of generativity, which eventuates in a quasi generative self, accumulating products and accomplishments from a safe distance.

This concept of selfhood and generativity follows the classical dyad of the Greek myth of the warrior-hero Odysseus and the woman-in-waiting Penelope, Keller's root metaphor for the erroneous and misleading idealization of separation and "separative" selfhood. (She replaces "separate" self with "separative," to indicate the fallacy and impossibility of the former). Odysseus represents the "self-enclosed subject, remaining self-identical throughout its exploits in time," unaffected by its relations, busy in its heroic accomplishments.[16]

To spin and wait upon the hero's return from adventure, and to support the appearance of independence, Penelope develops a self that literally and figuratively is able to dissolve into the more substantive self of the man. She becomes what Levinson calls a "transitional figure," a mere "component" of the man's self-structure.[17] Woman is artist Shel Silverstein's "giving tree," or "missing piece"—not much by herself, useful only as she provides for and resolves a man's incompletion, and dependent upon the selfhood of men (husband or son) for her very being. *The Giving Tree* gives until she has nothing left but an old stump.[18]

This classic pair, Odysseus and Penelope, built upon the mistaken presupposition of separate, independent selfhood, repeats itself in American myths (Daniel Boone, the Lone Ranger) and, more precisely, in every particular relationship between man and woman, and also in divine images. Even the God of classical Christian theology exemplifies the fear of maternal merger. God *Himself*—"this God could take only the pronoun *He*"—is the ultimate separate object, self-sufficient, and safe from change and influence in His complete omnipotence.[19] He embodies the supreme case of a restricted generativity. How does such a God actually give birth, one of life's most changing events? It is no wonder the Christian tradition has struggled with the relationship between God and Christ.

Several psychologists, such as Daniel Stern, Heinz Kohut, and John Bowlby, have been more successful than Keller in articulating the developmental foundations for the recovery of an alternative vision of connected selfhood, although only a few, like Jessica Benjamin and Jean Baker Miller, have attended to the complications of social and gender dynamics. However, none of them considers, as Keller does, the importance of religious and mythic images in human conceptions of selfhood. Keller confirms that we need a broader theoretical foundation that will include and move beyond psychology, as I have attempted to do in this book, to address moral and religious dimensions of selfhood. Separative selfhood is an ideal that religious and mythic stories have long upheld.

Nonetheless, these psychologists support the claim that human growth does not involve a movement from dependence to independence. Rather, growth entails learning more and more sophisticated modes of relating, with a movement from immature dependencies to more mature dependencies and attachments. Disputing the pervasive interpretation that a child develops through separation from an undifferentiated, hazardous entanglement with the mother, to ever increasing heights of individuation, Stern proposes that infants differentiate themselves from birth. Early development, he believes, "is not primarily devoted to . . . independence or autonomy or individuation—that is, getting away and free from the primary caregiver. It is equally devoted to the seeking and creating of intersubjective union with another." While the child must face separation issues on one level of self-experience, new forms of being with another must proceed in other domains.[20]

In this view, rather than symbolizing a dangerous return to primitive symbiosis, the ability to unite with another signifies a developmental advance. Attachment, nurture, and dependency are essential throughout life. People do not outgrow dependencies and attachments; they differentiate and learn more adequate ways of relating to others. Separation and independence, then, are not the primary developmental tasks that we had supposed. Authentic individual development, as Baker Miller asserts, proceeds "*only* by means of affiliation."[21]

These psychological theories force us to stop and think about our preconceptions about selfhood. For so long, we have taken for granted the ideal of development as an increase in self-sufficiency and self-reliance. These theories represent an underrated, but necessary side of human nature that has surfaced as women feel, think, and talk. This may not explain exhaustively the roots of restricted interpretations and enactments of generativity, or the problems that some men have with affiliations. But it does position the conversation within a broader cultural context, one characterized by a deep ambivalence about connection, care, and, by extension, ambivalence about the literal embodiment of a powerful mode of nurturing generativity in the pregnant woman and mother. It also may account for the social forces that relativize the woman's procreative role and privatize the value of caring. Even as we reappropriate values and the rights of women, women themselves will need to struggle with their ingrained antipathy toward themselves, their mothers, and their own potential or real motherhood that the myths and religious images have only further perpetuated.

Congregations as Holding Environments

Congregations have an important role in challenging the fears and related antipathies toward women and the connections they embody. I have made some suggestions about what mainline congregations could be offering that I want to amplify. I implied that congregations have at least three distinct, but interrelated roles in addressing work and family as creative theological dilemma: (1) a descriptive, or pastoral role (this is how life is these days); (2) a normative, or prophetic role (this is how life should be); and (3) a programmatic, or proclaiming role (here are a few ways to get there). On the one hand, these activities cannot really be so sharply separated from one another. On the other hand, each act deserves its own delineated place.

While congregations must attend to important religious and ethical visions of the good life, they must avoid moving to this second action too quickly, before basic understanding is reached. This is a danger for many conservative and evangelical churches. At the same time, they must not forget about forging normative judgments on life-styles. This is an equally tempting peril for many mainline congregations that wish to stress their openness and inclusivity, but then fail to adopt a clear position on critical family issues. Finally, dialogue must not remain at an esoteric or theoretical level, which is more the nature of the second, normative step, while ignoring the third step of down-to-earth recommendations.

Congregations provide a fitting forum for listening and reflecting on the time pressures, work load, and dilemmas of families today. This first step, that of simply knowing the concerns that lie before members, exposes a few core problems: the "conspiracy of silence," as Janet Fishburn calls it, that enshrouds what happens in the family lives of members.[22] And, I must add, the work lives of members; and the apprehensions that surround really listening to the struggles, desires, and ideas of women.

Many mainline clergy and church members have relegated family and work problems to the private realm. They seldom question deeply embedded conventions about family privacy and unwritten rules about what can and cannot be discussed. During "Joys and Concerns" in a typical small-church worship service, certain events, like anniversaries, deaths, acceptable illness and hospitalizations are mentioned, but many authentic concerns, such as divorce, infertility, abortion, domestic stress and violence, teen-parent conflicts, vocational conflicts and choices, are taboo. As Fishburn points out, however, clergy can influence the topics of conversation in the congregation more than they know. Given the problems that most adults face, preaching on the previously taboo crises of generativity is an utter necessity.

There is a real need to provide a "holding environment," a safe, dependable, predictable, trustworthy, sustaining space, which will allow open communication about the current gender, familial, relational, marital, intergenerational, and vocational strife of everyday life for nearly everyone. Conversations initiated through study groups, workshops, retreats, growth groups, house-church gatherings, and sermons must include the voices of both women and men of different ages, and must listen to people's concerns about the many changes in postmodern life-styles. They must look at present problems and at conventional answers, as well as the assumed religious doctrines.

In general, we tend to underestimate the immense anxieties that surround these issues, especially when changes in images of generativity, work, and family mean giving women new voice and authority, and diminishing the assumed priority and prerogatives of men and men's work. What happens when, as an editorial on abortion in *The Christian Century* requested of the National Conference of Catholic Bishops, we ask men "to retreat from public debate for a while"?[23] What happens when we claim that only mothers can know certain things, or that fathers ought to enter the domestic world for a while? If nothing else, for many men, women's equal participation in life remains an intrusion and a hassle. But more, the "sheer audacity," family theorist Morris Taggart honestly confesses, "of introducing a WOMAN as . . . commentator and fellow yearner" calls "everything . . . into question. . . . How can I deal with the anxiety that comes from feeling like a guest in (what I had assumed was) my own house?"[24]

Some of this apprehension is also intergenerational. Since most congregations are communities of many generations, members are most resistant to changes of any kind that expose generational differences. And changes in gender relations today do just that. Fishburn does an excellent job of identifying two different groups in many mainline congregations, to which members and clergy must remain sensitive: those born after, and those born prior to World War II. By and large, the latter group assumes, even if its members do not practice, a homogeneous, unified moral code. Among other things, this moral code prohibits masturbation, premarital intercourse, extramarital intercourse, and homosexuality, and it discourages interracial marriage, divorce, and even discussion of suicide, adultery, children out of wedlock, or other misfortunes. The younger generation is less likely to be imbued with most of these same moral ideals, professing a relative acceptance for many, if not all, of the behaviors that those born before World War II forbid or dispute. For most of the younger people, "no moral issue has the kind of black-and-white clarity . . . that it had for those who came of age before 1960."[25]

People across the generations may never fully understand or accept the other's worldview. Just recognizing and talking aloud about generational differences in beliefs about work and family, however, can go a long way toward increasing understanding. This is particularly true in an aging congregation, with a young minister whose vocational, sexual, and familial choices differ. Usually, people prefer to operate as if nothing has changed. But a great deal has changed, and people must notice and talk about the overt and hidden value gaps. Older members must grant greater allowance and acceptance to the younger members whose work and family lives follow new moral codes, in which sexual relations have changed, in which the woman is no longer the "Keeper of the Springs," in which the man has more responsibilities than "bringing home the bacon," and in which unexpected, unheard-of complications arise.[26] Greater awareness on the part of the younger generation of the things at which older members may take offense or experience disappointment is also needed.

Given the deep-seated nature of these apprehensions, pure rational discussion is inadequate to the task of intellectual and practical change. Change will require a new level of engagement, conflict, and empathy that many mainline congregations and families are bound to find most trying. But congregations, with their mix of generations, with their opportunities for informal gatherings and fellowship, with their mediating position between persons, families, and community, and with their moral traditions and scriptures, provide an especially fertile community for a kind of dialogue that cannot now be found anywhere else in our society, even within families themselves.

Congregations as Communities of Prophets and Visionaries

Of course, talking about "how life is these days" will push people to ask difficult normative questions about "how life should be." As the first step of listening, brainstorming, and holding has implied, a second equally challenging and critical step for mainline congregations is to deliberate over moral values and visions. First of all, men and women need new ways to think about their commitments to work. Congregations have a crucial prophetic role in confronting the values of a materialistic "Protestant" work ethic that puts profits before people. Clergy and members know that there is more to life than money, or they would not be worshiping. But just like Moses's people, religious people today need occasional or continual reminders, especially in America's gadget-oriented, product-hungry society. On this score, the needs of children must no longer be our lowest priority, the jobs related to children our lowest status, worst paid positions, or caring for children something of little value. As bell hooks contends, we must guarantee the "right of children to effective child care by parents and other childrearers," with the "restructuring of society so that women do not exclusively provide that care."[27]

Congregations also must begin to attend to, recognize, and proclaim the implicit connections between the interests of communities and families, and the interests of economics and politics. They need to critique the social and economic norms of care which artificially separate public material productivity from private procreativity, nurturance, and tending, rewarding the former and disregarding and devaluing the latter. On a minor scale, they can value the latter and encourage people to try to adapt the workplace to themselves and to the values of new life, nurturance, care, and faith, rather than continuing to adapt to male- and market-defined values, job schedules, and demands. I will mention some policy implications of this below.

People also need new ways to think about their commitments to families. Congregations play an instrumental role in fostering parental inclinations, broadly conceived, and in widening the circles of caring labor. If parenting is an act of faith, and even a sort of ministry of service, congregations must assign value to what parents, and all those who offer care in other forms, contribute, and must work to ease their burdens. As I suggest throughout this book, this must go hand-in-hand with a reevaluation of religious ideals of love and mutuality. Congregations can begin by simply talking about the use and abuse of power, both inside and beyond their walls. This is a task to which, a few decades ago, most families and congregations gave little, if any, time. Yet it is an invaluable step in human consciousness about relationships, freedom, and responsibility. There is much that can be said on this, from the power dynamics between children and adults within families and congregations (especially in terms of sexual abuse), to the power dynamics between husband and wife, mother and father. I limit my remarks to the latter.

If it is primarily, or partly, within the family and the congregation that children first come to have a sense of themselves, their relations with others, and their relation to God, an experience that is foundational to moral and spiritual development, then it makes all the difference in the world whether that experience is one of unequal altruism and one-sided self-sacrifice on the part of women and mothers, or one of justice, mutuality, and reciprocity. Political scientist Susan Moller Okin makes this point powerfully in *Justice, Gender, and the Family:*

What is a child of either sex to learn about fairness in the average household with two full-time working parents, where the mother does, at the very least, twice as much family work as the father? What is a child to learn about the value of nurturing and domestic work in a home with a traditional division of labor, in which the father either subtly or not so subtly uses the fact that he is the wage earner to "pull rank" on or to abuse his wife? What is a child to learn about responsibility for others in a family in which, after many years of arranging her life around the needs of her husband and children, a woman is faced with having to provide for herself and her children but is totally ill-equipped for the task by the life she agreed to lead, has led, and expected to go on leading? [28]

What will a child learn? A child will learn a distorted sense of justice, trust, equality, and vulnerability, one that requires sacrifices of women that are not required of men. If children are to develop a commitment to love, justice, and just institutions, in particular, they must spend their formative years in an environment and in institutions where love and justice are practiced. To Okin, I must add: The family is by no means the only place where injustice is learned and inordinate sacrifice is required, but it is one of the primary places. And families alone cannot institute equality in the tasks of caring labor in families when work structures, social institutions, and dominant ideologies all work against it. But if we want to liberate and transform lives, the redistribution of power in the contested terrain of the family is critical.

As I have argued, with children, the elderly, the sick, and others in need, self-giving is a necessary and inevitable part of life. But its unequal distribution between men and women is not. Mainline churches need to confirm this. They need to advocate greater justice between men and women in the home, as well as greater care in the workplace. This means changing distorted definitions of the "good mother" that equate goodness with self-sacrifice, and dated definitions of the conventional family that rely so heavily on the domestic labors of women. It means praising the virtues of "good enough" mothers who give of themselves without losing themselves, and of "good enough" families and fathers who share the burdens as justly as possible.

In general, it will not be an easy task to debunk negative views of dependency and personal needs, and the high esteem in which most congregations and pastors still hold "disinterested love" and self-sacrifice. Nor will it be easy to challenge the inhumane, impersonal structures and pressures of almost all work environments and the economic norms that put products and profits before persons. But, based on biblical and theological principles, congregations must participate in the needed movement toward greater justice at home and greater care in the workplace. Of utmost importance, they must reclaim and offer new interpretations of biblical passages that have been wrongly used and abused by fundamentalist traditions to support oppressive gender relations, familial relations, and views of women. Resources that were not available even a few years ago, like *The Women's Bible Commentary*, are now available and are invaluable in this process. Ultimately, as Fishburn's *Confronting the Idolatry of Family* reminds us, "Protestants need to hear the good news that family life and work life do not have to be the ultimate loyalties of Christians."[29] If anything, women have made family life a false idol, while men have worshiped work life, and both these idolatries have proved to be the scourge that Jesus declared.

Congregations as the Living Body

None of these discussions should be removed from the real life of the living Body or from the different needs of different parts of the body of believers. Discussions in the first two areas should always point toward a third movement of programming and restructuring, which will vary from community to community, depending upon circumstances. The following comments, therefore, are suggestive of some of the possibilities.

Congregations themselves must model changes in the internal distribution of their own caring labors. Although it is most difficult to change actual programmatic features, the restructuring of tasks previously divided along gender lines is important. Sunday school classes, for example, normally relegated to women, usually the mothers of the church, might be co-taught by female and male teams, who may or may not be parents. Youth and men's groups can help with coffee hour or funeral meals on as regular a basis as women's groups. Broadly speaking, congregations cannot continue to move women into new positions of authority without also valuing their former contributions, and urging men to take on some of those tasks. Congregations can also conscientiously oppose the tendency of women to become "giving trees" by thinking twice before relying on women and mothers to do the necessary chores. They may need to allow for an initial labor shortage among members and alter traditional programs and structures to accommodate the changed lives of many members.

Most women's work loads would be cut dramatically, however, if men made stronger commitments to children and families in the home. Congregations can oppose the social trends and conventional pressures that alienate boys and men from the activities of nurture, and even help them develop the skills required to care for the needs of dependent others. This means the mundane task of teaching men and the young, especially young boys, how to engage in egalitarian relationships, how to tend to the chores of children, relationships, and domesticity. Younger families might study what a healthy parental leave would be like, help people to institute policies in their workplaces, and support men in their responsibility to make use of those policies. Women and men might debate the inevitable problems of egalitarian relationships and share their strategies for distributing household chores, an accomplishment that can be most demanding and time-consuming for many couples. They might share ways to undercut the heightened time-crunch, to limit and control the pressures of extracurricular activities, work, and career advancement in general.

Congregations also stand in a good place to help create "good enough" communities that ease the load by providing avenues of mutual aid, assure women other means of self-worth, and expand the network of caregivers essential to a child's health. A wonderful example is the Roman Catholic tradition of naming godparents who often assume responsibilities for guiding, nurturing, and caring for children. Whatever happened to the religious tradition of "adopting" children in other religious communities? What has happened to the importance of images of adoption that figure so centrally in the relationship between Israel and God in general? These traditions merit resurrection. If churches are to be communities of people who "suffer with one another," as Herb Anderson contends, then they must work to offer living networks in which intergenerational relationships are cultivated, and parents are "relieved of sole responsibility" for the faith and development of their children. When this happens, argues Fishburn, it will be "easier to see that the American ideal of a self-sufficient family is not only impossible; it is undesirable."[30]

As an integral part of this third activity, congregations must seek to understand and, when appropriate, influence institutional and political decisions and policies, and legislation that supports children, parents, and a variety of current family forms. In almost everything I read on the problems of work and families, similar proposals are offered, despite sometimes widely divergent political stances. If nothing else, congregations must become much more aware of the nature of public policies and more adept at providing educational and supportive networks for securing necessary changes. Clergy and members need to consider seriously several measures before us.[31]

A reallocation of governmental priorities and resources is suggested. Policies for raising the personal tax exemptions allowed for dependent children, which have progressively eroded since 1948, and for spending less on military buildup and more on parenting and child care have been presented. Divorce laws also have come under closer scrutiny. Foremost in needed policies are the changes advocated by many people to insure the economic well-being of children and mothers. Some propose making payments from the absent parent, often the father, a collection process, similar to Social Security taxes.

There are other public policy needs that are pressing. We need more "family friendly" workplaces. This would include family-leave policies, child-care services, and flexible schedules and definitions of promotion. We need educational institutions that design their programs to affirm shared parenting and respond to the constraints of dual-income families, single parents, stepfamilies, and commuter marriages. We need male participation in these institutions, and in other institutions, such as day-care centers, so that children do not grow up thinking that only women are demoted to these apparently less valued, less profitable tasks.

Until unjust domestic arrangements are restructured so that the primary burden does not rest on women, we also must find ways to protect the vulnerabilities of women and ensure equal benefits. Where the one person, usually the woman and mother, remains economically dependent on the spouse, Susan Moller Okin and others have suggested "equal legal entitlement to all earnings coming into the household," with employers making out checks equally divided between the earner and the partner.[32] The partner is thereby reimbursed for the domestic services upon which both the earner and the employer depend.

Some of these proposals are more drastic than others. Some, like Okin's equal legal entitlement, have complicated and problematic implications, are open to abuse, and are based on a regrettable lack of trust between spouses. Some will take extensive work, planning, and funding, whereas others will, as Sylvia Hewlett likes to say, give us the "biggest bang for our buck" in the long run, costing less now than the alternative consequences.[33] All are designed, however, to alter the conventional avenues of generativity in work and in families, for women, men, and children. Power inequities between women, men, and children will not change, other than through such consistent systemic reordering.

At the same time, as I have said from the beginning, none of these proposals will have much lasting impact without a deeper desire for change on the part of American men and women. None of these public policies will be very successful without a personal and cultural crusade to deconstruct and restructure mature adult generativity. As Keller states, the changes require "more than a few considerate shifts of rhetoric and lifestyle. What is required is nothing less than our lives."[34] In the meanwhile, while no concrete steps, no strategies of intervention, no new support group will answer all the problems, many interim designs, when seen as part of a broader reconstruction of modern ideals of work and family, have a viability that demands their implementation. It is not just a strategic matter of sharing labors fairly. It is also a matter of reconsidering what it means to be a generative person in society at large.

We have tended to address the mechanics—women have joined educational systems, work empires, and men's clubs previously closed to them; some employers have instituted parental leaves, and the government has debated a minimalistic leave policy. However, superficial adjustments, when implemented apart from a critique of the dominant American values and beliefs about work and family, come at the expense of self and society.

Public policy and domestic changes require closer listening to children, mothers, and fathers, and they require careful, thoughtful response. They require teaching boys, from childhood on, that fatherhood and caring generativity have value and meaning. They require giving these activities moral and religious significance, and giving greater value to children and families than to work. They require a willingness on the part of men and women to give up economic advancements—a better job, a higher status, a bigger house—in order to give presence, time, and energy to children. They require rejecting market definitions of value, and, at one and the same time, establishing the value of the work of human caring, even if it may mean, in some unique cases, giving it greater market value. In our economic era, Hilda Scott says that it may be necessary to make caring labor a "legitimate economic category, with its own criteria of value and its own rewards for both women and men."[35]

In the end, however, from a theological perspective, we must argue that some forms of caring for human life can never be purchased and should never be quantified in material- or product-oriented ways. It is not easy or possible to reduce the requirements and contributions of caring labor, in terms of human connection, to economic-exchange values and costs. The I-Thou relationships of families and children cannot, and should not, be divided, organized, systematized, rationalized, bought, arranged, or bargained over in the same way as other kinds of labor. When maternal feminist theology calls for a world in which women and men can work in fulfilling ways *and* participate in families, and urges the re-valuation of caring labor that such a change will require, it calls us to a prophetic stance: to recognize the waters in which we swim—a society that devalues caring labor and those who perform its tasks—and to walk against the current. If a few join in, perhaps together the tide will turn. Perhaps some day, "Every valley shall be lifted up, and every mountain and hill be made low; the uneven ground shall become level, and the rough places a plain" (Isa. 40:4).

This would have been a nice place to end this book, but the reality is this: My life goes on amidst the ambiguities and mysteries of living, as do the lives of others who find themselves caught up in related or divergent dilemmas. This book, like life, was never intended as a tidy project. We can only live by etching in some rough proposals, like this final chapter, and then hope for the best. Of course, a few stones moved are a few stones closer to lifting up the valleys and leveling the mountains, so that the life for which we have been created comes a bit closer in view.

NOTES

Preface

1. I would like to extend appreciation to the publishers of some of my past work. This book builds upon several essays: "Produce or Perish: A Feminist Critique of Generativity," *Union Seminary Quarterly Review* 43(1989):201-21;
"Produce or Perish: Generativity and New Reproductive Technologies," *Journal of the American Academy of Religion* LIX(1991):39-69;
"Let the Children Come," *Second Opinion* 17(July 1991):10-25;
"Women Who Work and Love: Caught Between Cultures," *Women in Travail and Transition: A New Pastoral Care* (Minneapolis: Fortress, 1991), pp. 63-85;
"Returning to the Mother's House: Feminism's Orpahs," *The Christian Century* (April 17, 1991), pp. 428-30;
"Epistemology or Bust: A Maternal Feminist Knowledge of Knowing," *Journal of Religion* 72(April 1992):229-47.

Introduction

1. Alicia Suskin Ostriker, "Propaganda Poem: Maybe for Some Young Mamas," *The Mother/Child Papers* (Boston: Beacon, 1980), p. 44.
2. "Preface," *Feminism, Children, and the New Families*, ed. Sanford M. Dornbusch and Myra H. Strober (New York: Guilford, 1988), p. x.
3. Adrienne Rich, *On Lies, Secrets, and Silence: Selected Prose 1966–1978* (New York: W. W. Norton, 1979), p. 38.
4. Ibid.

Chapter One. Motherhood and the Theological Pie

1. Anita Shreve, *Remaking Motherhood: How Working Mothers Are Shaping Our Children's Future* (New York: Faucett Columbine, 1987), p. 6.
2. T. Berry Brazelton, *Working and Caring* (Reading, Mass.: Addison-Wesley, 1985), pp. xv-xxiii.
3. Carolyn G. Heilbrun, *Writing a Woman's Life* (New York: W. W. Norton, 1988), p. 48.
4. Toni Morrison, Interview with Claudia Tate, *Black Women Writers at Work*, ed. Claudia Tate (New York: Continuum, 1963), pp. 117-31.
5. Jacqueline Jones, *Labor of Love, Labor of Sorrow: Black Women, Work, and the Family from Slavery to the Present* (New York: Basic Books, 1986).
6. Katie Geneva Cannon, "Surviving the Blight," *Inheriting Our Mother's Gardens: Feminist Theology in Third World Perspective*, ed. Letty M. Russell, Kwok Pui-lan, Ada María Isasi-Díaz, and Katie Geneva Cannon (Philadelphia: Westminster Press, 1988), pp. 75-90.
7. Evelyn Nakano Glenn, "From Servitude to Service Work: Historical Continuities in the Racial Division of Paid Reproductive Labor," *Signs* 18(Autumn 1992):1-43.
8. Marie Ferguson Peters, "Parenting in Black Families with Young Children: A Historical Perspective," *Black Families*, 2nd Ed., ed. Harriette Pipes McAdoo (Newbury Park, Calif.: Sage, 1988), pp. 228-41.
9. Toinette M. Eugene, "Sometimes I Feel Like a Motherless Child: The Call and Response for a Liberational Ethic of Care by Black Feminists," *Who Cares?: Theory, Research, and Educational Implications of the Ethic of Care*, ed. Mary M. Brabeck (New York: Praeger, 1989), p. 45.

10. Hilda Scott, *Working Your Way to the Bottom: The Feminization of Poverty* (London: Pandora, 1984), pp. x, 3.
11. Ibid., p. x.
12. *Who Cares?* ed. Brabeck.
13. Robert N. Bellah, Richard Madsen, William M. Sullivan, Ann Swindler, and Steven M. Tipton, *Habits of the Heart: Individualism and Commitment in American Life* (Berkeley: University of California Press, 1985).
14. Bonnie Thorton Dill, "Our Mother's Grief: Racial Ethnic Woman and the Maintenance of Families," *Journal of Family History* 13(1988):415-31.
15. Amy Rossiter, *From Private to Public: A Feminist Exploration of Early Mothering* (Toronto, Ontario: The Women's Press, 1988), p. 270.
16. Barbara Katz Rothman, *Recreating Motherhood: Ideology and Technology in a Patriarchal Society* (New York: W. W. Norton, 1989); Ann Dally, *Inventing Motherhood: The Consequences of an Ideal* (New York: Schocken Books, 1982); Kathleen Gerson, *Hard Choices: Women Decide About Work, Career, and Motherhood* (Berkeley: University of California Press, 1986); Rosemary Curran Barciauskas and Debra Beery Hull, *Loving and Working: Reweaving Women's Public and Private Lives* (Bloomington, Ind.: Meyer Stone, 1989); Patricia W. Lunneborg, *Women Changing Work* (New York: Bergin & Garvey, 1990).
17. *New Men, New Minds: Breaking Male Tradition,* ed. Franklin Abbott (Freedom, Calif.: Crossing Press, 1987); Anthony Astrachan, *How Men Feel: Their Response to Women's Demands for Equality and Power* (Garden City, N.Y.: Doubleday & Co., 1986); Joseph H. Pleck, *Working Wives, Working Husbands* (Beverly Hills, Calif.: Sage Publications, 1985); Kyle D. Pruett, *The Nurturing Father* (New York: Warner Books, 1987).

Chapter Two. Generativity in Male Theory and Men's Lives

1. Ellen M. Umansky, "Creating a Jewish Feminist Theology: Possibilities and Problems," *Anima* 10(Spring Equinox 1984):133-34.
2. Susan Niditch, "Genesis," *The Women's Bible Commentary,* ed. Carol A. Newsom and Sharon H. Ringe (Louisville: Westminster/John Knox, 1992), pp. 10-25.
3. Barbara Ehrenreich and Deirdre English, *For Her Own Good: 150 Years of the Experts' Advice to Women* (New York: Doubleday, 1978), p. 3.
4. Ibid., p. 4.
5. Naomi Weisstein, "Psychology Constructs the Female," *Woman in Sexist Society: Studies in Power and Powerlessness,* ed. Vivian Gornick and Barbara K. Moran (New York: Basic Books, 1971), p. 133.
6. Sigmund Freud, "Female Sexuality," *Sexuality and the Psychology of Love,* ed., with an introduction by Philip Rieff (New York: Collier Books, 1963), pp. 200-201.
7. E. Jacobson, "Development of the Wish for a Child in Boys," *Psychoanalytic Study of the Child* 5(1950):139-52, cited by John Munder Ross, "Beyond the Phallic Illusion: Notes on Man's Heterosexuality," *The Psychology of Men,* ed. Fogel, Saree, and Siebert (New York: Basic Books, 1986), pp. 50-51.
8. Erik H. Erikson, "Womanhood and the Inner Space (1968)," *Woman and Analysis: Dialogues on Psychoanalytic Views of Feminity,* ed. Jean Strouse (Boston: G. K. Hall, 1985), p. 310; initially published as "Inner and Outer Space: Reflections on Womanhood," *Daedalus* 93(1964):582-606.
9. Erik H. Erikson, *Insight and Responsibility: Lectures on the Ethical Implications of Psychoanalytic Insight* (New York: W. W. Norton, 1964), pp. 131-32.
10. Erik H. Erikson, "Once More the Inner Space: Letter to a Former Student," *Women and Analysis,* ed. Jean Strouse., pp. 321-22.
11. Erikson, *Insight and Responsibility,* p. 132.
12. Erikson, "Once More the Inner Space," p. 332.
13. Erikson, "Womanhood and the Inner Space," p. 303.
14. Ibid., p. 296.
15. Ibid., p. 306.
16. Pamela Daniels, "Birth of the Amateur," *Working It Out: 23 Writers, Artists, Scientists, and*

Scholars Talk About Their Lives and Work, ed. Sara Ruddick and Pamela Daniels (New York: Pantheon Books), p. 61.

17. Erikson, *Insight and Responsibility*, p. 130.
18. Erikson, "Womanhood and the Inner Space," p. 308.
19. Ibid., p. 295.
20. Ibid.; *Insight and Responsibility*, p. 131; Erikson, *Childhood and Society*, 35th Anniversary Ed. (New York: Norton, 1968 [1950]), p. 267.
21. Erikson, "Once More the Inner Space," pp. 337-39.
22. Don S. Browning, *Generative Man: Psychoanalytic Perspectives* (New York: Delta, 1975).
23. Don S. Browning, *Pluralism and Personality: William James and Some Contemporary Cultures of Psychology* (Lewisburg, Penna.: Bucknell University Press, 1980), pp. 20-22; *Religious Thought and the Modern Psychologies* (Philadelphia: Fortress, 1987), pp. 5-6, 29-31.
24. Erikson, *Insight and Responsibility*, pp. 231, 233.
25. Ibid., p. 67; *Childhood and Society*, p. 267; *Identity: Youth and Crisis* (New York: Norton, 1968), p. 138.
26. Daniel J. Levinson, with Charlotte N. Darrow, Edward B. Klein, Maria H. Levinson, and Braxton McKee, *Seasons of a Man's Life* (New York: Ballantine, 1978), p. 9.
27. Ibid., p. 109.
28. Jean Baker Miller, *Toward a New Psychology of Women* (Boston: Beacon, 1976), p. 49.
29. Pamela Daniels, "Dream vs. Drift in Women's Careers: The Question of Generativity," *Psychology of Women: Selected Readings*, 2nd Ed., ed. Juanita H. Williams (New York: Norton, 1985), p. 427.
30. Douglas C. Kimmel, *Adulthood and Aging: An Interdisciplinary Developmental View* (New York: Wiley & Sons, 1974), pp. 189-90, 244-45.
31. George Vaillant, *Adaptation to Life* (Boston: Little, Brown, 1977), cited by Carol Gilligan, *In a Different Voice: Psychological Theory and Women's Development* (Cambridge: Harvard University Press, 1982), pp. 153-55.
32. Gerda Lerner, *The Creation of Patriarchy* (New York: Oxford University Press, 1986).
33. Michelle Stanworth, "Reproductive Technologies and the Deconstruction of Motherhood," *Reproductive Technologies: Gender, Motherhood, and Medicine*, ed. Michelle Stanworth (Minneapolis: University of Minnesota, 1987), pp. 26-27.
34. *Chicago Tribune*, September 18, 1988.
35. Stanworth, "Reproductive Technologies," pp. 13, 26.
36. Janice G. Raymond, "The Spermatic Market: Surrogate Stock and Liquid Assets," *Reproductive and Genetic Engineering* 1(1988):68.
37. Richard McCormick, "Abortion: The Unexplored Middle Ground," *Second Opinion* 10(March 1989):45.
38. Nancy Chodorow and Susan Contratto, "The Fantasy of the Perfect Mother," *Rethinking the Family*, ed. Barrie Thorne with Marilyn Yalom (New York: Longman, 1982), p. 71.
39. Brian Knowles, "Job vs. Family: Striking a Balance," *Focus on the Family* (June 1991):3.
40. Barbara Brandt, "Less is More: A Call for Shorter Work Hours," *Utne Reader* (July/August 1991):81.
41. John C. Raines and Donna C. Day-Lower, *Modern Work and Human Meaning* (Philadelphia: Westminster, 1986), p. 97.
42. Ruth Sidel, *On Her Own: Growing up in the Shadow of the American Dream* (New York: Viking, 1990).
43. Raines and Day-Lower, *Modern Work*, pp. 15, 96-102.
44. Brandt, "Less is More," pp. 82, 85.
45. Robert Bly, *Iron John: A Book About Men* (Reading, Mass.: Addison-Wesley, 1990).
46. Jan Halper, *Quiet Desperation: The Truth about Successful Men* (New York: Warner Books, 1989); James E. Dittes, *The Male Predicament: On Being a Man Today* (San Francisco: Harper & Row, 1985); James B. Nelson, *The Intimate Connection: Male Sexuality, Masculine Spirituality* (Philadelphia: Westminster, 1988).
47. Levinson, *Seasons*, p. 241
48. Gilligan, *Different Voice*, p. 12.

49. See Carol E. Franz and Kathleen White, "Individuation and Attachment in Personality Development: Extending Erikson's Theory," *Gender and Personality: Current Perspectives on Theory and Research,* ed. Abigail Stewart and Brinton Lykes (Durham: Duke University Press, 1985), pp. 137-68.
50. Browning, *Generative Man,* pp. 181 (his emphasis), 157.
51. Ibid., p. 7.
52. Erikson, *Life Cycle,* p. 68.
53. Browning, *Generative Man,* p. 164 (emphasis added).

Chapter Three. Generativity in Feminist Theory and Women's Lives

1. Erik H. Erikson, "Womanhood and the Inner Space (1968)" *Woman and Analysis: Dialogues on Psychoanalytic Views of Feminity,* ed. Jean Strouse (Boston: G. K. Hall, 1985), p. 317.
2. Sylvia Ann Hewlett, *A Lesser Life: The Myth of Women's Liberation in America* (New York: William Morrow, 1986), pp. 179-80.
3. Ibid., pp. 184-85.
4. Martha Weinman Lear, "The Second Feminist Wave," *New York Times Magazine,* March 10, 1968.
5. See Dale Spender, *Women of Ideas (and What Men Have Done to Them)* (London: Ark, 1983); Gerda Lerner, *The Creation of Feminist Consciousness: from the Middle Ages to 1870* (New York: Oxford University Press, 1993).
6. Pamela D. Couture, *Blessed Are the Poor?: Women's Poverty, Family Policy, and Practical Theology* (Nashville: Abingdon Press, 1991), pp. 143-44, 146-47.
7. Betty Friedan, *The Feminine Mystique* (New York: Dell, 1963); Simone de Beauvoir, *The Second Sex* (New York: Random House, 1952).
8. Elizabeth Fox-Genovese, *Feminism Without Illusions: A Critique of Individualism* (Chapel Hill: University of North Carolina Press, 1991), p. 2.
9. Judith Stacey, "Sexism by a Subtler Name: Postindustrial Conditions and Postfeminist Consciousness in the Silicon Valley," *Socialist Review* (November/December 1987):7-11.
10. Flora Davis, *Moving the Mountain: The Women's Movement in America Since 1960* (New York: Simon & Schuster, 1991), p. 279.
11. Arlie Hochschild and Anne Machung, *The Second Shift* (New York: Viking Penguin, 1989), pp. 11-12.
12. Susan Faludi, *Backlash: The Undeclared War Against American Women* (New York: Crown, 1991), pp. xviii, xx.
13. Mary Hunt, "Anne McGrew Bennett: Feminist Theological Pioneer," *Journal of Feminist Studies in Religion* 4(Fall 1988):84.
14. National Research Council, *Summary Report: Doctorate Recipients from United States Universities, 1987–1992;* United States Department of Education, National Center for Education Statistics, *Digest of Education Statistics, 1986–1992,* cited by Frank Crouch, "U.S. Doctorates in Religion and Theology Make Little Progress Toward Achieving Gender Parity," *Religious Studies News* (Summer 1993):9.
15. Judith Stacey, "Victims of The Family," *Bulletin of the Park Ridge Center* 6(January 1991):24.
16. Hewlett, *A Lesser Life,* p. 19.
17. Ibid., p. 369.
18. Interview with Hewlett, *Publishers Weekly* (July 12, 1991)50.
19. Sylvia Ann Hewlett, *When the Bough Breaks: The Cost of Neglecting Our Children* (New York: Basic Books, 1991), p. 47-50, 143-46.
20. Marian Wright Edelman, *The Measure of Our Success: A Letter to My Children and Yours* (Boston: Beacon, 1992), p. 15.
21. Barbara Katz Rothman, *Recreating Motherhood: Ideology and Technology in a Patriarchal Society* (New York: W. W. Norton, 1989), pp. 26-28 (and Part I in general).
22. Ibid., p. 20.
23. R. A. Easterlin and F. M. Crimmins, "Recent Social Trends: Changes in Personal Aspirations of American Youth," *Sociology and Social Research* 72(1988):217-23, cited by Larry L. Bumpass, "What's Happening to the Family?" *Demography* 4(November 1990):492.

24. See Mary Stewart Van Leeuwen, *Gender and Grace: Love, Work and Parenting in a Changing World* (Downers Grove, Ill.: Intervarsity, 1990) in the Reform tradition; Judith Plaskow, *Standing Again at Sinai: Judaism from a Feminist Perspective* (San Francisco: Harper & Row, 1990) in the Jewish tradition; Lisa Sowle Cahill, *Between the Sexes: Foundations for a Christian Ethics of Sexuality* (Philadelphia: Fortress, 1985) in the Roman Catholic tradition.

25. bell hooks, *Feminist Theory: From Margin to Center* (Boston: South End Press, 1984), p. 133.

26. See Cheryl Townsend Gilkes, "The Roles of Church and Community Mothers: Ambivalent American Sexism, or Fragmented African Familyhood?" *Journal of Feminist Studies in Religion* 2(1986):41-59.

27. Iris M. Young, "Humanism, Gynocentrism and Feminist Politics," *Women's Studies International Forum* 8(1985):173-83. Young cites Beauvoir, *The Second Sex*, and Shulamith Firestone, *The Dialectic of Sex* (New York: William Morrow, 1970).

28. Young cites Susan Griffin, *Women and Nature* (New York: Harper & Row, 1978); Mary Daly, *Gyn/Ecology* (Boston: Beacon, 1978); Carol Gilligan, *In a Different Voice* (Cambridge: Harvard University Press, 1981); Mary O'Brian, *Reproducing the World* (Boulder, Col.: Westview, 1989); Sara Ruddick, "Maternal Thinking," *Feminist Studies* 6(Summer 1980); and several works by Julia Kristeva and Luce Irigaray.

29. O'Brian, *Reproducing the World*, p. 10.

30. Karen Offen, "Defining Feminism: A Comparative Historical Aproach," *Signs: Journal of Women in Culture and Society* 14(1988):157.

31. Young, "Humanism, Gynocentrism and Femnist Politics," p. 177.

32. Toni Morrison, "What the Black Woman Thinks About Women's Lib," *New York Times Magazine*, August 22, 1971, cited by Davis, *Moving the Mountain*, p. 363.

33. Nancy F. Cott and Ellen Carol Dubois, "Comment and Reply" to Karen Offen, "Defining Feminism," *Signs: Journal of Women in Culture and Society* 15(1989):203-4.

34. Judith Stacey, "Are Feminists Afraid to Leave Home?:The Challenge of Conservative Pro-Family Feminism," *What Is Feminism?:A Reexamination*, ed. Juliet Mitchell and Ann Oakley (New York: Pantheon, 1986), pp. 208-37.

35. Stacey, "Sexism by a Subtler Name?" p. 24.

36. Nancy F. Cott, *The Grounding of Modern Feminism* (New Haven: Yale University Press, 1987), p. 50.

37. Ruth Sidel, *On Her Own: Growing up in the Shadow of the American Dream* (New York: Viking, 1990), p. 193.

38. Stacey, "Sexism by a Subtler Name?" p. 22.

39. Mary Fainsod Katzenstein, "Feminism Within American Institutions: Unobtrusive Moblization in the 1980s," *Signs: Journal of Women in Culture and Society* 16(Autumn 1990):27-28.

40. Stacey, "Sexism by a Subtler Name?" p. 8.

41. Davis, *Moving the Mountain*, pp. 492-93.

42. Elaine Bell Kaplen, "On the Backs of Our Sisters," *The Women's Review of Books* 10(June 1993):12-13, a review of Mary Romero, *Maid in the U.S.A* (New York: Rutledge Press, 1992).

43. Adrienne Rich, Foreword, *Working It Out: 23 Writers, Artists, Scientists, and Scholars Talk About Their Lives and Work*, ed. Sara Ruddick and Pamela Daniels (New York: Pantheon Books, 1977), p. xvi.

44. This refers to Adrienne Rich's important distinction between the rich experience of being a mother and the oppressive institution of motherhood as constructed under patriarchy, in *Of Woman Born: Motherhood as Experience and Institution* (New York: W. W. Norton, 1976).

45. Betty Friedan, *The Second Stage* (New York: Summit Books, 1981, 1986), p. 47.

Chapter Four. Orpah's Untold Story

1. Delores S. Williams, *Sisters in the Wilderness: The Challenge of God-Talk* (Maryknoll, New York: Orbis, 1993), pp. 2-6.

2. Phyllis Trible, *God and the Rhetoric of Sexuality* (Philadelphia: Fortress, 1978), p. 196.

3. Denise Lardner Carmody, *Biblical Woman: Contemporary Reflections on Scriptural Texts* (New York: Crossroad, 1988), p. 36.

4. Trible, *God and the Rhetoric of Sexuality*, p. 172.

5. Renita J. Weems, *Just a Sister Away* (San Diego: LuraMedia 1988), p. 27.
6. Trible, *God and the Rhetoric of Sexuality*, p. 172; Weems, *Just a Sister Away*, p. 27.
7. Amy Rossiter, *From Private to Public: A Feminist Exploration of Early Mothering* (Toronto, Ontario: The Women's Press, 1988), p. 11; Sara Ruddick, *Maternal Thinking: Toward a Politics of Peace* (Boston: Beacon, 1989), p. 7; Sylvia Ann Hewlett, *A Lesser Life: The Myth of Women's Liberation in America* (New York: William Morrow and Co., 1986), p. 18; Tuula Gordon, *Feminist Mothers* (New York: New York University Press, 1990), p. 53.
8. Valerie Saiving (Goldstein), "The Human Situation: A Feminine View," *Journal of Religion* (April 1960):108; reprinted in *Womanspirit Rising: A Feminist Reader in Religion*, ed. Carol P. Christ and Judith Plaskow (San Francisco: Harper & Row, 1979). Citations are from the original text.
9. "A Conversation with Valerie Saiving," *Journal of Feminist Studies* 4(Fall 1988):100.
10. Ibid., pp. 100, 111
11. Ibid., p. 102.
12. Ibid., pp. 108-9 (emphasis added).
13. Saiving, "The Human Situation," pp. 103, 105.
14. Ibid., p. 108.
15. Elisabeth Schüssler Fiorenza, *In Memory of Her: A Feminist Theological Reconstruction of Christian Origins* (New York: Crossroad, 1984), p. 349.
16. Julia Kristeva, "Stabat Mater," *The Kristeva Reader*, ed. Toril Moi (New York: Columbia University Press, 1986), p. 161.
17. Carolyn G. Heilbrun, *Writing a Woman's Life* (New York: W. W. Norton, 1988).
18. Introduction, *Womanspirit Rising: A Feminist Reader in Religion*, ed. Christ and Plaskow, pp. 7-9.
19. Introduction, *Weaving the Visions: New Patterns in Feminist Spirituality*, ed. Judith Plaskow and Carol P. Christ (New York: Harper & Row, 1989), p. 1.
20. Saiving, "The Human Situation," p. 105.
21. Christ and Plaskow, Introduction, *Womanspirit Rising*, p. 12; Carol P. Christ, "Spiritual Quest and Women's Experience," *Womanspirit Rising*, ed. Christ and Plaskow, pp. 240, 234.
22. Carol P. Christ, "Why Women Need the Goddess: Phenomenological, Psychological, and Political Reflections," *Womanspirit Rising*, ed. Christ and Plaskow, p. 281.
23. Adrienne Rich, *Of Women Born* (New York: Bantam Books, 1976), p. 290, cited by Naomi R. Goldenberg, "Archetypal Theory and the Separation of Mind and Body: Reason Enough to Turn to Freud?" *Weaving the Visions*, ed. Plaskow and Christ, p. 249.
24. Plaskow and Christ, *Weaving the Visions*, pp. 10, 173 (their emphasis).
25. Sallie McFague, "God as Mother," *Weaving the Visions*, ed. Plaskow and Christ, pp. 139-50. This chapter comes from a section of a chapter by the same title in *Models of God: Theology for an Ecological, Nuclear Age* (Philadelphia: Fortress, 1987).
26. Paula Gunn Allen, "Grandmother of the Sun: The Power of Woman in Native America," *Weaving the Visions*, ed. Plaskow and Christ, pp. 22-23, 26-27.
27. Delores S. Williams, "Womanist Theology: Black Women's Voices," *Weaving the Visions*, ed. Plaskow and Christ, p. 183.
28. Ibid., pp. 180, 182.
29. Anne Carr and Elisabeth Schüssler Fiorenza, Editorial, *Concilium: Motherhood: Experience, Institution, Theology* (Edinburgh, Scotland: T & T Clark, 1989), p. 4.
30. Saiving, "The Human Situation," p. 108 (her emphasis).
31. Christine Gudorf, "Parenting, Mutual Love, and Sacrifice," *Women's Consciousness, Women's Conscience: A Reader in Feminist Ethics*, ed. Barbara Hilkert Andolsen, Christine E. Gudorf, and Mary D. Pelauer (San Francisco: Harper & Row, 1985), pp. 175-91; Sally Purvis, "Mothers, Neighbors, and Strangers: Another Look At Agape," *Journal of Feminist Studies in Religion* 7(Spring 1991):19-34; Pamela D. Couture, *Blessed Are the Poor?:Women's Poverty, Family Policy, and Practical Theology* (Nashville: Abingdon Press, 1991); McFague, *Models of God;* Beverly Wildung Harrison, "The Power of Anger in the Work of Love: Christian Ethics of Women and Other Strangers," *Union Seminary Quarterly Review* 36(1981):41-57, published in expanded form in *Making the Connections: Essays in Feminist Social Ethics* (Boston: Beacon,

1985), pp. 3-21; Margaret A. Farley, *Personal Commitments: Beginning, Keeping, Changing* (San Francisco: Harper & Row, 1986); Catherine Keller, *From a Broken Web: Separation, Sexism, and Self* (Boston: Beacon, 1986); Mary E. Hunt, *Fierce Tenderness: A Feminist Theology of Friendship* (New York: Crossroad, 1991); Carter Heyward, *Touching Our Strength: The Erotic Power and the Love of God* (San Francisco: Harper & Row, 1989); Kathryn Allen Rabuzzi, *The Sacred and the Feminine: Toward a Theology of Housework* (New York: Seabury, 1982); *Motherself: A Mythic Analysis of Motherhood* (Bloomington: Indiana University Press, 1988).

32. Gene Outka, *Agape: An Ethical Analysis* (New Haven: Yale University Press, 1972), p. 272, cited by Purvis, "Mothers, Neighbors, and Strangers," p. 23.

33. Purvis, *Mothers, Neighbors, and Strangers*, p. 19.

34. Søren Kierkegaard, *Works of Love: Some Christian Reflections in the Form of Discourses,* trans. Howard Hong and Edna Hong (New York: Harper Torchbooks, 1962), p. 328 (caps in the original), cited by Purvis, "Mothers, Neighbors and Strangers," p. 21.

35. Purvis, "Mothers, Neighbors and Strangers," pp. 26-28.

36. Ibid., p. 31.

37. Gudorf, "Parenting, Mutual Love, and Sacrifice," p. 191.

38. Couture, *Blessed Are the Poor,* pp. 9-10.

39. Ibid., chap. 7.

40. George Bernard Shaw, *The Quintessence of Ibsenism* (New York: Hill & Wang, 1922), p. 139, cited by Adrienne Rich, *On Lies, Secrets, and Silence: Selected Prose 1966–1978* (New York: W. W. Norton, 1979), p. 34.

41. Harrison, "The Power of Anger," p. 51.

42. Mary O'Brian, *The Politics of Reproduction* (Boston: Routledge & Kegan Paul, 1989), p. 13.

Chapter Five. Generativity Crises of My Own

1. Nadya Aisenberg and Mona Harrington, *Women of Academe: Outsiders in the Sacred Grove* (Amherst: University of Massachusetts Press, 1988), p. 6.

2. John Naisbitt and Patricia Aburdene, *Megatrends 2000* (Morrow, 1990).

3. Aisenberg and Harrington, *Women of Academe*, pp. 26, 23.

4. Ibid., pp. 27-29.

5. Ibid., p. 133.

6. Pamela Daniels, "Dream vs. Drift in Women's Careers: The Question of Generativity," *Psychology of Women: Selected Readings*, 2nd Ed., ed. Juanita H. Williams (New York: W. W. Norton, 1985), pp. 435.

7. Mirra Komzrovsky, *Women in College: Shaping New Feminine Identities* (New York: Basic Books, 1986), p. 253.

8. Bonnie J. Miller-McLemore, "Am I a Woman? Alienation Versus Omnipotentiality," unpublished paper, May 1977.

9. Heilbrun, *Writing a Woman's Life*, pp. 37-38

10. Miller-McLemore, "Am I a Woman?"

11. Sara Ruddick, "A Work of One's Own," *Working It Out: 23 Writers, Artists, Scientists, and Scholars Talk About Their Lives and Work*, ed. Sara Ruddick and Pamela Daniels (New York: Pantheon Books), p. 134.

12. Aisenberg and Harrington, *Women of Academe*, pp. 111-12.

13. See Philip Blumstein and Pepper Schwartz's extensive study of thousands of couples, *American Couples* (New York: Morrow, 1983), pp. 324, 115, cited by Susan Moller Okin, *Justice, Gender, and the Family* (New York: Basic Books, 1989), p. 140.

14. William Countryman, *Dirt, Greed, and Sex: Sexual Ethics in the New Testament and Their Implications for Today* (Philadelphia: Fortress, 1990), p. 260.

15. Bronwyn Davies, *Frogs and Snails and Feminist Tales: Preschool Children and Gender* (Boston: Allen & Unwin, 1989), pp. ix, 133-37.

16. Judith Stacey, *Brave New Families: Stories of Domestic Upheaval in Late Twentieth Century America* (New York: Basic, 1990), pp. 258, 259, 260.

17. Cynthia Fuchs Epstein, *Deceptive Distinctions: Sex, Gender, and the Social Order* (New Haven: Yale University Press, 1988), p. 13.

18. Virginia Woolf, *A Room of One's Own* (New York: Harcourt Brace Jovanovich, 1957), pp. 22-23.

19. Mary Guerrera Congo, "The Truth Will Set You Free, But First It Will Make You Crazy," *Sacred Dimensions of Women's Experience,* ed. Elizabeth Dodson Gray (Wellesley, Mass.: Roundtable, 1988), pp. 78-79.

20. Robbie Davis-Floyd, "Pregnancy and Cultural Confusion: Contradictions in Socialization," *Cultural Constructions of "Woman,"* ed. Pauline Kolenda (Salem, Wis.: Sheffield, 1988), p.16.

21. Penelope Washbourn, *Becoming Woman: The Quest for Wholeness in Female Experience* (New York: Harper & Row, 1977), p. 2.

22. Sally B. Purvis, "Mothers, Neighbors, and Strangers: Another Look At Agape," *Journal of Feminist Studies in Religion* 7(Spring 1991):28.

23. John C. Raines and Donna C. Day-Lower, *Modern Work and Human Meaning* (Philadelphia: Westminster, 1986), pp. 18, 52.

24. Ulrich Beck, *Risk Society: Toward a New Modernity,* trans. Mark Ritter (London: Sage Publications, 1992), pp. 103-50.

25. Amy Rossiter, *From Private to Public: A Feminist Exploration of Early Mothering* (Toronto, Ontario: The Women's Press, 1988), p. 13.

26. Sara Maitland, *Why Children?* ed. Stephanie Dowrick and Sibyl Grundberg (London: Women's Press, 1980), p. 79, quoted by Tuula Gordon, *Feminist Mothers* (New York: New York University Press, 1990), p. 44.

27. Ruddick, "A Work of One's Own," p. 128-46.

28. Mary Becker, "Maternal Feelings: Myth, Taboo, and Child Custody," *Review of Law and Women's Studies* 1(1992):167.

29. Countryman, *Dirt, Greed and Sex,* p. 260.

30. Carol Gilligan, *In a Different Voice: Psychological Theory and Women's Development* (Cambridge: Harvard University Press, 1982), p. 149.

31. Frank A. Johnson and Colleen L. Johnson, "Role Strain in High Commitment Career Women," *Journal of the American Academy of Psychoanalysis* 4(1976):15-16.

32. Celia Gilbert, "The Sacred Fire," *Working It Out,* ed. Ruddick and Daniels, pp. 318-19.

33. Anita Shreve, *Women Together, Women Alone: The Legacy of the Consciousness-Raising Movement* (New York: Fawcett Columbine, 1989).

34. See David Heller, *The Children's God* (Chicago: University of Chicago Press, 1986).

35. Robert G. Kemper, "Where Have All the Assumptions Gone?" *The Chicago Theological Seminary Register* 77(1987):5-6.

36. Sharon Watkins, "Disciples Women in 1993: Serving Potlucks and Pulpits," *The Disciple: Journal of the Christian Church* 131(May 1993):8-11 (Disciples of Christ).

37. Mary J. Gennuso, "Letter to the Editors," *Journal of Feminist Studies in Religion* 5(1989):101-2.

38. Guerrera Congo, "The Truth Will Set You Free," p. 78.

39. Elisabeth Schüssler Fiorenza, *In Memory of Her: A Feminist Theological Reconstruction of Christian Origins* (New York: Crossroad, 1983), pp. 347-48

Chapter Six. Behold the Mother

1. Phyllis Chesler, *With Child* (New York: Berkeley, 1981), p. 133; Mary Gordon, *Men and Angels* (New York: Ballantine, 1985), p. 399.

2. Sara Ruddick, *Maternal Thinking: Toward a Politics of Peace* (Boston: Beacon, 1989), p. 53. Literature on lesbian mothers is growing. See, for example, Cheri Pies, *Considering Parenthood: A Workbook for Lesbians* (San Francisco: Spinsters/Aunt Lute, 1985); *A Lesbian Parenting Anthology,* ed. Sandra Pollack and Jeanne Vaughn (Ithaca, N.Y.: Firebrand Books, 1987).

3. Julia Kristeva, "Un Nouveau Type d'intellectuel: Le dissident," *Tel Quel* 74(Winter 1977):6-7, quoted by Susan Rubin Suleiman, "Writing and Motherhood," *The (M)other Tongue: Essays in Feminist Psychoanalytic Interpretation,* ed. Shirley Nelson Garner, Claire Kahane, and Madelon Sprengnether (Ithaca, N.Y.: Cornell University Press, 1985), pp. 352, 368.

4. Pauline Bart, quoted in Debra Anna Luepnitz, *The Family Interpreted: Feminist Theory in Clinical Practice* (New York: Basic Books, 1988), p. 167.

5. Mary Becker, "Maternal Feelings: Myth, Taboo, and Child Custody," *Review of Law and Women's Studies* 1(1992):136.

6. Nel Noddings, *Caring: A Feminine Approach to Ethics and Moral Education* (Berkeley: University of California Press, 1984), pp. 1-2.

7. Tillie Olsen, *Silences* (New York: Delta, 1965), pp. 19, 31-32.

8. Mary Field Belenky, Blythe McVicker Clinchy, Nancy Rule Goldberger, and Jill Mattuck Tarule, *Women's Ways of Knowing: The Development of Self, Voice, and Mind* (New York: Basic Books, 1986).

9. Francine Prose, "Confident at 11, Confused at 16," *The New York Times Magazine,* January 7, 1990, a review of *Making Connections: The Relational Worlds of Adolescent Girls at Emma Willard School,* ed. Carol Gilligan, Nona P. Lyons, and Trudy J. Hanmer (Cambridge: Harvard University Press, 1990).

10. Belenky, Clinchy, Goldberger, and Tarule, *Women's Ways of Knowing,* pp. 35-36, 142-43.

11. Mary Guerrera Congo, "The Truth Will Set You Free, But First It Will Make You Crazy," *Sacred Dimensions of Women's Experience,* ed. Elizabeth Dodson Gray (Wellesley, Mass.: Roundtable, 1988), p. 76.

12. Marilyn Chapin Massey, "The Vocation of the Feminine Soul," *Criterion* 29(Winter 1990):16-17.

13. Ruddick, *Maternal Thinking,* p. 11.

14. Mary O'Brian, *Reproducing the World* (Boulder, Col.: Westview, 1989), p. 8.

15. Riane Eisler, *The Chalice and the Blade* (San Francisco: Harper & Row, 1987), pp. 20-21.

16. Sara Ruddick, "Maternal Thinking," *Mothering: Essays in Feminist Theory,* ed. Joyce Treblicot (Totowa, New Jersey: Rowman and Allanheld, 1983), pp. 213-30.

17. Beverly W. Harrison, "Theology of Pro-Choice: A Feminist Perspective," *Abortion: The Moral Issues,* ed. Edward Batchelor, Jr. (New York: Pilgrim, 1982), p. 220.

18. Susan R. Grayzel, "Teaching Women's Peace Studies: Thinking About Motherhood, War, and Peace," *The Journal for Peace and Justice Studies* 2(1990):105.

19. Nancy J. Chodorow and Susan Contratto, "The Fantasy of the Perfect Mother," *Rethinking the Family: Some Feminist Questions,* ed. Barrie Thorne with Marily Yalom (New York: Longman, 1982), pp. 54-75.

20. Kristeva, "Un Nouveau Type d'intellectuel," quoted by Suleiman, "Writing and Motherhood," p. 360.

21. Elisabeth Schüssler Fiorenza, "In Search of Women's Heritage," *Weaving the Visions: New Patterns in Feminist Spirituality,* ed. Judith Plaskow and Carol P. Christ (New York: Harper & Row, 1989), p. 31.

22. See, for example, Elisabeth M. Tetlow, *Women and Ministry in the New Testament* (New York: Paulist, 1980); Ben Witherington III, *Women in the Minstry of Jesus* (New York: Cambridge University Press, 1984); Virginia Ramey Mollenkott, *Women, Men, and the Bible* (Nashville: Abingdon Press, 1977).

23. Elisabeth Schüssler Fiorenza, "Women in the Early Christian Movement," *Womanspirit Rising: A Feminist Reader in Religion,* ed. Carol P. Christ and Judith Plaskow (New York: Harper & Row, 1979), p. 88.

24. Phyllis Trible, *God and the Rhetoric of Sexuality* (Philadelphia: Fortress, 1978), pp. 15-21.

25. Phyllis Trible, "Eve and Adam: Genesis 2–3 Reread," *Womanspirit Rising,* ed. Christ and Plaskow, p. 74; Susan Niditch, "Genesis," *The Women's Bible Commentary,* ed. Carol A. Newsom and Sharon H. Ringe (Louisville: Westminster/John Knox, 1992), p. 13.

26. Lisa Sowle Cahill, *Between the Sexes: Foundations for a Christian Ethics of Sexuality* (Philadelphia: Fortress, 1985), p. 84.

27. Ibid., p. 55.

28. Mary Stewart Van Leeuwen, *Gender and Grace: Love, Work, and Parenting in a Changing World* (Downers Grove, Ill.: Intervarsity, 1990), pp. 44-45.

29. Cahill, *Between the Sexes,* p. 98.

30. Suleiman, "Writing and Motherhood," p. 362.

31. Ruddick, "Maternal Thinking," p. 213.

32. Julia Kristeva, "Stabat Mater," *The Kristeva Reader,* ed. Toril Moi (Columbia University Press, 1986), p. 166.
33. Gordon, *Men and Angels,* pp. 113, 217.
34. Kristeva, "Stabat Mater," pp. 178-79; Alice S. Rossi, "A Biosocial Perspective on Parenting," *Daedalus: Journal of the American Academy of Arts and Sciences* 106(Spring 1977):24.
35. Marian Wright Edelman, *Families in Peril: An Agenda for Social Change* (Cambridge, Mass.: Harvard University Press, 1987), p. viii.
36. N. Murai, and N. Murai, "A Study of Moods in Pregnant Women," *Tohoku Psychological Folia* 34(1975):10-16 and A. Jarrahi-Jadeh et al., "Emotional and Cognitive Changes in Pregnancy and Early Puerperium," *British Journal of Psychiatry* 115(1969):797-805, cited by Sheri Fenster, Suzanne B. Phillips and Estelle R. G. Rapoport, *The Therapist's Pregnancy: Intrusion in the Analytic Space* (Hinsdale, N. J.: 1986), p. 1.
37. Sally Mugabe, "High Fertility Hampers Women's Status," *Popline: World Population News Service* 9(June 1987):1-2, cited in "Giving Birth," *Sacred Dimensions of Women's Experience,* ed. Gray, p. 50.
38. Virginia Woolf, *A Room of One's Own* (New York: Harcourt Brace Jovanovich, 1957), p. 116.
39. Joseph Conrad, quoted in Olsen, *Silences,* pp. 12, 34.
40. Interview with Mary Gordon, *Chicago Tribune,* December 3, 1989.
41. J. Giles Milhaven, "A Medieval Lesson on Bodily Knowing: Women's Experience and Men's Thoughts," *Journal of the American Academy of Religion* 57(Summer 1989):355.
42. Beverly Wildung Harrison, "The Power of Anger in the Work of Love: Christian Ethics for Women and Other Strangers," *Union Seminary Quarterly Review* 36(1981):45, 48.
43. The hormone "oxytocin acts upon the basket cells around the alveoli, causing them to constrict, and . . . squeeze out the milk in the phenomenon known as 'milk let-down'" (R. Berde, *Recent Progress in Oxytocin Research* [Springfield, Illinois, 1959], cited by Rossi, "A Biosocial Perspective," p. 17).
44. Milhaven, "A Medieval Lesson on Bodily Knowing," p. 358; see also Milhaven, "Thomas Aquinas on Sexual Pleasure," *Journal of Religious Ethics* 5(1977):157-81.
45. Ruddick, "Maternal Thinking," p. 219.
46. *Introduction to The (M)other Tongue,* ed. Garner, Kahane, and Sprengnether (Ithaca, N.Y.: Cornell University Press, 1985), pp. 23-24.
47. Noddings, *Caring,* p. 30; Belenky, Clinchy, Goldberger, and Tarule, *Women's Ways of Knowing,* p. 122.
48. Genia Pauli Haddon, *Body Metaphors: Releasing God-Feminine in Us All* (New York: Crossroad, 1988), pp. 11-12.
49. Noddings, *Caring,* pp. 31-35.
50. Harrison, "The Power of Anger," pp. 44, 47-48.
51. John MacMurray, *Persons in Relation* (London: Faber and Faber, 1961), pp. 49, 51.
52. Ibid., p. 50.
53. bell hooks, *Feminist Theory: From Margin to Center* (Boston: South End Press, 1984), p. 135.
54. Gordon, *Men and Angels,* p. 163
55. Ibid., pp. 399-400.

Chapter Seven. According to the Pace of the Children

1. I am indebted to Susan B. W. Johnson, minister at Hyde Park Union Church of Chicago, for drawing my attention to the Genesis 33 passage, "according to the pace of the children." This theme will be developed also in *Regarding Children,* a book Johnson is writing with Herbert Anderson as part of a series on Family Living in Pastoral Perspective (Westminster/John Knox, 1994).
2. Amy-Jill Levine, "Matthew," *Women's Bible Commentary,* ed. Carol A. Newsom and Sharon H. Ringe (Louisville: Westminster/John Knox, 1992), p. 259.
3. For example, Robert Coles, *The Moral Life of Children* (Boston: Houghton Mifflin, 1986); *The Spiritual Life of Children* (Boston: Houghton Mifflin, 1990).
4. Sara Ruddick, "A Work of One's Own," *Working It Out: 23 Writers, Artists, Scientists, and*

Scholars Talk About Their Lives and Work, ed. Sara Ruddick and Pamela Daniels (New York: Pantheon Books), pp. 140-41.

5. Mary Gordon, interview in *Chicago Tribune,* December 3, 1989.
6. Hans Jonas, "Contemporary Problems in Ethics from a Jewish Perspective," *Journal of Central Conference of American Rabbis* (January):27-39, cited by Leon Kass, "On Dignity in Death: A Commentary on Ramsey," *The Hastings Center Studies* 2(May 1974)75.
7. Stanley Hauerwas, "Having and Learning How to Care for Retarded Children: Some Reflections," *Ethics in Medicine: Historical Perspectives and Contemporary Concerns,* ed. S. J. Reiser, A. J. Dyck, and W. J. Curran (Cambridge, Mass.: MIT Press, 1977), p. 633.
8. Wendy M. Wright, "Living the Already But Not Yet: The Spiritual Life of the American Catholic Family," *Warren Lecture Series in Catholic Studies,* No. 25, University of Tulsa, March 21, 1993.
9. Elizabeth Ann Dreyer, "Asceticism Reconsidered," *Weavings: A Journal of the Christian Spiritual Life* 3(1988):14.
10. Sara Ruddick, "Maternal Thinking," *Mothering: Essays in Feminist Theory,* ed. Joyce Treblicot (Totowa, N. J.: Rowman & Allanheld, 1983), pp. 215, 217, 223-24.
11. Idania Fernandez, letter cited by Mary Guerrera Congo, "The Truth Will Set You Free, But First It Will Make You Crazy," *Sacred Dimensions of Women's Experience,* ed. Elizabeth Dodson Gray (Wellesley, Mass.: Roundtable, 1988), p. 83.
12. Erik H. Erikson, *The Life Cycle Completed: A Review* (New York: W. W. Norton, 1982), p. 80.
13. Penelope Washbourn, *Becoming Woman: The Quest for Wholeness in Female Experience* (New York: Harper & Row, 1977), pp. 97-98.
14. Erik H. Erikson, *Insight and Responsibility: Lectures on the Ethical Implications of Psychoanalytic Insight* (New York: W. W. Norton, 1964), p. 132; *Life Cycle Completed,* p. 68.
15. Sallie McFague, *Models of God: Theology for an Ecological, Nuclear Age* (Philadelphia: Fortress, 1987), p. 104; Stanley Hauerwas, *Suffering Presence: Theological Reflections on Medicine, the Mentally Handicapped, and the Church* (Notre Dame, Ind.: University of Notre Dame Press, 1986), pp. 144, 147.
16. Robert Jay Lifton, *Life of the Self: Toward a New Psychology* (New York: Basic Books, 1976), p. 81; "On Death and Death Symbolism: The Hiroshima Disaster," *The Phenomenon of Death: Faces of Mortality,* ed. Edith Wyschogrod (New York: Harper and Row, 1973), pp. 93-94.
17. Hilary Rose, "Hand, Brain, and Heart: A Feminist Epistemology for the Natural Sciences," *Signs: Journal of Women in Culture and Society* 9(1983):83.
18. Erik H. Erikson, *Childhood and Society* (New York: W. W. Norton, 1963 [1950]), p. 268.
19. Bill Moyers, interview with T. Berry Brazelton, *A World of Ideas: Conversations with Thoughtful Men and Women About American Life Today and the Ideas Shaping Our Future,* ed. Betty Sue Flowers (New York: Doubleday, 1989), pp. 146-47.
20. Guerrera Congo, "The Truth Will Set You Free," pp. 76-77.
21. Christine Gudorf, "Parenting, Mutual Love, and Sacrifice," *Women's Consciousness, Women's Conscience: A Reader in Feminist Ethics,* ed. Barbara Hilkert Andolsen, Christine E. Gudorf, and Mary D. Pelauer (San Francisco: Harper & Row, 1985), p. 176.
22. Ibid., pp. 181-82.
23. Ibid., pp. 103, 173.
24. Ibid., pp. 182, 186.
25. Elisabeth Badinter, *Mother Love, Myth and Reality: Motherhood in Modern History* (New York: Macmillan, 1981).
26. Diane E. Eyer, *Mother-Infant Bonding: A Scientific Fiction* (New Haven: Yale University Press, 1993).
27. Jessica Benjamin, *The Bonds of Love: Psychoanalysis, Feminism, and the Problem of Domination* (New York: Pantheon, 1988), pp. 82, 114.
28. Dorothy Dinnerstein, *The Mermaid and the Minotaur: Sexual Arrangements and Human Malaise* (New York: Harper & Row, 1976), p. 25.
29. Mary Gordon, *Good Boys and Dead Girls and Other Essays* (New York: Viking, 1991), p. 247.
30. Elizabeth Schüssler Fiorenza, *In Memory of Her* (New York: Crossword, 1984), p. 350; Delores S. Williams, "The Salvation of Growth," *The Christian Century* (October 10, 1990), p. 899.

31. Elizabeth Janeway, *Cross Sections* (New York: William Morrow, 1982), cited in bell hooks, *Feminist Theory: From Margin to Center* (Boston: South End Press, 1984), p. 143.

32. Amelie Oksenberg Rorty, "Dependency, Individuality, and Work," *Working It Out,* ed. Ruddick and Daniels, p. 44.

33. Nancy Chodorow, *The Reproduction of Mothering: Psychoanalysis and the Sociology of Gender* (Berkeley: University of California Press, 1978) and *Feminism and Psychoanalytic Theory* (New Haven: Yale University Press, 1989); Dinnerstein, *The Mermaid and the Minotaur.*

34. Alice S. Rossi, "A Biosocial Perspective on Parenting," *Daedalus: Journal of the American Academy of Arts and Sciences* 106(Spring 1977):25.

35. Mercy Amba Oduyoye, "Poverty and Motherhood," *Motherhood: Experience, Institution, Theology,* ed. Anne Carr and Elisabeth Schüssler Fiorenza (Edinburgh, Scotland: T & T Clark, 1989), pp. 23-24.

36. Eileen Ogintz, "French Translate Day-Care into Low-Cost Quality," *Chicago Tribune,* November 8, 1989.

37. Patricia Hill Collins, *Black Feminist Thought: Knowledge, Consciousness, and the Politics of Empowerment* (New York: Routledge, 1991), pp. 119-20.

38. Ibid., p. 122.

39. McFague, *Models of God,* p.105.

40. Janet Fishburn, *Confronting the Idolatry of Family: A New Vision for the Household of God* (Nashville: Abingdon, 1991), p. 121.

41. McFague, *Models of God,* p. 105.

42. Ibid., p. 120.

Chapter Eight. Returning to the Mother's House and Mending the Web

1. Audre Lorde, *Sister Outsider: Essays and Speeches* (Freedom, Calif.: The Crossing Press, 1984), pp. 78, 77.

2. Danna Nolan Fewell and David M. Gunn, " 'A Son is Born to Naomi!': Literary Allusions and Interpretation in the Book of Ruth," *Journal for the Study of the Old Testament* 40(1988):99-100, 102.

3. Phyllis Trible, *God and the Rhetoric of Sexuality* (Philadelphia: Fortress, 1978), p. 169.

4. Ibid.

5. Amy-Jill Levine, "Ruth," *The Women's Bible Commentary,* eds. Carol A. Newsom and Sharon H. Ringe (Louisville: Westminster/John Knox, 1992), p. 80.

6. Barbara Katz Rothman, *Recreating Mothering: Ideology and Technology in a Patriarchal Society* (New York: W. W. Norton, 1989), pp. 34, 30.

7. Edward F. Campbell, Jr., *Ruth: A New Translation with Introduction, Notes, and Commentary* (New York: Doubleday, 1975), p. 79.

8. Renita J. Weems, *Just a Sister Away* (San Diego: LuraMedia, 1988), p. 33.

9. Ibid., pp. 28-29.

10. Debby Kearney, "Many Reasons to Give Thanks," *New Beginnings* 5(May-June 1989):86.

11. Carol Gilligan, *In A Different Voice: Psychological Theory and Women's Development* (Cambridge: Harvard University Press, 1982).

12. Ibid., pp. 100, 98 (emphasis added).

13. Jean Baker Miller, *Toward a New Psychology of Women* (Boston: Beacon, 1976), pp. 22-23, 25-26.

14. Catherine Keller, *From a Broken Web: Separation, Sexism, and Self* (Boston: Beacon, 1986).

15. Daniel J. Levinson, with Charlotte N. Darrow, Edward B. Klein, Maria H. Levinson, and Braxton McKee, *Seasons of a Man's Life* (New York: Ballantine, 1978), p. 239.

16. Keller, *From a Broken Web,* p. 8.

17. Levinson, *Seasons,* p. 109.

18. Shel Silverstein, *The Giving Tree* (New York: Harper & Row, 1964) and *The Missing Piece* (New York: Harper & Row, 1976).

19. Keller, *From a Broken Web,* p. 35

20. Daniel N. Stern, *The Interpersonal World of the Infant* (New York: Basic Books, 1985), p 10.

21. Baker Miller, *Toward a New Psychology,* p. 83.

22. Janet Fishburn, *Confronting the Idolatry of Family: A New Vision for the Household of God* (Nashville: Abingdon, 1991), p. 141.
23. Susan Maloney, S.N.J.M., "Catholic Bishops and the Art of Public Moral Discourse," *The Christian Century*, May 9, 1990, p. 486.
24. Morris Taggart, "Epistemological Equality as the Fulfillment of Family Therapy," *Women in Families: A Framework for Family Therapy*, ed. Monica McGoldrich, Carol M. Anderson, and Froma Walsh (New York: W. W. Norton, 1989), p. 110.
25. Fishburn, *Confronting the Idolatry of Family*, p. 30.
26. Ibid., p. 20.
27. bell hooks, *Feminist Theory: From Margin to Center* (Boston: South End Press, 1984), p. 140.
28. Susan Moller Okin, *Justice, Gender, and the Family* (New York: Basic Books, 1989), pp. 23-24.
29. Fishburn, *Confronting the Idolatry of Family*, p. 180.
30. Ibid., pp. 172, 174; citing Herbert Anderson, "Christian Themes for Family Living," *Dialog* 28(Summer 1989):172.
31. See, for example, Elaine Ciulla Kamarck and William A. Galston, with essays by Robert J. Shapiro and Margaret Beyer, "Putting Children First: A Progressive Family Policy for the 1990s," published by The Progressive Policy Institute, Washington, D.C., September 27, 1990, pp. 7-8, 21-33.
32. Okin, *Justice, Gender, and the Family*, pp. 180-81.
33. Sylvia Ann Hewlett, *When the Bough Breaks: The Cost of Neglecting Our Children* (New York: Basic Books, 1991), p. 243.
34. Keller, *From a Broken Web*, p. 4.
35. Hilda Scott, *Working Your Way to the Bottom: The Feminization of Poverty* (London: Pandora, 1984), p. xi.

BIBLIOGRAPHY

❦ ❦ ❦

Anderson, Herbert, and Susan B. W. Johnson. *Regarding Children*. Philadelphia: Westminster/John Knox, 1994.

Badinter, Elisabeth. *Mother Love: Myth and Reality*. New York: Macmillan, 1981.

Barciauskas, Rosemary Curran, and Debra Beery Hull. *Loving and Working: Reweaving Women's Public and Private Lives*. Bloomington, Ind.: Meyer Stone, 1989.

Becker, Mary. "Maternal Feelings: Myth, Taboo, and Child Custody." *Review of Law and Women's Studies* 1(1992):133-222.

Belenky, Mary Field, et al. *Women's Ways of Knowing: The Development of Self, Voice, and Mind*. New York: Basic Books, 1986.

Berry, Mary Frances. *The Politics of Parenthood: Child Care, Women's Rights, and the Myth of the Good Mother*. New York: Viking, 1993.

Billinsky, Andrew. *Climbing Jacob's Ladder: The Enduring Legacy of African-American Families*. New York: Simon & Schuster, 1992.

Brabeck, Mary M., ed. *Who Cares?: Theory, Research, and Implications of the Ethic of Care*. New York: Praeger, 1989.

Browning, Don S. *Generative Man: Psychoanalytic Perspectives*. New York: Delta, 1975.

Cahill, Lisa Sowle. *Between the Sexes: Foundations for a Christian Ethic of Sexuality*. Philadelphia: Fortress, 1985.

Cancian, Francesca M. *Love in America: Gender and Self-Development*. Cambridge: Cambridge University Press, 1987.

Carmody, Denise Lardner. *Biblical Woman: Contemporary Reflections on Scriptural Texts*. New York: Crossroad, 1988.

Carr, Anne, and Elisabeth Schüssler Fiorenza, eds. *Concilium: Motherhood: Experience, Institution, Theology*. Edinburgh, Scotland: T & T Clark, 1989.

Chodorow, Nancy J. *The Reproduction of Mothering: Psychoanalysis and the Sociology of Gender*. Berkeley: University of California Press, 1978.

_____. *Feminism and Psychoanalytic Theory*. New Haven: Yale University Press, 1989.

Chodorow, Nancy J., and Susan Contratto. "The Fantasy of the Perfect Mother." *Rethinking the Family: Some Feminist Questions*, ed. Barrie Thorne, with Marilyn Yalom, 54-75. New York: Longman, 1982.

Christ, Carol P., and Judith Plaskow, eds. *Womanspirit Rising: A Feminist Reader in Religion*. San Francisco: Harper & Row, 1979.

Coles, Robert. *The Moral Life of Children*. Boston: Houghton Mifflin, 1986.

_____. *The Spiritual Life of Children*. Boston: Houghton Mifflin, 1990.

Coontz, Stephanie. *The Social Origins of Private Life: A History of American Families, 1600–1900*. London: Verson, 1988.

_____. *The Way We Never Were: American Families and the Nostalgia Trap*. New York: Basic Books, 1992.

Couture, Pamela D. *Blessed Are the Poor?: Women's Poverty, Family Policy, and Practical Theology*. Nashville: Abingdon Press, 1991.

Dally, Ann. *Inventing Motherhood: The Consequences of an Ideal*. New York: Schocken Books, 1982.

Davies, Bronwyn. *Frogs and Snails and Feminist Tales: Preschool Children and Gender*. Boston: Allen & Urwin, 1989.

Davis, Flora. *Moving the Mountain: The Women's Movement in America Since 1960*. New York: Simon & Schuster, 1991.

Dill, Bonnie Thorton. "Our Mother's Grief: Racial Ethnic Women and The Mainte-nance of Families," *Journal of Family History* 13(1988):415-31.

Dornbusch, Sanford M., and Myra H. Strober, eds. *Feminism, Children, and the New Families*. New York: Guilford, 1988.

Edelman, Marian Wright. *Families in Peril: An Agenda for Social Change*. Cambridge, Mass.: Harvard University Press, 1987.

Edwards, Richard. *Contested Terrain: Transformation in the Workplace in the Twenti-eth Century*. New York: Basic Books, 1979.

Erikson, Erik H. *Childhood and Society*. New York: Norton, [1950] 1963.

_____. "Womanhood and the Inner Space." *Woman and Analysis: Dialogues on Psychoanalytic Views of Feminity*, ed. Jean Strouse. Boston: G. K. Hall, 1985 [1968], 291-319.

_____. "Once More the Inner Space: Letter to a Former Student." *Women and Analysis: Dialogues on Psychoanalytic Views of Feminity*, ed. Jean Strouse. Boston: G. K. Hall, 1985 [1974], 320-40.

_____. *The Life Cycle Completed: A Review*. New York: W. W. Norton, 1982.

Faludi, Susan. *Backlash: The Undeclared War Against Women*. New York: Crown, 1991.

Farley, Margaret A. *Personal Commitments: Beginning, Keeping, Changing*. San Fran-cisco: Harper & Row, 1986.

Fox-Genovese, Elizabeth. *Feminism Without Illusions: A Critique of Individualism*. Chapel Hill: University of North Carolina Press, 1991.

Gerson, Kathleen. *Hard Choices: Women Decide About Work, Career, and Motherhood*. Berkeley: University of California Press, 1986.

Glaz, Maxine, and Jeanne Stevenson Moessner, eds. *Women in Travail and Transition: A New Pastoral Care*. Minneapolis: Fortress, 1991.

Bibliography

Goldscheider, Frances K., and Linda Waite. *New Families, No Families? The Transformation of the American Home.* Berkeley: University of California Press, 1991.

Gordon, Tuula. *Feminist Mothers.* New York: New York University Press, 1990.

Gudorf, Christine E. "Parenting, Mutual Love, and Sacrifice." *Women's Consciousness and Women's Conscience: A Reader in Feminist Ethics,* ed. Barbara Hilkert Andolsen, Christine E. Gudorf, and Mary D. Pellauer, 175-91. San Francisco: Harper & Row, 1985.

Harrison, Beverly W. *Making the Connections: Essays in Feminist Social Ethics.* Boston: Beacon, 1985.

_____. "The Power of Anger in the Work of Love: Christian Ethics of Women and Other Strangers." *Union Seminary Quarterly Review* 36(1981):41-57.

Hewlett, Sylvia Ann. *When the Bough Breaks: The Cost of Neglecting Our Children.* New York: Basic Books, 1991.

hooks, bell. *Feminist Theory: From Margin to Center.* Boston: South End Press, 1984.

Jones, Jacqueline. *Labor of Love, Labor of Sorrow: Black Women, Work, and the Family from Slavery to the Present.* New York: Basic Books, 1986.

Keller, Catherine. *From a Broken Web: Separation, Sexism, and Self.* Boston: Beacon, 1986.

Kitzinger, Sheila. *Women as Mothers: How They See Themselves in Different Cultures.* New York: Random House, 1978.

Kristeva, Julia. "Stabat Mater." *The Kristeva Reader,* ed. Toril Moi. New York: Columbia University Press, 1986.

Lazarre, Jane. *The Mother Knot.* Boston: Beacon, 1976.

Lerner, Gerda. *The Creation of Feminist Consciousness, from the Middle Ages to 1870.* New York: Oxford University Press, 1993.

Lorde, Audre. *Sister Outsider.* Trumansburd, N.Y.: Crossing, 1984.

Massey, Marilyn. *Feminine Soul: The Fate of An Ideal.* Boston: Beacon, 1985.

McAdoo, Harriette Pipes, ed. *Black Families,* 2nd ed. Newbury Park, Calif.: Sage, 1988.

McFague, Sallie. *Models of God: Theology for an Ecological, Nuclear Age.* Philadelphia: Fortress, 1987.

Miller-McLemore, Bonnie J. "Epistemology or Bust: A Maternal Feminist Knowledge of Knowing." *Journal of Religion* 72(April 1992):229-47.

_____. "Let the Children Come." *Second Opinion* 17(July 1991):10-25.

_____. "Produce or Perish: A Feminist Critique of Generativity." *Union Seminary Quarterly Review* 43(1989):201-21.

_____. "Produce or Perish: Generativity and New Reproductive Technologies." *Journal of the American Academy of Religion* LIX(1991):39-69.

_____. "Returning to the Mother's House: Feminism's Orpahs." *The Christian Century* (April 17, 1991), 428-30.

_____. "Women Who Work and Love: Caught Between Cultures." *Women in Travail and Transition: A New Pastoral Care,* ed. Maxine Glaz and Jeanne Stevenson Moessner, 63-85. Minneapolis: Fortress, 1991.

Mintz, Steven, and Susan Kellogg. *Domestic Revolutions: A Social History of American Family Life.* New York: Free Press, 1988.

Newsom, Carol A., and Sharon H. Ringe, eds. *The Women's Bible Commentary.* Louisville: Westminster/John Knox, 1992.

Noddings, Nel. *Caring: A Feminine Approach to Ethics and Moral Education.* Berkeley: University of California Press, l984.

O'Brian, Mary. *Reproducing the World: Essays in Feminist Theory.* Boulder, Col.: Westview, 1989.

Okin, Susan Moller. *Justice, Gender, and the Family.* New York: Basic Books, 1989.

Olsen, Tillie. *Silences.* New York: Delta, [1965] 1978.

Ostriker, Alicia Suskin. *The Mother/Child Papers.* Boston: Beacon, 1980.

Patton, John, and Brian H. Childs. *Christian Marriage and Family: Caring for Our Generations.* Nashville: Abingdon Press, 1988.

Plaskow, Judith. *Standing Again at Sinai: Judaism from a Feminist Perspective.* San Francisco: Harper & Row, 1990.

Plaskow, Judith, and Carol P. Christ, eds. *Weaving the Visions: New Patterns in Feminist Spirituality.* New York: Harper & Row, 1989.

Purvis, Sally. "Mothers, Neighbors, and Strangers: Another Look At Agape." *Journal of Feminist Studies in Religion* 7(Spring 1991):19-34.

Raines, John C., and Donna C. Day-Lower. *Modern Work and Human Meaning.* Philadelphia: Westminster, 1986.

Rich, Adrienne. *Of Woman Born: Motherhood as Experience and Institution.* New York: W. W. Norton, 1976.

_____. *On Lies, Secrets, and Silence: Selected Prose 1966–1978.* New York: W. W. Norton, 1979.

Rossiter, Amy. *From Private to Public: A Feminist Exploration of Early Mothering.* Toronto, Ontario: The Women's Press, 1988.

Rothman, Barbara Katz. *Recreating Motherhood: Ideology and Technology in a Patriarchal Society.* New York: W. W. Norton, 1989.

Ruddick, Sara. *Maternal Thinking: Toward a Politics of Peace.* Boston: Beacon, 1989.

Ruddick, Sara, and Pamela Daniels, eds. *Working It Out: 23 Writers, Artists, Scientists, and Scholars Talk About Their Lives and Work.* New York: Pantheon Books, 1977.

Russell, Letty M., et al. eds. *Inheriting our Mother's Gardens: Feminist Theology in Third World Perspective.* Philadelphia: Westminster Press, 1988.

Saiving, Valerie. "The Human Situation: A Feminine View." *Journal of Religion* (April 1960:100-12).

Bibliography

Schüssler Fiorenza, Elisabeth. *In Memory of Her: A Feminist Theological Reconstruction of Christian Origins.* New York: Crossroad, 1984.

Scott, Hilda. *Working Your Way to the Bottom: The Feminization of Poverty.* London: Pandora, 1984.

Shreve, Anita. *Remaking Motherhood: How Working Mothers Are Shaping Our Children's Future.* New York: Faucett Columbine, 1987.

Sidel, Ruth. *Women and Children Last: The Plight of Poor Women in Affluent America.* New York: Viking, 1986.

_____. *On Her Own: Growing Up in the Shadow of the American Dream.* New York: Viking, 1990.

Soelle, Dorothee, with Shirley A. Cloyes. *To Work and To Love: A Theology of Creation.* Philadelphia: Fortress, 1984.

Stacey, Judith. "Are Feminists Afraid to Leave Home?: The Challenge of Conservative Pro-Family Feminism." *What Is Feminism?: A Reexamination,* ed. Juliet Mitchell and Ann Oakley, 208-37. New York: Pantheon, 1986.

_____. *Brave New Families: Stories of Domestic Upheaval in Late Twentieth-Century America.* New York: Basic Books, 1990.

Thorne, Barrie, ed., with Marilyn Yalom. *Rethinking the Family: Some Feminist Questions.* New York: Longman, 1982.

Tilly, Louise A., and Joan W. Scott. *Women, Work, and Family.* New York: Routledge, 1978.

Trebilcot, Joyce, ed. *Mothering: Essays in Feminist Theory.* Savage, Md.: Rowman & Littlefield, 1983.

Trible, Phyllis. *God and the Rhetoric of Sexuality.* Philadelphia: Fortress, 1978.

Van Leeuwen, Mary Stewart. *Gender and Grace: Love, Work, and Parenting in a Changing World.* Downers Grove, Ill.: Intervarsity, 1990.

Van Leeuwen, Mary Stewart, with Annelies Knoppers, Margaret L. Koch, Douglas J. Schuurman, and Helen M. Sterk. *After Eden: Facing the Challenge of Gender Reconciliation.* Grand Rapids: Eerdmans, 1993.

Weems, Renita J. *Just a Sister Away.* San Diego: LuraMedia, 1988.

Williams, Delores S. *Sisters in the Wilderness: The Challenge of God-Talk.* Maryknoll, N. Y.: Orbis, 1993.

Young, Iris Marion. *Throwing Like a Girl, and Other Essays in Feminist Philosophy and Social Theory.* Bloomington, Ind.: Indiana University Press, 1990.